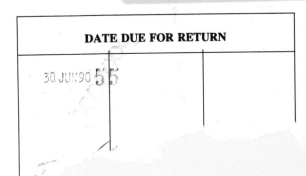

ES I R58

DEVELOPMENT OPTIONS
in the
NEW ZEALAND MOTOR CAR
ASSEMBLY INDUSTRY

W. D. ROSE

RESEARCH PAPER No. 16

of the

N.Z. Institute of Economic Research (Inc.)

P.O. Box 3479

WELLINGTON

N.Z. INSTITUTE OF ECONOMIC RESEARCH (INC.)

The N.Z. INSTITUTE OF ECONOMIC RESEARCH (INC.), founded in 1958, is an independent non-profit making Incorporated Society with a membership open to any person or corporate body. Its object is to increase knowledge of New Zealand's economic development through research, education and the training of research workers. It conducts research by its own staff and in co-operation with universities and kindred bodies. The general research work of the Institute is entirely financed by annual subscriptions from members. The views expressed in research publications are not necessarily those of members.

The Institute is under the direction of a Board of Trustees, partly elected by members and partly ex officio and co-opted.

CONTENTS

PREFACE

This study is the product of several years' research, interrupted frequently by the author's other responsibilities as Assistant Director and Editor of Quarterly Predictions. The ensuing delay in publication has however enabled informed people within and without the motor car assembly industry to appraise Mr. Rose's findings as the research proceeded. In a difficult area of economic analysis such as this, adequate time to consider the import of empirical observations and policy prescriptions is quite as essential as the basic facts.

Mr. Rose has ably synthesised the various, more or less unconnected, conclusions arrived at by research workers overseas concerning the fundamental economics of motor car assembly. To this he has added his own research, the first of its kind in New Zealand, to produce a definitive study of this key industry.

Without the ready co-operation of people in the industry and of public servants concerned with it, the research would not have been possible. I feel sure that all who have contributed to it in any way, Institute Members and the interested public generally, will find the analysis and conclusions illuminating and thought-provoking.

J. W. ROWE,
Director.

September, 1970.

ACKNOWLEDGEMENTS

A study of this size depends upon the co-operation and assistance of many people. I have been fortunate. Many people in industry, in government, and elsewhere, have given generously of their time over a long period.

I have had discussions with all but one of the motor assembly companies and with a number of important component manufacturers. Detailed questions have been answered and draft material commented upon. This study would not have been possible without their co-operation. Considerable help was given by members of government departments and other bodies. In particular thanks are due to the Departments of Statistics, Customs, and Industries and Commerce, the Treasury, the New Zealand Retail Motor Trade Association, the N.Z. Engineering and Related Trades Union, and the Canadian Government Trade Commisioner in New Zealand.

My professional colleagues, particularly those at this Institute, have been most helpful in resolving particular problems and in their comments upon my text. Particular thanks are due to the Director, Mr. J. W. Rowe for continual and ready assistance, and to Messrs. P. G. Elkan, C. Gillion, K. Lowen and A. J. van Zijl. Finally I must also thank the Institute itself for bearing the cost of this research over a long period.

W. D. ROSE.

1. INTRODUCTION AND SUMMARY

1. Introduction

In affluent societies the motor car is one of the commonest, and yet most expensive and prestigious of consumer durables. It forms an important part of the expenditure of the typical household and of society as a whole. At the same time motor car manufacture exhibits to an extraordinary degree the phenomenon of economies of scale; in general terms if we produce more cars we will produce them more cheaply. The same phenomenon is present in motor car assembly but to a lesser extent.

These two characteristics have confronted smaller affluent nations such as New Zealand with an acute dilemma. They share the high per capita demand for cars but lack the scale necessary for their most economic production. To import cars is to incur a high cost in overseas exchange: to produce them locally may mean a wasteful use of local labour and capital which could more profitably be employed in other industries.

In practice the dilemma has been resolved by cutting the car in two. Those parts which are most subject to economies of scale are imported from the major international motor car producers whilst other parts are produced locally and incorporated in the locally assembled car. Then as the scale of the domestic industry increases, production is slowly extended to include more and more items that were previously imported.

The world motor industry comprises a small number of international corporations. The national policy maker seeking an increase in local content is in effect attempting to alter the internal production patterns of those corporations by inducing them to buy or make locally parts which they would prefer to import. He may attempt this by decree or by changing the pricing point at which the corporations assess the economics of local production.

Policy makers have invented many combinations of these two approaches but in the last analysis the viability of any particular policy depends upon the underlying technical, economic, commercial and political relationships.

This study examines the New Zealand motor car assembly industry and assesses the nature of production economies in motor car manufacture and assembly. Its purpose is to illuminate the policy issues which surround attempts to secure an increased level

7

of local production. It is hoped that in doing so some light is also thrown on the more general policy issues faced by small economies in the process of industrialization.

The following paragraphs summarise this research paper. The side headings are those of the various chapters.

2. A Brief History of the Industry

The New Zealand motor assembly industry has a long history. From the advent of the motor car, ocean freight costs and tariffs encouraged local body building. In 1932 Coates, the then Minister of Finance, introduced the forerunner of the present tariff which offers concessional duty rates on unassembled cars. Coates' tariff encouraged the establishment of most of the major units of the present industry, apart from General Motors which had already set up a plant in 1926.

Motor cars have been subject to import licensing in most years since the war but there have been several attempts by Government to match the demand for new cars. To date these have been unsuccessful and at the time of writing the outcome of the current initiative in this direction remains uncertain.

Since its establishment the industry has been encouraged to increase local content. The encouragement has been modest with the exception of a few years in the early 1960's when additional import licences were offered to firms achieving specified increases in local content. As well as inducing a small increase in local content these schemes enabled several new small assembly plants to be set up. In recent years trans-Tasman trade in automotive products has been developed. There have also been a number of proposals to produce cars embodying very high levels of New Zealand content. To date none of these have come to fruition.

3. The Industry Today

The motor car assembly industry, which is one of the larger manufacturing industries, comprises nine companies, three of which are subsidiaries of overseas companies. One company assembles cars in two plants, the rest each have one plant. Three quarters of the cars produced are assembled in factories in the Hutt Valley, and most of the others are assembled in Auckland.

Motor car assembly is not highly capital intensive, and assembly work is mainly unskilled. The industry has a very high rate of labour turnover which adversely affects productivity. On the other hand this factor together with national rather than plant unionisation probably contributes to the industry's peaceful industrial relations.

8

The annual production of motor cars has fluctuated markedly since the war with a peak level of 58,000 units being reached in 1964-65. This seems certain to be exceeded in 1970-71. Imported components account for the major part, about 60 per cent, of the wholesale value of cars assembled in New Zealand. This compares with an import content of 71 per cent in the early post-war years, since when the proportion of materials purchased locally has risen, from 10 to 14 per cent of the wholesale price of a car. Nevertheless, if account is taken also of the imports required for the manufacture of components the motor vehicle assembly industry had a higher import content than any other industry specified in the 1959-60 inter-industry study. In the post-war period the level of manufacturing surplus in the industry increased from 6 to 9 per cent of the wholesale price of a car.

4. The Comparative Cost of New Zealand Assembly

The motor assembly companies achieve considerable savings in freight and duty by assembling in New Zealand. Together these savings more than offset the higher assembly costs incurred in New Zealand plants. On the basis of data supplied by seven of the assembly companies it appears that the New Zealand wholesale price of an overseas assembled car is about 8 per cent more than that of one assembled locally. In the absence of the protective duty the New Zealand wholesale price of an overseas assembled car would be about 3 per cent less than that of its locally assembled equivalent. The comparison would be still less favourable if there was no freight saving and it is tentatively concluded that the manufacturing cost of local assembly and local components is about twice that of the same operations when carried out by the overseas supplier industry.

This cost disability is however almost fully offset by the saving in freight. A comparison of the local resources used in assembly with the overseas exchange saved shows that the cost of saving a dollar of overseas exchange in motor assembly is about $1.31. This compares favourably with the average performance of the manufacturing sector. It also contrasts dramatically with the $2.50 estimate made by the 1967 World Bank Mission, an estimate which appears to have taken inadequate account of the freight savings consequent on local assembly.

5. Policy Instruments Affecting the Motor Industry

The motor car assembly industry operates in an environment affected by the tariff, import licensing, and price control. Whilst the British Preferential Tariff provides a strong incentive to assembly, the rate of duty on components is so low that it provides little incentive to increase local content unless this is dictated by a change in the tariff "determinations" prohibiting the import of a specified component for use in assembly. The draconic nature of this latter weapon prohibits its use. The main incentive to increased local content has been provided by import licensing but this has been weakened by the recurrent prospect of relaxation.

6. Motor Car Assembly

Many factors influence the productivity of an assembly plant. Two of the more important are the extent to which its capacity is used and the number of models which are produced in it. As noted, the assembly industry is not capital intensive so that the potential for reducing unit capital costs by adopting shiftwork is not great. It is felt that additional problems in labour management and recruitment would offset any such gains. As plant size increases, capital intensity can be expected to rise and at some point this would make shiftwork profitable. This point is probably well in excess of the largest plant at present operating in New Zealand.

Over the years the industry volume of output has fluctuated widely, largely in response to government regulation, so that varying use has been made of its capacity. As about $7\frac{1}{2}$ per cent of the industry's costs are fixed, lesser use of capacity is likely to raise unit costs and it is estimated that a fall in usage from 100 to 60 per cent use of capacity could cause an increase of approximately 20 per cent in non material unit costs, or of about 3 per cent in the ex-factory cost of the whole vehicle.

In 1969 thirty-three different models of car were assembled in average production runs of 1,600 units. There is no doubt that this diverse pattern of production is expensive and it is estimated that a reduction to fifteen models, two each in the five largest plants, and one in each of the smallest plants, might lead to a $1-1\frac{1}{2}$ per cent fall in the ex-factory cost of the average car. This estimate reflects no more than the saving in assembly expenses in the present array of plants. It takes no account of possible savings in component costs or of the consequences of a radical rationalisation which would reduce the array of assembly plants.

7. The Effect of Scale in Assembly

For several reasons, motor assembly like most industrial processes, evidences economies of scale. That is to say, the unit cost of production tends to fall as the designed capacity of the plant is increased. So far as can be judged from overseas research and experience, significant economies are realised as plant capacity is increased up to 100,000 units per annum, a capacity five times that of the largest New Zealand plant.

It has been a major concern of this study to quantify the extent of the saving generated by increasing scale, in the range that is of relevance to New Zealand. On the basis of data drawn from a number of sources it is thought that unit operating costs (exclusive of component costs) could be as much as 20 per cent lower in an industry comprising only two assembly plants than in the industry as shaped at present. In turn this would mean a 3 per cent lower ex-factory cost and a 2 per cent lower retail price for locally assembled cars. This saving would be additional to those yielded by reduction in the array of models and any economies in component production.

8. Manufacture

The proportion of locally manufactured components used in assembly is small. It has increased since the war but is still less than one-fifth.

The cost of local components is on average in the range 1·6 to 2·0 times that of the deletion allowance, (the amount allowed as a credit by the overseas supplier for parts no longer supplied in the c.k.d. pack). Because the deletion allowance is, with some justification, usually less than the average overseas production costs of components and because it usually takes no account of freight savings a comparison of the cost of local production with the imported cost of overseas produced components gives a more favourable picture. On this latter basis the cost ratio appears to be, very approximately, about 1·25 in favour of overseas components.

Economies of scale continue to far higher levels in motor car manufacture than in assembly. Estimates vary but, at a minimum, an annual volume of 200,000 units is necessary to secure the major economies in conventional car production. There is a possibility that developing use of plastics may lower volume requirements.

International comparisons give clear evidence of the connection between scale, costs and labour productivity, and it is possible to derive a function relating the comparative cost of manufacture to the volume of production and the level of local content.

Finally this chapter reviews the section of the World Bank Report dealing with the New Zealand assembly industry. It is argued that this contains a number of serious errors which make it unsuitable as a basis for policy judgements about the industry.

9. Development Policies Followed Overseas

In the post-war period motor vehicle assembly and manufacture have spread around the world. In the capitalist economies, other than Japan, the usual pattern has been the development of subsidiary operations by the main international motor corporations often under pressure from the national governments.

The justification for this expansion arises from national industrial development policies. The nature of production economies has however conflicted with these wider aspirations. For optimum production a manufacturer needs a large market. In most instances the market of the industrialising country is small so that high cost production is a likely consequence. This problem is compounded by the likelihood that policies intended to induce one corporation to commence local manufacture will also encourage others to do so, thus dividing the market still further.

The policy maker interested in low cost motor car manufacture will thus be interested in restricting the range of vehicles produced and in serving as wide a market as possible. The former is difficult without direct licensing although Australia was a lucky exception in that initially only one international corporation undertook local manufacture.

More recently efforts have been made to enlarge the effective size of markets through bilateral agreements encouraging increased specialisation and trade between the automotive industries of pairs of the countries concerned.

One of the clearer lessons of international experience is that while it is a simple matter to force local manufacture it is difficult to obtain a fully satisfactory pattern of production within the new industry.

10   A Suggested Policy

Limited scale has been the main factor militating against an increase in the local content of cars assembled in New Zealand. This problem has been compounded by the fragmented state of the New Zealand industry. In the current decade a substantial growth in the annual production of cars is likely, particularly if government is able to release the overseas exchange required to match demand for them. This together with the increasing possibilities of international exchange of parts enabling greater specialization suggests that some increase in content will be economically attainable during the current decade.

After an examination of tariff and other policy alternatives it is concluded that the British Preferential Tariff on assembled cars should be increased to 30 per cent whilst that on components for use in local assembly of cars should be increased markedly from the present $6\frac{1}{4}$ per cent to a level of 20 per cent at present content levels. Provision should be made for a progressive decline in the tariff rate as local added value is increased. The general effect of the proposed tariff changes is to extend to all stages of assembly and manufacture a uniform, 35 per cent, level of effective protection. An unsought consequence of the proposed tariff changes would be an increase in the final cost of cars. It is proposed that sales tax should be reduced to offset this.

It is also suggested that the policy focus be broadened to include promotion of automotive exports on an equal footing with import substituting increases in local content. Finally, it is suggested that the present discriminatory tariff against motor cars from countries other than the United Kingdom and Australia be reduced to the minimum level consistent with treaty obligations.

2. A BRIEF HISTORY OF THE INDUSTRY

2.1 Origins

The New Zealand motor car assembly industry has been fostered by distance and protection; distance because the high cost of shipping a fully built up car encouraged local assembly; and protection, because successive governments have used the tariff to supplement the natural protection of high transport costs. Motor body building evolved from coachbuilding and up to the advent of the steel body in the 1930's, the square body fitted atop the chassis and behind the engine, was built, as were the coaches, of timber framing, plywood, metal panelling, and upholstery. Not only were the techniques common, the early body building industry shared the protection granted to vehicles as diverse as drays, perambulators and bicycles under the 1895 tariff. Complete vehicles were dutiable at 20 per cent ad valorem whilst materials to be used in local manufacture were admitted free.

In 1907 a new tariff itemized motor vehicles for the first time and drew a pattern which, in its essentials, has persisted. Assembled motor vehicles were to be dutiable at an ordinary rate of 20 per cent but a schedule of exemptions provided for the free entry of chassis whether attached to a vehicle or not. Effectively the local body building industry could import its materials free and enjoyed protection on body building. The war tariff of 1915 removed this protection and substituted a flat 10 per cent tariff on body and chassis, but protection was reintroduced in 1921 when an additional variable specific duty was imposed on assembled bodies. For bodies having canopies the duty was £15.

This measure appears to have assisted the industry through a difficult transition. The number of motor vehicle bodies built increased rapidly, from 527 in 1918-19 (the earliest year for which there are statistics) to 2545 in 1923-24. Over the same period production of wagons, drays, dog carts, etc., declined.

In 1924 a trade journal eulogizing the industry as fulfilling "orders for roadsters, touring types, sports models, coupes, sedans, and limousines, all equipped with equal satisfaction" suggested that "the busy times of the industry can be credited to a measure of tariff protection, for which the manufacturers are grateful, and they are hopeful that the results so far achieved in the provision of employment for many men will make the Government and Parlia-

14

ment feel justified in a reasonable additional protection which would be reflected in a proportional expansion of the industry."[1]

The nature of the industry changed radically when, in 1926, the first substantial motor vehicle assembly plant in New Zealand was established at Lower Hutt by General Motors New Zealand Limited. This decision reflected both the particular circumstances of the New Zealand market and more general questions of company policy. Commenting on this period Sloan, President of the parent company, recalled, "in the long run our European export and distribution systems were threatened by economic nationalism We continued to press our export business there as well as we could and we backed up this position by building up assembly plants in several European countries."[2] The same consideration led General Motors to build several plants in South America and plants in South Africa, Australia, and New Zealand.

Although one Australian critic likened the Australian plant to a glorified meccano set and one New Zealand member of Parliament questioned whether the assembly of cars came within the category of an industry at all, the New Zealand plant was a major innovation in New Zealand's manufacturing development. The new plant assembled the chassis as well as the body, used some local materials and operated on a scale far beyond anything that had gone before. For eight years it remained the only large assembly plant in New Zealand and during that time produced more than 25,000 vehicles.

Perhaps of more significance than the immediate increase in local manufacture was the firm commitment to continuing activity implied by the General Motors investment; a theme which was emphasized in company literature. In the short run the company saved on transport costs and duty and strengthened its position in a market which had developed a strong preference for the larger North American cars.

The dominance of North American cars on the New Zealand market (in 1929 19,000 of the 23,000 passenger vehicles and chassis imported came from North America) occasioned criticism from a number of sources on the ground that it prejudiced New Zealand's trading relationship with Britain. In 1927 the specific duty on bodies was replaced by an ad valorem duty of 10 per cent on the first £200 by value of the whole car in an attempt to reduce the effective duty on smaller, particularly British, cars. The Minister of Finance, Downie Stewart, also hoped that the tariff would encourage other companies to start assembly in New Zealand. None did, and shortly the great depression temporarily removed any such possibility.

2.2 The Coates' Tariff

Quite apart from the depression the motor body building industry was subject to more fundamental pressures. The parent industry was consolidating and reducing the range of models. Fuller advantage was being taken of the potential of mass production techniques and most importantly the major part of the body was now made of pressed steel. At the same time freight costs on completed cars were reducing so that the protection accorded by distance diminished.

These developments foreshadowed the demise of body building as a separate industry, at least so far passenger cars were concerned, and in the six years to March 1933 only 7,600 of the 64,300 cars imported were fitted with New Zealand bodies. In 1934 a Tariff Commission reported to Parliament that the industry was ill suited to New Zealand conditions and suggested the ending of protection. The Commission thought that assembly of cars was suited to New Zealand and that because of freight and other savings the industry could be carried on economically without special protection. A British preferential tariff of 15 per cent was suggested.

Coates, the Minister of Finance, was not so sanguine and introduced a tariff which distinguished between assembled and unassembled vehicles. Fully assembled cars from Britain were to be dutied at 15 per cent and c.k.d. (completely knocked down or more accurately, unassembled) cars at 5 per cent. For non-British cars the rates were to be 50 and 60 per cent. Further, the Minister was to determine what constituted an unassembled car and in 1935, following discussions with the British Society of Motor Manufacturers and Traders, at which the major companies agreed to assembly in New Zealand, Coates issued the first c.k.d. determination.

The 1935 determination defined a c.k.d. car as one in which the chassis frame was assembled and the engine and gear box, but no other parts, attached. Other elements such as the scuttle and windscreen assembly, and the body shell, could be assembled and primed. Upholstery materials could be cut to shape but not sewn. There was no restriction on the range of components that could be imported as part of the c.k.d. pack, the determination dealing solely with the degree of assembly that could be undertaken.

The Customs determination, the agreement with the United Kingdom companies, and recovery from the depression led to a rapid expansion of the New Zealand industry. Two New Zealand distributing companies, Todd Motors and Dominion Motors, set up plants and began assembly of the main cars for which they held franchises (Rootes and Chrysler and the Nuffield group respectively). Ford followed General Motors' lead and established a subsidiary assembly company. Total imports of cars rose from 3,000 in 1933 to 28,000 in 1938, and the number of units assembled locally increased from about 300 in 1933 to 19,000 in 1938.

Expansion was not without its problems. In particular a number of manufacturers, including those in the upholstery trade, found the new industry a poor substitute for the protected market of the old motor body building trade. In 1939 the Customs determination was amended so that hide leathers, upholstery textiles and flock, and other kinds of upholstery padding could no longer be imported as part of a c.k.d. pack. Batteries were also to be excluded. At the same time the permitted degree of overseas assembly was reduced. Welded panels could no longer be soldered, filled or trimmed, and body shells could not be painted.

The decision to exclude certain items from the definition of a c.k.d. pack was an important innovation. The protection afforded the local manufacturer of an item excluded by the determination was much greater than the 10 per cent difference between duty rates for assembled and unassembled cars, for to include such an item was to render the entire pack liable to the higher duty rate.

At the end of the decade an exchange crisis led to the imposition of quantitative import controls and although the allocations for the first six-month licensing period were on a par with previous levels war swiftly reduced the allocation to nil.

2.3 The Post-war Years 1945-57

During the war few cars entered New Zealand, and the aftermath of the war was a shortage, which has persisted. During most of the post-war period car imports have been subject to quantitative controls which have in general favoured local assembly. As in many other instances import controls have proved a more powerful and pervasive protective instrument than has the tariff.

Several new plants began assembly after the war. Motor Assemblies, a company formed by several New Zealand distributors, had built its Christchurch plant before the war, but began assembly of Studebaker and Standard only after the war. Austin Distributors, a joint venture by Austin franchise holders, began assembly in Wellington in 1946. Finally in 1948 an Auckland firm, Jowett Motors (now Motor Industries (International)) began assembly of Bradford vans and Javelin cars. All three enterprises were New Zealand owned but one, Motor Assemblies, became a subsidiary of the Standard-Triumph Company of England in 1954.

During the five years 1946-50 imports of motor cars averaged 13,000 units a year, significantly less than the 24,000 average during the five boom years at the end of the 1930's. Slow recovery of the industry overseas, and local production and balance of payments problems, kept imports down. At the same time the dollar shortage meant that import licences were restricted in the main to British sources and this furthered the change in sourcing from American to British c.k.d. packs that had been encouraged by the tariff.

Table 1:

COUNTRY OF ORIGIN OF MOTOR CAR
IMPORTS TO NEW ZEALAND
(c.k.d. and built up)   (1000 units)

	Britain	Canada	U.S.A.	Australia	Other	Total
1927	2·1	2·3	6·1	—	0·3	10·9
1937	18·1	7·4	4·9	—	—	30·3
1947	13·7	4·7	1·0	—	—	19·4
1957	33·2	1·3	0·2	3·5	3·2	41·5
1967	28·6	0·4	0·6	15·6	7·5	52·8
1968–69	31·9	—	2·0	11·3	7·8	53·0

Source: New Zealand Motor Trade Yearbook, and New Zealand Trade Statistics.

Import licences were limited to use for c.k.d. imports but provision was made for dispensation in special cases. Such dispensations were widespread at first, but by 1949 more than 90 per cent of imports were for assembly in New Zealand.

In June 1948 production of motor tyres began and the Customs definition of a c.k.d. pack was amended to exclude tyres and tubes. In 1949 a further amendment excluded car radios.

The imposition of import licensing was not without its problems and led to widespread allegations of inequity. In November 1950 the Import Licensing Committee appointed by the newly-elected Holland administration reported that "it was impossible to identify any general principle or principles which had been followed over the years in the case of licences issued to the 'Big Five'. This lack of uniformity was especially apparent in the establishment of basic licences."[3] This report doubtless strengthened the government, which included amongst more important supporters groups traditionally opposed to protection, as well as a greater proportion of those most able to pay for a car, in its determination to remove controls when opportunity offered. Already, in May 1950, the government had announced that no-remittance licences would be issued for imports which the applicant could finance out of his own overseas funds. The scheme has continued up to the present.

The opportunity for more extensive action was not long delayed. The Korean wool boom led to a rapid rise in export receipts (wool

CHART 1. MOTOR CAR IMPORTS

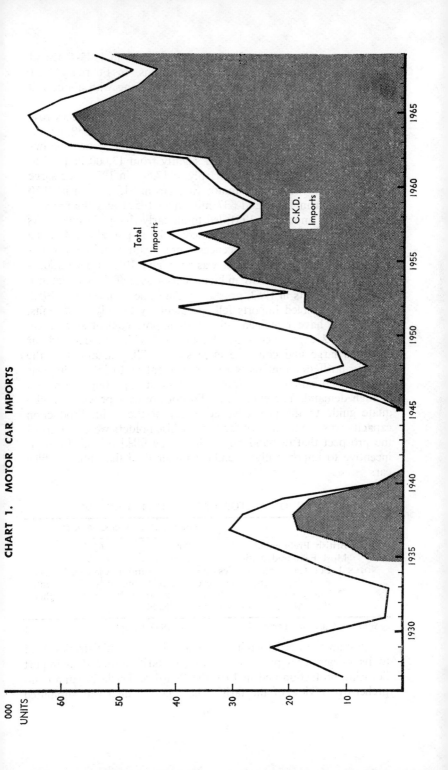

exports earned in 1950-51 five times as much as in 1945-46), and swung the balance of payments into surplus. In February 1951 motor car imports were freed from control along with about 700 other items.

The reaction was spectacular. Imports of assembled cars rose from 2,700 in 1950 to 14,100 in 1951, and 21,400 in 1952, as importers hurried to supply a starved market. At the same time imports of unassembled vehicles fell slightly from 13,000 in 1950 to 12,800 in 1951, and then rose sharply to 17,800 in 1952. The surge in overseas expenditure on motor cars (from $15 million in 1950 to $27 million in 1951, and $37 million in 1952) and the reduced level of c.k.d. imports in 1951, led to an early change in policy. As from March 1952 no built up cars could be imported and in June of the same year import licences were again required for unassembled vehicles. The boom was over and 1953 licence allocations were reduced to $18 million. This was sufficient to finance 17,700 c.k.d. units in 1953, practically the same number as in 1952, but fully assembled imports fell spectacularly to only 3,200 units. Motor cars have remained subject to import control since then. The 1951-52 experience showed that the backlog of demand for cars was large and could be expensive to fill, and also that the existing tariff differentials were not so great as to inhibit imports of assembled cars during a transition to open importing in a period of high demand. The experience did not however provide an adequate guide to the protective adequacy of the tariff. Production capacity was limited and so far as franchise holders were concerned the prospect that demand might shortly be filled provided a clear incentive to import fully assembled rather than than unassembled cars.

Table 2:

TARIFF ON MOTOR CARS—FROM JULY 1962

	Assembled	Unassembled
British Preferential	20%	6¼%
Most Favoured Nation	55%	45%

NOTES 1. For Canadian vehicles there are several intermediate tariff rates depending upon the degree of Commonwealth content.
2. The General Tariff which provides rates 20 per cent higher than M.F.N. rates is rarely applicable.

Source: Customs Tariff of New Zealand 1967 Chapter 87.

Despite the need to reimpose controls the administration held to its longer term policy of moving to tariff rather than import licensing protection and in 1956 the Board of Trade began a comprehensive review of the tariff. The report, which was submitted to Government just before the 1957 General Election, recommended a minor upward movement in tariff rates for motor cars but no change was made until 1961 when the tariff as a whole was revised.

2.4 A Period of Change 1958-1970

Towards the end of 1957 New Zealand's balance of payments deteriorated seriously. In December net overseas assets of the banking system fell below $100 million for the first time since the war, and at the end of the year stood at only about half the average level of the previous five years. The newly-elected Nash administration reimposed comprehensive import controls and replaced the previously published 1958 licensing schedule with one much more stringent.

Whereas the original schedule had provided for some increase in motor car imports above the record level of 1957, the new schedule cut allocations to 75 per cent of 1957 imports for c.k.d. packs and to 50 per cent for built up cars. In 1959 imports were reduced a little further.

The 1958 report of the Department of Industries and Commerce, which was something of a testament for the cause of manufacturing, identified the motor assembly industry as one in which expansion could be expected but limited its comments in detail to:

"Component parts of motor vehicles such as springs, radiators, tyres, batteries, pistons, piston rings, and mufflers, as well as upholstery and spray painting, are already supplied by New Zealand manufacturers. An expansion to other parts and a wider use of already manufactured parts could be considered."

This somewhat passive attitude towards development in the motor assembly industry probably reflected the consideration that the high import content and exchange cost of motor vehicles would not in the short run be significantly affected by any change in local content, and a judgement that as a luxury item motor car imports should be reduced substantially in a time of crisis.

In 1958 the Customs determinations were amended, for the first time since 1949, to exclude radiators and laminated undercarriage springs from c.k.d. packs for motor cars. During the next few years production began of a number of new components including oil filters and motor car heaters, but no move was made to require inclusion of these in locally assembled cars.

Then late in 1960, in announcing the 1961 Import Licensing Schedule, the Minister of Customs Mr Boord outlined a scheme designed to increase local content. Basic import allocations for 1961 were to be set at 100 per cent of 1960 entitlements but provision was made for additional issue of licences provided that specified levels of local content were achieved. (See Table 3.)

It is difficult to assess the effect of this scheme. The original ministerial statement made it clear that some companies were already above the 35 per cent requirement, and subsequent official estimates of the increase in local content that had been achieved under the scheme were ambiguous. In June 1961 Mr Marshall,

Table 3:

1960 INCENTIVE SCHEME

If local content increased to:	% increase in import licence allocation
35% by 30 June 1961	7½
37½% by 30 June 1961	10
40% by 31 December 1961	15

Source: Customs Department.

Minister of Industries and Commerce, announced that an additional 3,600 cars (an increase of about 12 per cent on 1960 imports of c.k.d. cars) should be available as a result of the incentive scheme and stated that "an increased New Zealand content of about 10 per cent has been obtained by the greater use of locally made parts and by a higher proportion of assembly work in New Zealand on imported components."[4]

In contrast the industrial production statistics suggest that, between 1960-61 and 1961-62, the New Zealand content of motor cars assembled in New Zealand increased from 351 parts per 1000 to 363, an increase of 4 per cent or, if we express content in the more usual sense of a percentage of total ex-factory cost, an increase in local content of only 1·2 per cent.

Although the incentive scheme was seen mainly as an inducement to increase the local content of established models, provision was made for the issue of c.k.d. licences for assembly of limited numbers of cars for other franchise holders. This scheme provided the basis for what was to become known as the "300 club", under which licences sufficient for 300 units could be issued for manufacturing proposals embodying a sufficiently high local content, with the prospect of larger allocations if higher content was achieved. There was also provision for holders of licences for built up units to transfer that entitlement for import of c.k.d. units. No specific rules as to degree of local content were declared, the question being open to negotiation in each particular case, but in general "300" proposals were not accepted unless the local content was set at approximately 40-44 per cent of ex-factory cost.

The "300 club" reflected the government's reaction to a number of pressures. The historical base of the licensing system prevented the entry of new units to the industry, and licence allocations, by discriminating against imports of assembled cars, had affected some franchise holders severely. In the wider field of international trade relations Government was under pressure to make some licensing provision for cars from the resurgent European industry which was unrepresented in New Zealand apart from the Volkswagen. This car had been assembled in Auckland by Motor Industries Ltd. (then V.W. Motors) since 1954 when they acquired the franchise in substitution for the Jowett Javelin, which had gone out of production. For a period, 1964-68, V.W.'s were imported from Australia but importation from Germany resumed in 1968 following the company's abandonment of Australian manufacture.

The effects of the "300 club" have been far reaching. Motor Industries has been a major beneficiary, undertaking the assembly of a number of lines which now comprise Fiat, Skoda and Simca. These have been assembled either on behalf of, or after takeover of, the franchise holder. The other established New Zealand-owned companies are also represented in the 300 club through assembly on behalf of independent franchise holders of marques related to the assemblers' main products. In addition the scheme enabled three new assembly operations. In 1960 New Zealand Motor Bodies, a long-established motor body building firm, undertook assembly of the Simca, but in 1964 lost this operation when the franchise holder was taken over by Motor Industries Ltd. In 1965 New Zealand Motor Bodies undertook assembly of the Datsun. Campbell Industries Ltd., a component manufacturer at Thames, in 1964 opened an assembly plant which now assembles Rambler, Peugeot, Toyota, Corolla, Isuzu and Renault cars, and in 1966 Steel Brothers began assembly of the Toyota Corona in Christchurch.

The most noticeable effect of the 300 club has been an increase in the number of assembly plants and in the number of models produced. Most of the new assembly operations are at the minimum level envisaged under the scheme and in general assemblers have found it cheaper to multiply the range of models assembled rather than to increase the depth of manufacture.

Although the 300 club had little effect upon the level of New Zealand content incorporated in the average car, it did increase the level of motor car production. Even more effective to this end was the expansion in no-remittance imports which occurred during 1961 largely as a result of the Government decision to advance from

23

1953 to 1958 the date before which overseas shares had to have been held to qualify under the scheme. In 1961 no-remittance imports totalled 7,727, almost twice the 1960 level, and total motor car imports increased from 32,400 to 35,400.

Exchange problems continued to restrain the Government from further increasing imports and the 1962-63 import licensing schedule held imports to 1961 levels, although in November 1962 the incentive scheme, which had been inoperative since December 1961, was revived with provision for increases in licence issue as set out in Table 4.

Table 4:

Increase in local content by 30 June 1963	% increase in import licence allocation above 1961
From 35 to 37½	2½
From 37½ to 40	5
„ „ „ 42½	7½
„ „ „ 45	10

Source: Customs Department.

The effect of this scheme was soon to be swamped. An improvement in the balance of payments (in the year ended March 1963 the Balance of Payments deficit was only $46 million, compared with $110 million in the previous year) encouraged the administration to make a determined attempt to match the demand for cars. The 1962-63 import licensing schedule provided for additional licences to be distributed under two schemes. The first of these, the bonus scheme, entailed granting additional licences to franchise holders according to the level of no-remittance business gained by them. Each no-remittance sale permitted an equivalent import on a remitting basis. Alongside of this the production incentive scheme set aside $5 million for distribution amongst the assembly companies in a manner related to the percentage increase above normal production achieved in the six months July to December 1963. Together the two schemes were expected to involve $9.5 million of additional licence issue.

The two schemes reflected Government's wish to enable differential growth under import licensing, which, operating from an historical base, tended to perpetuate the market share of each company. This problem had been faced before, in 1950, by the Board of Trade which reallocated some licences and this was followed by the brief exemption of motor cars from licensing, which permitted further change. Since then, however, the licensing system had, with the exception of the schemes designed to increase local content, followed a strict historical base.

24

No-remittance imports were heavily favoured under both schemes, directly by the bonus scheme, but also indirectly through the incentive scheme which, being geared to the actual level of production, was sensitive to increased no-remittance business. This is reflected in the changing share of the total market enjoyed by those companies having vehicles attractive to no-remittance purchasers. The principal beneficiary was General Motors, which scooped 51 per cent of the 1965 no-remittance market and whose Holden alone took 41 per cent of the market. This success was reflected in an increased share of the total market, General Motors' share increasing from 22 per cent in 1960 to 27 per cent in 1965. (See Table 5.)

Table 5:
SHARES OF THE MARKET—PERCENTAGE OF TOTAL REGISTRATIONS

	1950	1955	1960	1965	1969
Austin Distributors Federation	15	12	14	9	10
British Leyland Motor Corporation	8	6	6	3	5
Campbell Industries	—	—	—	1	4
Dominion Motors	16	14	15	13	11
Ford Motors	23	24	18	21	22
General Motors	19	22	22	27	22
Motor Industries	—	3	4	6	7
New Zealand Motor Bodies	—	—	—	1	1
Todd Motors	17	15	15	17	16
Steel Bros.	—	—	—	—	1
Other	2	5	6	3	2
TOTAL	100	100	100	100	100

NOTE: Marques are classified according to the company which assembled them whether or not that company held the franchise. Because registration statistics do not separate New Zealand and overseas assembled vehicles all figures are overstated to the extent of built-up imports, of marques which are in the main assembled in New Zealand. These will however in general be small. The entry, "other", includes all marques not assembled in New Zealand.

Source: New Zealand Motor Trade Yearbook and New Zealand Retail Motor Trade Association.

Under the stimulus of the two schemes, and increased allocations for built up cars, imports rose rapidly; 1964-65 and 1965-66 licence allocations were set at still higher levels and the opportunity taken to re-allocate licences on the basis of production during the 1964-65 period. In total, motor car imports increased by 74 per cent, from 38,000 to 66,000, between 1962 and the peak year 1965. The Government did not, however, satisfy the demand for cars.

Despite the large increase in imports demand still outran supply, and then, as balance of payments pressures again became evident, allocations for motor cars were cut successively in the 1966-67 and 1967-68 licensing schedules. The motor car boom of the early sixties was over. Retrenchment also led to the cessation of approval for new projects under the 300 club, which had been modified in 1965 so that manufacturers, to qualify under the scheme, had to include a specified list of components rather than achieve a particular percentage of local content.

Although the 1967 exchange crisis did not lead to a general industrialization drive as did the 1958 crisis, there have been a series of innovations and proposals for major change. Late in 1966 Motor Industries International began production of a utility vehicle, the Trekka, designed in New Zealand and embodying a high New Zealand content around a Skoda engine and transmission. During 1967 several far-reaching proposals were made, the principal one being to build a fibreglass bodied, medium size car to a New Zealand content of 60 per cent (rising to 90 per cent), initially around a Ford engine. This was proposed by an Auckland firm, Anziel Limited, which drew on the technical and design resources of a small English manufacturer, the Reliant Company, which has assisted similar projects in Turkey and Israel. Anziel did not find the path to local manufacture easy. Dependent on government approval for import licences for engines and other parts the company had to wait until late in 1968 for an approval from Government. When that came it was for a volume of licences very much less than the 2,000 previously stated by Anziel to be the minimum initial scale of operation under which the project would be viable. In a subsequent public statement[5] the Minister of Industries and Commerce said that he had told the company that if the first 300 cars it produced showed the New Zealand public wanted to buy the product and if the New Zealand content was between 70 and 80 per cent, then he did not see how the company could be refused licences for the 2500 units it had sought.

At the end of 1969 Anziel announced that it proposed to undertake a modified production programme as from July 1970, but then in March of that year, following the Government's announcement that it was stepping up the level of licence issue in an attempt to meet the demand for cars, Anziel shelved the project. It seems clear that a precondition for its success was a market for something like the 2,000 units sought by the company. The company which advanced its original proposal during the 1967 exchange crisis, envisaged that market as being provided behind the protection of import licensing. The exchange crises proved short lived and in the aftermath, and in the absence of any substantial tariff protection, the proposal looked much less attractive.

A similar proposal to manufacture a plastic body was made in 1967 by the American Borg-Warner Company which held discussions with some assembly companies and the Government. Later in the year the American Motor Corporation, looking for an assembly point which would qualify for preferential tariffs within the Commonwealth, proposed assembling Rambler cars at the Thames plant of Campbell Motors, for export to the West Indies. Neither of these proposals came to fruition.

Late in 1968 Rotarymotive Developments announced their intention to manufacture a small fibreglass passenger car powered by a locally designed and manufactured rotary engine. At time of writing the car, and its engine, were still under development.

In the United Kingdom, in 1968, the British Motor Corporation and Leyland Motors merged, as the British Leyland Motor Corporation. The merger culminated a series which brought together in the one firm many of the best known British marques, including Austin, Morris, Standard, Triumph, Rover, and Jaguar. The new company was faced with a diverse range of assembly plants in New Zealand, comprising the Dominion Motors' plants in Auckland, the Austin Distributors' plant in Lower Hutt, and the recently-built Standard-Triumph plant at Nelson.

Early in 1969 the president of the Corporation visited New Zealand seeking some rationalization of the Corporation's activities. In 1970 Dominion Motors and the main Austin franchise holders merged to form the New Zealand Motor Corporation. This company and the British Leyland Motor Corporation plan to set up a jointly-owned company to establish a new assembly plant to handle Morris and Austin vehicles. In the meantime the New Zealand Motor Corporation has announced an interim rationalization of model production between its Lower Hutt and Auckland plants. The rationalization plans have not so far affected the Nelson plant which is fully owned by the British Leyland Motor Corporation and which continues to assemble Triumph and Rover cars.

As New Zealand recovered from the exchange crisis of the late 1960's import licence allocations for motor cars were increased, by 15 per cent in 1968-69, and by 5 per cent in 1969-70. Then, in 1970, the Government, with a buoyant balance of payments behind it, once again set out to match the demand for cars. Substantial increases in import licences were announced so that imports were expected to rise to 80,000 units during 1970-71 as compared with an estimated 60,000 units in 1969-70. It remains to be seen whether this substantial increase will be sufficient to match demand, which must be presumed to be stimulated by buoyant internal economic conditions.

The last years of the 1960's also saw considerable activity in connection with Australia-New Zealand trade. The formal arrangements for the exchange of automotive components, established under the New Zealand-Australia Free Trade Agreement, are discussed subsequently. Here it is sufficient to note that this trend towards trans-Tasman industry co-ordination is likely to strengthen during the coming decade.

3. THE INDUSTRY TODAY

3.1 The Companies

Motor vehicle assembly is one of the larger manufacturing industries, employing 2 per cent of the manufacturing labour force, generating 3 per cent of the net value of factory output, and contributing 4 per cent of gross value. The high ranking of the industry on the last measure reflects a high usage of materials, particularly imports. In 1968-69 imports of unassembled motor vehicles cost $51.5 million c.d.v. This was $6\frac{1}{2}$ per cent of total imports.

The motor car assembly industry comprised (as at July 1970) the nine companies listed in Table 6. Three of them, General Motors, Ford, and the British Leyland Motor Corporation, are subsidiaries of overseas companies. The remainder are New Zealand owned, of which three, the New Zealand Motor Corporation, Motor Industries, and New Zealand Motor Bodies, are public companies. There is little public information on the financial operations of most of the companies. Comprehensive public information is limited to statistics of vehicle registrations and the industrial production statistics of the Government Statistician. These latter refer to assembly of all motor vehicles, not only cars, and include a number of establishments which do not assemble motor cars.

The existence of several important locally-owned companies contrasts with the situation in many other countries where it is usual for the more important assembly operations to be carried out in plants in which the supplying company has an interest. In Australia, for example, each of the American big four (three of whom have English subsidiaries), the independent British Leyland Motor Corporation, the German Volkswagen and the French Renault companies, all operate their own assembly plants. The New Zealand situation, which is paralleled in South Africa, has its origins in history, but its continuance results from the operation of import licensing. Import licences for motor cars are specific as to marque (no other licences are so tied) and thus ensure to the established franchise holder the sole right to import that marque of car. This being so an overseas supplier interested in establishing his own assembly operation can only do so by taking over the franchise holding company or companies, not an easy task if the company concerned is private with a concentrated shareholding.

Table 6:

THE NEW ZEALAND MOTOR CAR ASSEMBLY INDUSTRY

Name of Company	Location of Assembly Plant	Nature of Company	Year in which Assembly Began (1)	Marques Assembled 1969	1969 Registrations (2) 000	Franchise Holder
General Motors New Zealand Limited	Upper Hutt	Subsidiary of U.S. Company	1926	Holden Vauxhall	4·8 7·0 ――― 11·8	General Motors
Ford Motor Company of New Zealand Limited	Lower Hutt	Subsidiary of Canadian Company	1936	Ford	11·5	Ford Motor Company
New Zealand Motor Corporation Limited Dominion Motors Plant Auckland		New Zealand Public Company	1938	Morris Riley Wolseley (3)	5·0 0·3 0·2 ――― 5·6	N.Z. Motor Corporation N.Z. Motor Corporation N.Z. Motor Corporation (for North Island only)
Austin Plant	Petone		1946	Austin B.M.C. Wolseley (3)	4·6 0·2 0·5 ――― 5·3	N.Z. Motor Corporation Cossens and Black South Island Motors
Total, New Zealand Motor Corporation					10·9	
Todd Motor Industries Limited	Lower Hutt	New Zealand Private Company	1935	Chrysler Hillman Singer Sunbeam	3·2 4·1 0·7 0·4 ――― 8·5	Todd Motors Todd Motors Allied Motors N.Z. Ltd. Todd Motors

Company	Location	Company type	Year	Marque	Registration %	Franchise holder
Motor Industries (International) Limited	Auckland	Wholly owned subsidiary of Motor Holdings Limited, a New Zealand Public Company	1948	Fiat Simca Skoda Volkswagen	1·3 0·4 0·6 1·5 —— 3·8	Torino Motors Ltd. In each case the franchise is held by a sister company of Motor Industries (International) Ltd.
British Leyland Motor Corporation of N.Z. Ltd.	Nelson	Subsidiary of U.K. Company	Ch/ch 1946 Nelson 1966	Triumph Rover	2·2 0·3 —— 2·5	British Leyland Motor Corporation of N.Z.
Campbell Industries Limited	Thames	New Zealand Private Company	1964	Toyota Corolla Isuzu Peugeot Rambler Renault	0·7 0·4 0·4 0·2 0·3 —— 1·9	Consolidated Motor Industries H. H. Moller Ltd. Campbell Motor Imports Ltd. ,, ,, ,, ,, ,, ,,
Steel Bros. (Addington) Limited	Christchurch	New Zealand Private Company	1965	Toyota Corona	0·6	Consolidated Motor Industries
New Zealand Motor Bodies Limited	Auckland	New Zealand Public Company	1960	Datsun	0·6	Nissan Motor Distributors (N.Z.) Ltd., Auckland

NOTE ON TABLE 6:
1. The year given is that in which c.k.d. motor car assembly was begun. Many of the firms listed were, however, operating before the date shown.
2. Registration figures are derived from analyses of motor car registrations by the New Zealand Retail Motor Trade Association. The figures do not refer to assembly and will generally be higher than the number of vehicles assembled. Marques are grouped according to the company assembling and not according to franchise holder. Registrations of marques not assembled in New Zealand totalled 1255 in 1969 out of a total registration of 53,325.
3. Wolseley cars were assembled by both Austin and Dominion Motors Plants but registration data do not differentiate the two operations. The entries in the above table are based on information from the companies concerned.

Many of the international corporations initially opted out of local assembly operations. But as time made clear the permanence of industrial development policies, and the likelihood that policies initially designed to encourage assembly would lead on to local manufacture, many of the corporations changed attitudes. The official Ford history records this change as it affected that company during the 1950's:

"The feeling in Dearborn now was that the Corporation, like General Motors, should move towards a full ownership of all its foreign activities. Officials felt that overseas operations had got out of hand by being developed abroad and that with 100 per cent ownership could be brought back into the fold. If a foreign company were American owned in its entirety, nothing could interfere with its being operated in the manner most profitable to the home office. Dividend and expansion policy could be shaped without deference to minority stockholders."[1]

In New Zealand, Ford had, of course, long since followed General Motors' example. The independent British and Continental groupings did not.

3.2 Location

Geographically, the assembly industry is highly concentrated. Four of the largest plants, accounting for 72 per cent of the 1969 level of registrations, are situated in the Hutt Valley, and three, accounting for 19 per cent of the market, assemble in Auckland. The remaining three plants are in Nelson, Thames, and Christchurch.

The factors influencing location are diverse but three stand out; inward shipping for c.k.d. packs; the cost of distributing assembled vehicles to the New Zealand market; and labour supply. With the exception of the Campbell Industries plant at Thames, all assembly plants are situated at or near to a major port, and in the case of the Thames plant the possibility of coastal sea transport from Auckland has enabled negotiation of special rail freights.

Outward distribution is more complex. Motor cars sell on a national market and the cost of transport is likely to be minimized by locating the plant centrally. This factor, along with the advantage of being near the government, encouraged the early concentration of the industry in the Hutt Valley, but the gradual shift in population towards Auckland has altered the balance of the advantage. Auckland and Wellington are now fairly closely matched in terms of locational advantage[2] and most firms envisage that the balance will shift still further in Auckland's favour. This is reflected in the general presumption that the proposed New Zealand Motor Corporation plant will be established in Auckland.

Table 7:
LOCATION OF ASSEMBLY PLANTS

	1969 Registrations 000	%
Hutt Valley		
General Motors	11·8	
Ford	11·5	
Todd	8·5	
Austin Distributors	5·5	
	37·3	72
Auckland		
Dominion Motors	5·4	
Motor Industries	3·8	
New Zealand Motor Bodies	0·6	
	9·8	19
Nelson		
Standard-Triumph	2·5	5
Thames		
Campbell Motors	1·9	4
Christchurch		
Steel Brothers	0·6	1
	52·1	100

Since the Austin plant was established in 1946, in war surplus buildings, no new plants have been established in Wellington, whilst assembly lines have been set up in Auckland, Thames, Nelson and Christchurch. The Auckland operations and the Thames plant were built around existing dealerships and related manufacturing. The location of the British Leyland Motor Corporation plant in Nelson depended to a large extent on government, which was anxious to find some use for the buildings originally intended for the ill-fated cotton mill. The company was induced to put its new plant into Nelson only after guarantees of regular overseas shipping and negotiation of special rail freights.

The difficult labour situation in the Hutt Valley has also provided a disincentive and the prospect of an ample supply of unskilled labour enhanced the attractions of locations such as Nelson and Thames. Nevertheless, despite the generally unskilled nature of assembly work, the industry does recognise a range of acquired skills, and plants in Auckland and the Hutt Valley tend to call upon a common pool of experienced workers. To move away from the main centres may cause problems, as for example, when Standard Triumph (now B.L.M.C.) shifted its plant from Christchurch to Nelson and found it necessary to transfer a number of their assembly staff.

3.3 Employment

In 1967-68 the motor assembly industry employed 3,666 persons. The composition of total employment is shown in Table 8.

Table 8:

EMPLOYMENT IN MOTOR VEHICLE ASSEMBLY
INDUSTRY 1967-68

	Males	Females	Total
Managers and overseers	186	2	188
Accountants, clerks, etc.	240	76	316
Professional and Technical	45	2	47
Wage earning employees	2,782	333	3,115
	3,253	413	3,666

Source: N.Z. Industrial Production Statistics, 1967-68, Industry 464.

This industry excludes the New Zealand Motor Bodies assembly plant, the predominant activity of that company being motor body building, and includes a number of assembly units not engaged in motor car assembly.

Motor vehicle assembly does not require many highly-skilled workers but much of the work is semi-skilled. There is however no comprehensive data on the skills employed, and in discussions with various establishments and the main union involved there was wide variation in usage of the term.

One small assembly plant, employing about 130 people, suggested that amongst these the following could be classified as skilled: 5 welders, 2 panel beaters plus 1 sub-foreman, 7 spray painters, the trim foreman, the trim cutter and 2 machinists, and at the final stage 5 mechanics and one foreman. In all this gave a total of 25 or about 20 per cent of the labour force. One of the larger companies suggested a similar proportion and this and another company estimated that about 10 per cent of the labour force had some form of technical qualification.

Much assembly work is semi-skilled and the main industrial award[3] grants assemblers, defined as "workers who are substantially

34

engaged in assembling the parts of new motor vehicles", a 1.9c per hour margin over process workers, who are defined as "workers engaged on repetition work on any automatic, semi-automatic, or single purpose machine, or any machine fitted with jigs, gauges or other tools rendering operations mechanical . . ."

The semi-skilled learn their skills on the job. Competence will generally be acquired in a day or two but the experience of most firms is that performance improves over a period of two to three months. Most firms recognize this in their engagement and wage payment policies. One firm, for example, provides for assemblers to advance on foreman's recommendation from $1.02 per hour to $1.13½ during the first few months of employment. The company also offers higher initial rates to experienced workers. In contrast the award offers little recognition of skill. Under it the minimum rate for an assembler increases from 88.6 cents to 89.2 cents per hour after three months' service.

Labour turnover is generally regarded as a problem. In the year ended October 1969 terminations of employment in the vehicle and cycle manufacturing industry were equal to 94 per cent of the industry's payroll, compared with only 46 per cent for the all industries total, and outranking all but a few of the 66 industries surveyed by the Department of Labour.

The New Zealand motor assembly industry, unlike many of its counterparts overseas, has a long record of industrial peace. This probably reflects two factors. First, the high rate of turnover just discussed, and secondly, the fact that assembly line workers are in the main organized under national unions.

Rapid labour turnover inhibits the building of strong group and union loyalties, despite the existence of unqualified preference clauses in the main awards. It also reduces the prospect of tensions being generated amongst workers tied to mass production lines, tensions which have made the overseas industry something of a sociologists' paradise. This prospect is also reduced by the New Zealand industry's much lower degree of automation and job standardization.

The most important union in the motor assembly industry is the N.Z. Engineering and Related Trades Union. This represents the bulk of assembly line workers but shares jurisdiction in Wellington with the Coach and Motor Body Workers' Union. Other trades such as electricians, storemen and packers, clerical workers and drivers have their own unions. National representation of the main body of assembly workers and the fact that the principal award is national in scope means that industrial conflicts tend to be resolved on an industry-wide basis, so reducing the likelihood of direct action at a particular plant. This situation contrasts markedly with that in the United Kingdom, for example, where most unions are limited to particular plants.

3.4 Capital Investment

The industrial production statistics show that at March 1969 the value of fixed assets employed in motor vehicle assembly was, at historical depreciated cost, land and buildings, $11.1 million, and plant machinery and equipment, $4.6 million, giving a total of $15.7 million.

Because the official statistics are valued at historical depreciated cost they provide no guide to the present worth of fixed assets. They do however suggest, when compared with similarly valued data for other industries, that the car assembly industry is not particularly capital intensive. The value of fixed assets per person employed in motor vehicle assembly was $4,513 at the end of 1968-69, compared with an average value of $4,384 for all manufacturing industries in 1967-68. Overseas studies of small-scale assembly industries, such as those in South Africa[4] and Ireland[5] have commented also on the relatively low capital intensity of assembly. Even the fully integrated automotive industries of the larger industrial countries are not capital intensive relative to manufacturing as a whole. In the United Kingdom for example it was estimated that in 1954 the value of fixed assets, at replacement cost, was the same in the motor, cycle and aircraft industries as the average of all manufacturing industries.[6]

In the course of interviews with the New Zealand companies estimates of the present worth of existing assembly plants were sought. Such estimates were obtained from most companies, on varying bases, including actual cost for recently-completed establishments, recent insurance valuations, and even takeover offers. When related to the capacity of the various plants these displayed a consistent pattern and were used to estimate capital values for those firms from which estimates had not been forthcoming. The estimates relate to assembly establishments only, but, as factory buildings often include the head offices of the company, the coverage is probably wider than that of the industrial production statistics, which ask for "assets used in manufacturing side of your business only." They will not however include distribution systems beyond the main establishment.

On this basis the current capital value of fixed assets in the New Zealand motor assembly industry was estimated to be about $35 million in 1967, which is equivalent to about $8,000 per person employed.

Dependent as it is on supply of c.k.d. packs, the industry has a fairly high level of inventories. There are no official figures for inventories in the motor vehicle assembly industry alone, but for transport manufacturing industries as a whole, 1966-67 inventories averaged $30 million. Most of this comprised raw materials and it is likely that the assembly industry, whose material usage is 48 per cent of the group total, held a similar proportion of inventories.

Taken together with the estimate of the current worth of fixed assets this suggests a total investment of about $50 million in 1967, or between $11,000 and $12,000 per person. This is consistent with the General Motors statement that their new Trentham plant involved investment of $14,730 per person.[7]

As has been noted, balance sheet information is not available for the major units of the industry so that it is not possible to estimate its total worth. This situation contrasts with that in most other countries where balance sheet data for all major units is public information. Under New Zealand law most of the largest units have not been required to publish financial statements either because they are fully owned subsidiaries of overseas companies, or because they are private companies. In the case of the former, publication of accounts is required as from the first of January 1971, in terms of the Companies Amendment Act 1969.

3.5 Motor Vehicle Production

The post-war period has been one of rapid expansion in motor vehicle assembly. Activity resumed in the 1946-47 production year and was soon close to pre-war levels. In 1949-50 employment in the industry passed the peak level of 1937-38. From 1949-50 to 1957-58 the value of motor vehicle assembly output increased fairly evenly at an annual average rate of 16 per cent, or 11 per cent in volume terms.

Production fell sharply during 1958-59 and 1959-60 with the reintroduction of comprehensive import controls, and then increased rapidly, at average annual rates of 15 per cent in value and 14 per cent in volume, until 1965-66. In 1966-67 the value of output rose by only 4 per cent whilst the volume of production fell by 4 per cent. Both value and volume of output fell by 15 per cent in 1967-68. In 1968-69 the value of output fell by 1 per cent whilst volume fell by 7 per cent.

In 1968-69 the New Zealand industry assembled 44,600 cars, 3,000 vans, and 3,000 trucks, along with other vehicles such as buses, tractors, and motor scooters. (Appendix A. Table 3 shows the number of vehicles assembled since the war.)

The value of output in 1968-69 was $86.4 million, the main elements of which are shown in Table 9.

Table 9:

COST OF MOTOR VEHICLE PRODUCTION 1968-69

	Total Cost $m	Parts per 1000
Imported c.k.d. components	53·7	622
Other materials	12·3	142
Other expenses	5·2	61
Salaries and wages	8·3	97
Manufacturing surplus	6·9	79
Value of production	86·4	1,000

Source: Industrial Production Statistics 1968-69. For more detailed analysis on basis of 1967-68 data see Appendix A Table 4.

Table 9 values production at factory door and so excludes value added by subsequent transport, wholesale, and retail operations. As many assembly companies also operate as distributors the above summary presents only a partial view of their operations. Also, because many assembly plants buy from and sell to related companies, the prices for c.k.d. components and the value of production quoted in Table 9 may not be determined "at arm's length" and may well be influenced by wider considerations of company policy. Despite these limitations the data relates directly to the assembly operation with which this study is concerned.

Imported components comprise the major part (622 parts per thousand) of the final cost of a vehicle produced in New Zealand. New Zealand sourced materials and other expenses, apart from wages, account for 203 parts per thousand of the final cost. Salaries and wages and manufacturing surplus (which is equivalent to profit before tax) account for 187 parts per thousand of total cost.

Grouping of the industry into three size groups reveals some significant differences between companies. Table 10, which is based on 1965-66 tabulations specially supplied by the Department of Statistics, divides the industry into three groups of companies; the biggest four, which on the basis of registrations in 1965 and 1966, were probably General Motors, Ford, Todd Motors, and Dominion Motors; the fifth to seventh largest, the composition of this group being uncertain, apart from Austin Distributors and Motor Industries, because companies assembling vehicles other than motor cars may have had higher levels of production than Standard-Triumph, which was shifting location; and finally, the remaining companies.

Table 10:
COST OF MOTOR VEHICLE PRODUCTION 1965-66
FOR THREE GROUPS OF COMPANIES

	The four largest Companies	The 5th to 7th largest Companies	Other Companies
Value of production as percentage of industry total	79	16	5
Value of motor cars assembled as percentage of value of output	80	82	23
Cost of production, parts per 1000			
Imported c.k.d. components	614	645	524
Other materials	143	136	221
Other expenses	36	37	42
Salaries and wages	104	129	97
Manufacturing surplus	103	52	117
Value of production	1,000	1,000	1,000

Source: Tabulations specially supplied by Department of Statistics.

The two largest groups account for 98 per cent of all motor cars assembled and 93 per cent of vans and trucks. Whereas in the larger groups motor car production accounted for 80 per cent of total production, the smallest companies concentrated on truck, van and other assembly operations. Motor cars accounted for only 23 per cent of the output of this latter group. This different composition of output explains the lower usage of c.k.d. components in the smaller establishments, as trucks and other utility vehicles generally use less knocked down body panels, which comprise a major part of the value of motor car c.k.d. packs. (It is also possible that this reflects a statistical anomaly in that truck cabs are not entered as c.k.d. components for tariff purposes. This may be reflected in the statistical returns of truck manufacturers.)

The proportion of the value of production accounted for by manufacturing surplus is noticeably less in the group of 5th to 7th largest companies. This lower level of surplus reflects several factors, the principal amongst which are likely to be the influence of smaller scale upon costs of production, a lower level of investment per person engaged, the presence in the group of the principal assembler of continental cars (c.k.d. packs which are dutiable at higher rates), and, if the group includes Standard-Triumph, as it probably does, profitability would have been affected by that company's transfer of operations. It is also possible that Austin Distributors which was unique in that it was co-operatively owned by regional franchise holders follows a different pricing policy from other companies.

There are a number of differences between the operations of overseas and locally domiciled companies. Table 11 shows that a

Table 11:

MOTOR VEHICLE ASSEMBLY INDUSTRY 1963-64

	Overseas Companies	Local Companies	Total
Cost of production, parts per 1000			
Imported c.k.d. materials	591	665	622
Other materials	131	134	132
Other expenses	31	28	30
Salaries and wages	86	125	103
Manufacturing surplus	161	47	114
Value of production	1000	1000	1000
Value of production $m	48·5	34·8	83·4
%	58	42	100
Employment 000	1·7	2·2	3·9

Source: R. Deane. Overseas Investment in New Zealand.

larger proportion of the value of production arises from wage and salary payments in local companies. This reflects a higher level of employment per unit of output in local companies, and comparison with Table 10 suggests that this difference is concentrated in the middle group of companies on the size classification. It does not appear to result from labour intensive assembly of vehicles other than cars, vans or trucks, in the smaller establishments. This being so the difference is probably attributable to variations in labour productivity related to size of plant.

The value of c.k.d. imports is relatively less important in overseas companies. This is almost certainly related to the higher relative level of manufacturing surplus. It is common practice for affiliates of overseas companies, in any industry subject to import licensing, to write down the value of imports so as to stretch import licence entitlements, and to earn a higher profit in New Zealand, such profit being freely remittable under present policies.

In this context it is significant that General Motors and Ford were the first to opt for the price control formula which bases the New Zealand price for U.K. vehicles upon the overseas retail price, rather than on the actual cost of assembling an imported c.k.d. pack.

The direct import content of motor vehicles assembled in New Zealand has tended to fall in the post-war period. In 1948-49, the first year for which information is available, c.k.d. components represented 754 parts per thousand of the total value of motor

CHART 2. COSTS OF ASSEMBLY

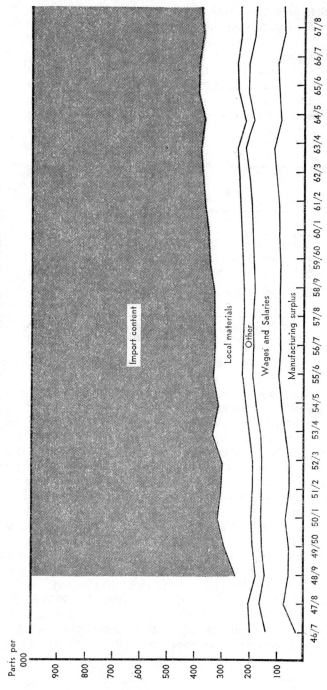

vehicle production, whereas in 1966-67 this proportion had fallen to 615 parts per thousand. (See Chart 2.) A trend line[8] fitted to the data for the period to 1968-69 shows an annual reduction in the proportion of c.k.d. parts to total production of 5·5 parts per thousand. Inspection of Table 12 and Chart 2 show that this decline in direct import content is complemented by increases in most other elements of total cost, particularly by increases in use of local materials and manufacturing surplus. During the post-war period

Table 12:

COST OF MOTOR VEHICLE PRODUCTION

	Three year averages, parts per 1000		
	1948/49 —1950/51	1956/58 —1959/60	1966/67 —1968/69
Imported c.k.d. components	714	669	621
Other materials	100	109	140
Other expenses	34	39	51
Salaries and wages	94	98	102
Manufacturing surplus	58	85	86
Value of Production	1,000	1,000	1,000

Source: Industrial Production Statistics—see Appendix A, Table 3 and Table 6 for details during full post-war period.

the upward trend in usage of local materials has averaged an annual rate of 2·4 parts per thousand. The trend line equations confirm the inference suggested by Table 12 that changes in the use of local materials have been much more rapid in the latter part of the post-war period. During the decade to 1958-59 the trend of usage of local parts was slightly upwards, at an average annual rate of 1·0 parts per 1000 per annum, whilst in the period from 1958-59 to 1968-69 the usage of local materials increased on average by 3·1 parts per 1,000 per annum. This change reflects the drive for local content which shaped the environment of the industry during the last decade.

There has been a marked increase in manufacturing surplus relative to the total value of production. The increase has been uneven. In the years to 1953-54 manufacturing surplus averaged about 60 parts per thousand. It then rose rapidly over a few years and from 1954-55 to 1966-67 averaged more than 90 parts per thousand and reached a peak of 114 parts per thousand in 1963-64. In 1966-67 and 1968-69 it was less than 80 parts per thousand. The increased rate of surplus reflects two major influences. First the volume of production increased markedly during the middle years of the 1950's following the re-introduction of restrictions upon imports of assembled cars. In 1953 the volume of production index stood at 658 (on base 1956-57 = 1000), but by 1955 had increased to 1601. There is a general presumption that increased use of capacity will lower costs and lead to increased profits provided that selling prices can be sustained. Given the starved market conditions typical of the period, and price control, this latter assumption is warranted. Several companies and some officials have suggested that such increased use of capacity is the main cause of the noted increase in surplus. It has not been possible to test this assertion.

It is possible that the increase in surplus during the period arose in part from increased capital intensity. The inadequate nature of the available investment data precludes firm judgment on this but it seems unlikely that this factor has been important.

The increase in manufacturing surplus during the mid-1950's coincided with the introduction of the new price control formula which established New Zealand retail prices for United Kingdom vehicles by reference to overseas retail prices rather than on a cost plus basis. As mentioned earlier, the new formula increased the incentive to stretch import licence entitlements by the setting of low invoice values for c.k.d. packs imported by subsidiaries of overseas companies. It has not been possible to quantify the effects of this on the level of manufacturing surplus.

This latter factor also means that some part of the fall in the relative importance of the c.k.d. pack will have been due to a change in pricing policy. To this extent the reduction in import content suggested by the industrial production statistics as having occurred in the mid-1950's is illusory.

It is usual in discussing import usage in an industry to consider the extent to which the industry indirectly requires imports through its purchases from other industries. Although the motor vehicle assembly industry has since the second world war incorporated many local components, most of these embody imported materials, such as rubber for tyres and metal sheet for mufflers. The 1959-60 inter-industry study provides a basis for assessing the importance of such indirect usage of imports. According to that study direct imports to the motor vehicle industry comprised 614 parts per thousand of total output exclusive of indirect taxes. If account is taken also of indirect usage of imports, then the import usage of the industry is raised from 614 to 655 parts per thousand, i.e. an increase of 6·7 per cent. Considering that the industry's purchases from other sectors comprise 180 parts per thousand of total output, exclusive of indirect tax, there is an implicit import content in bought-in materials and services of about 23 per cent. This is an average figure and will mask a wide variation amongst the sectors supplying the assembly industry.

The motor assembly industry's usage of imports is the highest of any of the 110 industries described in the 1959-60 study. Table 13 lists the nine industries which in 1959-60 had direct and indirect

Table 13:
INDUSTRIES HAVING CUMULATED IMPORT COEFFICIENTS > 0·4 IN 1959-60

Industry	Cumulated Import Coefficients
84 Vehicle assembly	·655
57 Chemical fertilizer	·547
75 Nail making	·527
63 Petroleum and coal products	·434
35 Made-up textiles	·430
74 Wire working	·424
44 Venetian blinds	·424
15 Food preparations n.e.i.	·422
78 Farm machinery	·419
Average all industries	·191

Source: Inter-Industry Study of the New Zealand Economy 1959-60, Part 2, Table 2.2.
(Note: Data has been recalculated to exclude indirect taxes and subsidies.)

import coefficients greater than 400 parts per thousand of total output exclusive of indirect tax. It is rather startling to note that the motor vehicle assembly industry compares with the chemical fertilizer and nail making industries in terms of import usage, and implicitly in the degree of transformation of imported materials. The motor vehicle assembly industry thus remains highly import dependent.

3.6 Productivity

Productivity is the measure of the volume of output per unit of factor input (both labour and capital) and as such provides a suitable basis for comparing economic efficiency both through time and between firms and countries. Measurement of productivity is however difficult because the volume of output is an elusive concept, given a diverse and changing array of products, because it is difficult to combine measures of labour and capital inputs, and because of difficulties in measuring capital inputs. On this last point it has been commented:

44

"There does not seem to be any general solution to this problem. The basic fact is that capital in general has no physical units, and any arbitrary solution will pre-determine the answers."[9]

In the light of this difficulty most productivity studies have concentrated on changes in the volume of output per unit of labour input only which will approximate to a measure of total productivity,

"the more nearly proportional the increases of labor and other resources over time, and the smaller the relative weight of non-labour resources in total input."[10]

It has not proved practicable in this study to build up any time series relating to the level of capital inputs in the industry; indeed as we have noted to establish this measure even at one point of time presents major difficulties. Consequently the estimates presented below relate to changes in output per unit of labour input only.

Table 14:
INDICES OF VOLUME OF PRODUCTION, HOURS WORKED AND PRODUCTIVITY IN THE MOTOR ASSEMBLY INDUSTRY

	Volume of Production	Hours Worked	Productivity	Index of Engine Capacity
1949/50	1000	1000	1000	1000
1950/51	1149	1103	1042	982
1951/52	1334	1197	1114	1044
1952/53	1289	1203	1072	1165
1953/54	1335	1278	1045	1225
1954/55	1744	1595	1093	1243
1955/56	2152	1775	1212	1270
1956/57	2028	1798	1127	1281
1957/58	2172	1955	1111	1296
1958/59	1748	1484	1178	1274
1959/60	1501	1380	1088	1268
1960/61	1941	1682	1154	1313
1961/62	2109	1815	1162	1339
1962/63	2176	1972	1103	1347
1963/64	2935	2414	1216	1371
1964/65	3316	2645	1254	1405
1965/66	3269	2690	1215	1431
1966/67	3129	2612	1198	1457
1967/68	2657	2204	1206	1464
1968/69	2482	1996	1243	1421

Notes: Volume of production is the official index converted to base 1949/50 = 1000.

Hours worked calculated by assuming that each person employed worked 48 weeks of 38 hours and adding to this total overtime hours.

$$\text{Productivity} = \frac{\text{Volume of production}}{\text{Hours worked}} \times 1000$$

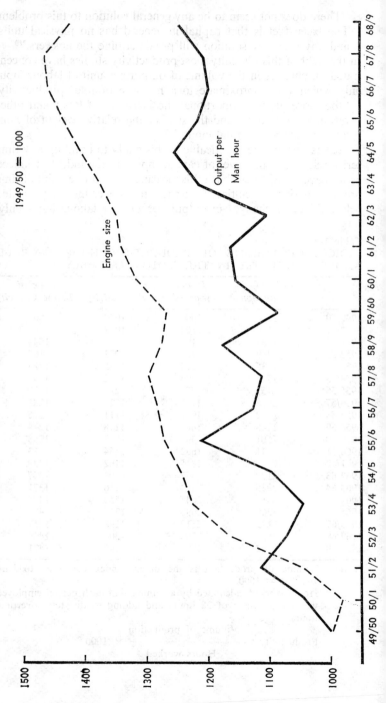

CHART 3. INDICES OF OUTPUT PER MAN HOUR AND OF ENGINE SIZE

1949/50 = 1000

Engine size

Output per Man hour

Moreover they assume that the average quality of labour input has remained constant through the period. It is possible that changes in technique have caused variation in the quality of labour required but any such change is probably small. Given the moderate capital intensity of the industry and the slow change in techniques it is unlikely that the relative importance of capital inputs has changed significantly over time, so that changes in labour productivity will approximate to changes in total productivity.

The industrial production statistics have, since 1949-50, included estimates of the volume of production in the vehicle assembly industry. The official index relies on a simple weighting of the number of vehicles produced and makes no allowance for changes in size or quality.

The same statistics record the average number of persons employed each year and the aggregate number of hours overtime worked. As the industry is one in which overtime working is important, and fluctuating, it is preferable to measure the volume of output against hours worked rather than numbers employed. Table 14 records the official volume of production index, the aggregate number of hours worked, and the derived index of productivity which is also displayed in Chart 3.

The productivity index shows a clear tendency to rise over the period. The series is however very erratic, as could be expected in an industry which experiences marked variations in production, especially as the productivity index takes no account of any lagged relationship between employment and output. A comparison of the average levels of productivity in the three initial and terminal years shows an increase of $15\frac{1}{2}$ per cent which equals an annual rate of 0·9 per cent.

Throughout the post-war period the average size of motor cars has tended to increase and the amount of work required at the assembly point can be expected to have increased on this account. It has however proved impossible to derive an appropriate measure of such change. The only related series which is available is that of average engine capacity, and an index of such changes has been derived from the record of horsepower and c.c. ratings recorded in the statistics of registrations prepared by the New Zealand Retail Motor Trade Association and the New Zealand Motor Trade Federation. The measure shown in Table 26 is approximate both because it is calculated from grouped data, and because the break in registrations from horsepower to c.c. ratings could only be bridged arbitrarily. As can be seen, there has been a very marked increase in average engine capacity over the period (the annual average increase has been 1·9 per cent), but it is not possible to infer from this what changes have been required in assembly effort. Different assemblers had different views as to the relationship between engine size and the labour required for assembly. We can however assume that larger cars will in general require some increase in assembly time, so that the observed increase in engine size suggests that productivity increased faster than measured by the index in Table 14. We cannot however estimate how much faster that increase has been.

4. THE COMPARATIVE COST OF NEW ZEALAND ASSEMBLY

A central element in assessing the economic efficiency of any operation is its comparative cost. If we are considering alternative ways of achieving the same end, and if considerations other than cost are neutral as between the alternatives, then we will choose the cheaper means. In practice the simple comparative cost criterion is difficult to apply because decision makers rarely believe that other things are equal. A higher cost of local assembly might be held to be justified because the industry has encouraged engineering skills or because it has provided employment or for any of a number of reasons. The Tariff and Development Board, for example,[1] has suggested fifteen criteria in addition to that of comparative cost and even those critics of the Board who give prime emphasis to the latter do not discount the others entirely.

Furthermore the term comparative cost is variously defined. For example the 1967 World Bank mission used it to mean "least comparative disadvantage" and thus implied that a comparison of the cost of manufacturing something in New Zealand and overseas was not in itself sufficient. Rather the World Bank report[2] suggested that "if by producing commodity a, the economy can save or earn one unit of foreign exchange at a lower cost of New Zealand dollars than by producing commodity b, then more resources should be drawn into the production of commodity a." Clearly under this criterion a simple comparison of the cost of overseas and local manufacture has no cardinal significance but is useful only in ordering one industrial operation amongst all others, an ordering which will only be possible if similar comparisons exist for all other industries.

There is a further difficulty. For an ideal comparison of economic efficiency between countries we would need to measure prices and profits as determined in freely-supplied and untrammelled markets. In fact this is not possible. The international industry is dominated by a few large producers whose pricing policies can be expected to depart from those that would be established in a market in which no single producer could influence the price at which his product was sold. Furthermore in New Zealand the supply of cars is restricted and prices are officially controlled. In total the oligopolistic nature of the industry (which arises directly from production economies) and the interference of the State means that any price comparison will depart to an unknown extent from the perfectly competitive ideal which in theory is the only one to carry normative significance in measuring economic efficiency.

Despite these limitations a comparison of overseas and local assembly costs is of central interest. Indeed, in the absence of import licensing, comparative costs, including transport costs, could be assumed to determine whether or not particular companies would continue to assemble vehicles in New Zealand, and to incorporate the present degree of local content, given present tariffs.

Historically, and apart from import licensing, the main incentive to assemble in New Zealand did not arise from any comparative manufacturing advantage. Rather a disadvantage on this account was offset by savings in freight costs and later by the effect of tariffs.

4.1 Freight and Duty Costs

The main cause of freight saving is that a c.k.d. vehicle occupies less space than an assembled one, but freight rates themselves also have some influence. C.K.D. packs are usually shipped in sets (practice varies but one company for example usually ships in sets of 24) which allows nesting of parts such as body panels. The resultant space savings are considerable. In one instance the space occupied per car falls from 8 measurement tons assembled to $3\frac{1}{4}$ tons unassembled. For this car the assembled version occupied 2·6 times the space occupied by its c.k.d. pack.[3]

In addition freight rates are cheaper for c.k.d. cars from most sources. This difference reflects the shipping companies' general preference for handling a conveniently boxed cargo (many lines set specifications for approved packs) but is also influenced by the bargaining power exercised by the assembly companies in favour of what is for them a relatively more important cargo. The combined power of the assembly companies, which account for 25 per cent of the cargo carried to New Zealand by the United Kingdom Conference Lines, together with the preparedness of at least one company to threaten independent chartering, has enabled freight increases for c.k.d. vehicles to be held down.[4] From 1956 to 1967 freight rates for c.k.d. cars increased by 47 per cent compared with an 85 per cent increase for general import cargoes.

Freight rates for cars shipped c.k.d. and assembled, from various points, are shown in Table 15 together with estimates of freight per vehicle. At current rates the saving in freight achieved by shipping c.k.d., ranges from about $100 per unit for cars

Table 15:
FREIGHT RATES AND COSTS, JULY 1970 $N.Z.

| | Freight rates per measurement ton | | Cost per Car* | | Difference | |
| | | | | | At current rates | If c.k.d. and assembled rates were equal† |
	c.k.d.	Assembled	c.k.d.	Assembled		
Imports from:						
United Kingdom or Northern Europe	24·55	34·20	83	308	225	137
United States, East Coast	31·02	50·89	105	458	353	174
Japan	13·70	21·52	47	194	147	77
Australia‡	18·20	18·20	62	164	102	102

* Calculated on basis of car occupying 3·4 measurement tons in c.k.d. form and 9·0 measurement tons assembled.
† The c.k.d. rate is assumed to apply to both c.k.d. and assembled vehicles.
‡ Roll-on roll-off Melbourne to Wellington.
  Source: Rates as quoted by the relevant shipping line or conference.

coming from Australia to about $350 for similar cars from the United States. The last column of the table shows that if freight rates for assembled cars were set at the same level as those for c.k.d. packs then the freight saving would generally be less and would vary less between countries. In thinking of the longer term economics of the freight alternatives the last column in the table is probably a better guide to the potential saving. The reason for the generally lower c.k.d. rates per ton reflects the bargaining power of the motor corporations in negotiating the rates for their more important cargo. There is little doubt that those companies would be able to secure more favourable rates for fully built-up cars were these to become a major cargo item.

In this context it is interesting to note that Japanese manufacturers have recently begun to use specially-designed bulk car carriers capable of carrying about 2000 fully-assembled cars. Because these vessels are owned by the companies concerned, there is no public information as to freight costs but it is reasonable to assume that technical developments in this field will lead to reduced costs. If so, the cost advantage of shipping c.k.d. could be reduced.

At current rates, the lowest unit saving is gained on the Australian run. This run is also unusual in that the rates for c.k.d. packs and assembled vehicles are the same (on conventional shipping from Australia, assembled vehicles actually have a small preference) so that freight savings depend solely on stowage factors.

Roll-on roll-off is in its infancy and companies are still experimenting with cargo packaging. Any resulting improvements are more likely to affect c.k.d. rather than assembled vehicles and so increase the freight advantage of the former.

The tariff provides substantial protection additional to that resulting from transport savings. The tariff sets rates of $6\frac{1}{4}$ and 20 per cent British Preferential, and 45 and 55 per cent Most Favoured Nation, for c.k.d. and assembled cars respectively. As can be seen from Table 16, these add significantly to the cost of the fully assembled import relative to a c.k.d. import. In 1968-69 the average current domestic value of c.k.d. packs from all sources was $842. On the basis of data supplied by the assembly companies it is reasonable to assume that the corresponding average value of an assembled vehicle would be $1063 c.d.v. For such a car the British Preferential tariff implies a duty of $53 if unassembled and $213 if fully built up. In other words, the decision to bring the car in built up rather than c.k.d. implies a $160 increase in duty. For cars from Most Favoured Nation sources the increase is much the same, $206, although the total amount of duty is very much greater.

Table 16:

TARIFF COSTS $

| | | Tariff Cost | |
	Average value of vehicle*	British Preferential	Most Favoured Nation
Unassembled cars	842	53	379
Assembled cars	1063	213	585
Increase in Duty	—	160	206

* The $842 is the average 1968-69 trade statistics value for c.k.d. cars. The $1063 is derived on basis of company data shown in Table 17.

$$\frac{\text{c.d.v. overseas assembled}}{\text{c.d.v. N.Z. assembled}} \times \text{average trade statistics value}$$

i.e. $\dfrac{660}{523} \times 842 = 1063$

4.2 A Comparison of Costs

In practice duty and higher transport costs fully offset additional costs incurred by assembly in New Zealand, as is shown by the information displayed in Table 17. The first two columns of this table are derived from information supplied by the Price Control Division of the Department of Industries and Commerce and refer to averages struck over three cars of comparable size whilst the

Table 17:
COMPARATIVE COST OF NEW ZEALAND AND OVERSEAS
ASSEMBLED CARS OF SAME MODEL
Costs as parts per 000 of wholesale price of New Zealand assembled car.

	Price Control Data Averages of 3:		Company Data Average of 12 examples from 7 companies
	Large Australian Cars	Small English Cars	
NEW ZEALAND ASSEMBLED			
CDV value	—	—	523
Freight etc. to New Zealand	—	—	50
CIFE value	600	587	573
Duty	32	28	41
Cost of landing	7	8	9
Assembly and component costs	289	306	296
Manufacturing and wholesale margin	72	71	81
Wholesale price	1,000	1,000	1,000
OVERSEAS ASSEMBLED			
CDV value	—	—	660
Freight etc. to New Zealand	—	—	160
CIFE value	790	844	820
Duty	134	141	154
Cost of landing	13	23	22
Local costs	—	—	2
Wholesale margin	121	83	86
Wholesale price	1,058	1,091	1,084

Sources: As stated in text.

NOTE: 1. The information supplied by the Price Control Division was based on October 1967, i.e. pre-devaluation costings. In deriving the above figures a simple devaluation adjustment to CIFE values was made, all other elements being held to the same level. In fact other costs will have changed and in particular in the period since devaluation a lower percentage margin has been allowed.
2. Two companies did not supply information on margins and in four of the examples the C.I.F.E. cost could not be divided into C.D.V. and freight costs. In these instances I have made my own estimates in the light of the other examples supplied to me.

third column is derived from information supplied by individual companies. In each case the wholesale price of the overseas assembled car is higher than that of the locally assembled car. This is also so for each of the twelve examples consolidated in column 3 although those examples are diverse with wholesale prices for overseas assembled cars ranging from less than 1 to almost 20 per cent above those of the same cars assembled locally.

This being so it is probable that with existing tariffs and costs most companies would find local assembly more profitable than overseas assembly and would continue to assemble in New Zealand even in the absence of import licensing. Three major qualifications must be made however.

First, the assembly and wholesale margins quoted reflect not only cost and demand factors, but also price control and import licensing. The latter, by limiting the supply of cars, creates a sellers' market and government controls prices in an attempt to prevent exploitation of this. The margin is thus effectively limited by price control variation in control formulae (these are discussed in section 5.3), and changing costs have led to a position where the margin is higher on overseas than on locally assembled cars. It is unlikely that this would persist in the absence of import licensing because in a full supply situation the market premium on an overseas assembled car is likely to be less than that permitted by the price control formulae. Further, inasmuch as margins can be looked on as a factory return or as a return on investment, the higher level of investment and activity required by local assembly suggests that a company considering local assembly would seek a higher margin than one considering importation of fully built up units. The margins shown in Table 17 are thus arbitrary, and it is likely that in an uncontrolled situation the wholesale price comparison would be less favourable to local assembly.

Secondly, the costs shown in Table 17 are those incurred at a particular degree of local content. Although the lower wholesale price for a locally assembled car suggests, even allowing for the preceding qualification, that it is profitable to assemble in New Zealand rather than overseas, the likelihood that marginal costs rise as local content increases means that a company might well opt for a lower degree of local content in the absence of the incentive provided by import licensing.

Thirdly, the observation that the motor companies would find local assembly preferable to importing assembled cars in the absence of import licensing needs to be qualified in respect of the period immediately following any relaxation of control. At such a time there would be a very strong incentive, as in the early 1950s, for companies to temporarily augment supply from their assembly plants with fully built up imports. Such importation would not, however, be in substitution for local assembly but would reflect the difficulty of gearing up production to cope with what was likely to be a short term surge in sales.

It is clear that the tariff is critical in the decision whether or not to assemble in New Zealand. Table 18, which compares the cost exclusive of duty, of overseas and local assembly, shows that in general it is more expensive to assemble locally than to import fully assembled cars. This is not, however, the case for three of the twelve company examples.

Table 18:
COMPARATIVE COST, EXCLUSIVE OF DUTY, OF NEW ZEALAND
AND OVERSEAS ASSEMBLED CARS OF SAME MODEL
Units as in table 17, i.e. wholesale price of New Zealand
assembled cars, inclusive of duty = 1000

| | Price Control Data Averages of 3: | | Company Data Average of 12 examples from 7 companies |
	Large Australian Cars	Small English Cars	
New Zealand assembled	968	972	959
Overseas assembled	924	950	930
Ratio $\dfrac{\text{N.Z. assembled}}{\text{overseas assembled}}$	1·05	1·02	1·03

For most cars local assembly would, in the absence of duty, be more expensive than importing fully built up cars and this taken together with the qualifications stated earlier, that the allowed margin on fully assembled imports seems disproportionately high in relation to that on c.k.d. vehicles and the presumption that marginal costs will increase with increasing local content, suggests that in the absence of protection many companies would prefer overseas to local assembly. Further, those companies that continued to assemble locally would want to reduce local content.

As noted earlier the recent World Bank Mission suggested that in assessing an import substituting industry's contribution to the economy it is relevant to compare the foreign exchange saved with the domestic costs incurred in saving it, and to compare this with the performance of other industries.[5] This suggestion relates to the distinction, commonly drawn by economists, between nominal and effective tariff rates.[6] Briefly this is that the nominal rate of a tariff will confer a higher effective rate of protection on the local manufacturing operation, unless the same or a higher rate of duty is imposed on imported materials. For example, suppose that a local manufacturer is importing materials worth $600 and adding New Zealand value of $500, giving a final product value of $1,100. Suppose also that the commodity can be imported at $1,000 and that a 10 per cent tariff is imposed to equalize the prices of the imported and locally produced commodities. In this example the nominal tariff is 10 per cent, but effectively it permits the manufacturer to add domestic value of $500 rather than $400, which would be the competitive maximum in the absence of a tariff. The effective rate of tariff is seen to be $\frac{500-400}{400}$, i.e., 25 per cent. The concept of the domestic cost of saving a dollar of overseas exchange is directly related. In the example a domestic cost of $500 is incurred in saving $400 overseas exchange (i.e. $1,000, the import cost of the finished produce, less $600 the import cost of materials for local manufacture), so that the domestic cost per dollar saved is $\frac{500}{400} = \$1.25$.

The concept is difficult to apply in practice because it does not conform closely to costs as normally measured by a manufacturer. For example, the World Bank Mission in its formulation suggests that the import saving should be measured net of the firm's domestic purchases of tradeable commodities and depreciation, both measured at import values. The data presented in Table 17 does, however, enable an approximation of exchange saved. This is presented in Table 19.

This shows the implicit cost of saving a dollar of overseas exchange as ranging from $1.23 in the Australian case to $1.09 in respect of cars from the United Kingdom. The mean value for

Table 19:

THE DOMESTIC COST OF SAVING OVERSEAS EXCHANGE

| | Price Control Data | | Company Data |
	Large Australian Cars	Small English Cars	Average of 12 examples from 7 companies
CIFE IMPORT COST			
Overseas assembled	790	844	820
New Zealand assembled	600	587	573
Saving in Exchange	190	257	247
DOMESTIC COSTS			
(Exclusive of duty)*			
New Zealand assembled	368	385	386
Overseas assembled	134	106	110
Additional New Zealand cost	234	279	276
Cost in N.Z. $ of saving			
$1 overseas exchange	1·23	1·09	1·12

* Domestic costs include cost of landing, assembly and other local costs, and margins.

the twelve company examples, most of which relate to the United Kingdom, is $1.12 (the range being $0.81—$2.38, see table 23). The higher ratio for Australia results from the smaller saving of exchange. In turn this reflects the lesser freight saving achieved in shipping c.k.d. packs from Australia. The table is limited to the data presented in Table 17, and so falls short of the desired measure, and this for three main reasons.

First, the saving in exchange takes no account of the import content of locally purchased materials, which have been included in the item assembly and component costs. This latter item also includes duties imposed on such indirect imports together with other indirect taxes entering into the cost of locally purchased materials. These factors mean that both the saving in exchange, and the local resource cost of achieving it are overstated. It would be appropriate to make some allowance for this. The 1959-60 inter-industry study suggests that indirect imports and indirect taxes comprise about 19 per cent and 6 per cent respectively of intermediate purchases.

Secondly, the estimate in Table 19 is less than ideal in its treatment of depreciation which in its economic sense is the measure of capital used up in production (and also of provision for its replacement). Two issues arise. First, it is likely that the depreciation included in our estimate is understated. As we have seen, the book value of capital assets as recorded seems to be well out of line with actual values ($15 million as compared with about $35 million in 1967-68) and depreciation can be expected to be similarly affected. In 1965-66 depreciation by the assembly industry was equal to 0·6 per cent of the factory door value of production. By 1967-68 this had risen sharply to 1·5 per cent, reflecting recent heavy investment, particularly that by General Motors. Because of the likelihood of high rates of initial depreciation it is probable that the 1967-68 official figure for depreciation is understated by less than is the capital value of assets. In this situation we could think of full economic depreciation as being equal to about 2·5 per cent of the value of production.

The second issue connected with depreciation is analogous to that of local purchases of materials. Capital goods used up in production will either have been produced by domestic factors of production, or imported. To the extent that they are imported they should be excluded from our measure of the New Zealand cost of production and also from the saving in imports. In 1959-60 imports accounted for a little less than one third of the direct and indirect cost of capital goods used in motor vehicle assembly.[7]

This figure is unlikely to have changed significantly during the following decade.

Thirdly and most importantly, the profit margins included in the domestic costs of overseas and locally assembled vehicles are incongruous. We have noted that the price control formula allows similar margins on both locally and overseas assembled cars but that, with the exception of sub-contracted assembly work, there is no allowance for a manufacturer's margin on local assembly. The two margins set in Table 17 and included in Table 19 are, in the economic sense at least, arbitrary. The direction of the adjustment required is clear, although its extent is not. A reasonable adjustment can, however, be made by distinguishing between the manufacturer's and the wholesaler's margin. There is no reason for assuming any significant difference between wholesale margins on overseas and locally assembled cars. If we assume that these are the same then our estimate of the additional domestic costs of local assembly will be unaffected by the rate of wholesale margin. This element can thus be ignored. Some manufacturing margin must be assumed; perhaps the most appropriate procedure would be to include a margin of 10 per cent on domestic assembly costs, as if the price control sub-contracted assembly margin applied to all assembly work.

In summary these qualifications suggest three adjustments to the data presented earlier.
1. Some allowance for the import and indirect tax content of materials, components, and services purchased by the motor assembly industry.
2. A separate estimate of depreciation, greater than is presently included in local assembly costs, the import content of which should be deducted from the calculated import saving, and the domestic content of which should be included in New Zealand value added.
3. A separate estimate of a manufacturing margin on all local assembly costs and no estimate of wholesalers' margin. This means in effect estimating the factory door rather than ex-wholesale price of the vehicle.

In total these adjustments have a significant effect on some of the relationships noted in the preceding tables. Table 20 shows in detail the effect of incorporating these assumptions for the average values derived from the twelve sets of company data, and Table 21 summarises the results of such analysis for all examples.

In each case the modified data suggests a less favourable performance by the New Zealand industry. Whereas the original ratio of costs of New Zealand to overseas assembly was in all but

Table 20:
MODIFIED COMPARATIVE COST DATA—AVERAGE FOR TWELVE EXAMPLES FROM SEVEN COMPANIES
Costs as parts per 000 of unmodified wholesale price of New Zealand assembled car.

	Original Data Table 17 Column 3	Adjustments to Data Indirect Imports* and Indirect Taxes	Depreciation†	Adjusted Data
NEW ZEALAND ASSEMBLED				
CIFE value	573	36	8	617
Duty	41	11		52
Cost of landing	9			9
Assembly and component costs	296	—47	(—15 +17)	251
Margin	81			30‡
Price ex-factory	1,000			959
OVERSEAS ASSEMBLED				
CIFE value	820			820
Duty	154			154
Cost of landing	22			22
Local costs	2			2
Margin	86			—‡
Price ex-wharf	1,084			998
RATIO OF WHOLESALE PRICES				
N.Z. assembled to Overseas assembled				
a. including duty	0·92			0·96
b. excluding duty	1·03			1·07
IMPORT COST				
Overseas assembled	820			820
New Zealand assembled	573			617
Saving in exchange	247			203
DOMESTIC COSTS (excluding duty)				
New Zealand assembled	386			290
Overseas assembled	110			24
Additional New Zealand cost	276			266
Cost in N.Z. $ of saving $1 overseas exchange	1·12			1·31

* Calculated as 19 and 6 per cent respectively of assembly and component costs less assumed wage and salary payments. Following the 1959-60 inter-industry study, wage and salary payments were assumed to equal

109 parts per 1000 of total inputs, inclusive of duty but exclusive of
sales tax. In this case (296—109) (0·19) = 36 and (296—109) (0·06) = 11.
† The effect of the adjustment is to substitute depreciation of 25 units
(8 import content, 17 domestic content) for the 15 units total as
measured in industrial production statistics in 1967-68.
‡ Manufacturing margin assumed to be 10 per cent of assembly and
component costs—wholesale margin ignored.

one case less than, and in one case equal to, 1·0, the adjusted
data shows three company examples, and the price control data
for Australian cars, as having a higher cost if assembled in New
Zealand. Implicitly continued assembly of these models would be
uncertain even with the considerable incentive provided by the
tariff.

The ratio of costs exclusive of duty is similarly affected and
in all but three cases assembly in New Zealand would be more
expensive than overseas.

The most spectacular changes occur in the cost of saving a
dollar of overseas exchange. In general, the estimated exchange
saving is reduced considerably and the estimate of the domestic
cost of saving that exchange is reduced only slightly. The ratio
estimates consequently increase, particularly in cases where the
exchange saving was already relatively small.

These results have been examined in the light of what is
known about other variables. There appears to be no significant
general relationship between them and the annual level of production or the level of import content, although in some particular
cases, including notably the extreme D3*, such factors explain
the very unfavourable result. There is, however, some variation
with respect to source. One of the higher ratios relates to an
Australian vehicle and in conjunction with the price control data
on Australian cars, suggests a higher cost of saving exchange than
in the case of cars sourced in the United Kingdom. The major
reason for this will be the difference in freight costs. As noted
in Table 15, the freight saving realised by shipping c.k.d. rather
than assembled vehicles is about $123 greater on imports from the
United Kingdom than from Australia. It is also quite possible
that the estimates supplied reflect undervaluation of imports. This
practice is, as we have noted, evident in the lower declared c.i.f.
than c.d.v. value of imports both c.k.d. and assembled, and results
primarily from the phenomenon of import licensing stretch. This
pattern would of course change in the absence of import licensing
but it is not possible to assess its importance.

* This example relates to a very small production run with special
problems, and the assembly operation is not typical.

Table 21:
COST RATIOS NEW ZEALAND AND OVERSEAS ASSEMBLED VEHICLES

| | N.Z. assembled / Overseas assembled | | | | Cost in N.Z. $ of saving $1 of overseas exchange | |
| | Including Duty | | Excluding Duty | | | |
Ratio of costs	Unadj.	Adj.	Unadj.	Adj.	Unadj.	Adj.
Price control data						
Large Australian	0·95	1·03	1·05	1·15	1·23	1·83
Small English	0·92	0·96	1·02	1·07	1·09	1·30
Average of 12 examples supplied by 7 companies*	0·92	0·96	1·03	1·07	1·12	1·31
Individual company examples†						
D1	0·84	0·87	0·93	0·96	0·81	0·89
D2	0·85	0·87	0·96	0·97	0·87	0·90
C1	0·86	0·89	0·96	0·99	0·87	0·95
F1	0·91	0·95	1·03	1·06	1·08	1·25
B	0·93	0·96	1·04	1·08	1·11	1·25
F2	0·94	0·98	1·05	1·09	1·21	1·42
F3	0·95	0·98	1·05	1·09	1·25	1·49
A	0·95	1·02	1·06	1·14	1·22	1·51
G	0·95	0·98	1·04	1·10	1·23	1·55
E	0·96	1·02	1·08	1·16	1·34	1·79
C2	0·97	1·00	1·11	1·16	1·59	1·95
D3	1·00	1·04	1·11	1·17	2·38	3·75

* Average company ratios were derived from consolidated company data and not as simple average of individual company ratios.
† Company codes were allocated according to date of receipt and so are irrelative to any company characteristics.

From the information available it is not sensible to attempt further explanation of the wide differences between the examples quoted. Obviously they reflect many influences. In any consideration of the industry it is necessary to bear in mind the diversity which underlies the industry average. It is also necessary to remember the limitations of the data on which Table 21 is based and the arbitrary nature of the adjustments made. The estimates are no more than approximate. Because of this, the individual company estimates are not discussed further, attention being confined to the three sets of average data.

The estimates presented in Tables 17 to 21 contrast markedly with those made by the 1967 World Bank Mission to New Zealand, which commented in paragraph 78 of its report:

"A vehicle which would cost NZ$2,000 c.i.f. may cost about NZ$3,200 when produced domestically. The 60 per cent is, however, only the nominal excess cost. At domestic content of

40 per cent, the *net* savings of imports are about NZ$800. If it costs NZ$2,000 in domestic resources to save NZ$800 worth of imports, the ratio of domestic to international costs in vehicle production is about 250 per cent on a net basis."

As we have seen, on the basis of our adjusted cost figures, derived from company data, the cost, exclusive of duty, of a domestically produced car averages 7 per cent above that of an overseas produced car, rather than 60 per cent as implied by the World Bank, and the ratio of domestic resource cost to import saving is on average 1·31 : 1 rather than 2·50 : 1 as implied by the World Bank. The conflict between these two sets of estimates is discussed more fully in Section 6.4.

Our original data in Table 17 contains estimates of the current domestic value (i.e. value in country of origin) of c.k.d. packs and of completed cars. Implicitly the difference between these, measures the cost incurred by the overseas company in assembly and in purchase or manufacture of parts which are not included in the c.k.d. packs, less any special costs associated with preparation of c.k.d. packs. The same sets of data show the assembly and component costs incurred in New Zealand assembly. This information is restated and compared in Table 22.

The results are striking and suggest that New Zealand direct manufacturing costs are more than twice as high as those in the country of origin of the motor vehicle. Moreover, as we have noted, local assembly costs include no profit margin, inclusion of which would raise the ratios significantly. Against this there are a number of problems raised by the pricing of c.k.d. packs and assembled vehicles, and the problem of additional costs incurred in preparing c.k.d. packs, consideration of which will have to be delayed until later in this report.

Table 22:
COST OF ASSEMBLY AND OF COMPONENTS SOURCED IN
NEW ZEALAND FOR LOCALLY ASSEMBLED CARS

	Average of 12 examples from 7 companies
Costs associated with overseas assembly:	
c.d.v. value of fully assembled car	660
c.d.v. value of c.k.d. pack	523
Cost of overseas assembly and components less	
extra costs incurred in preparing c.k.d. packs	137
Cost of New Zealand assembly and components	296
Ratio of New Zealand to overseas costs	2·16

Source: Table 17 above.

In total, however, these would not appear sufficient to negate the implication that the manufacturing cost of the New Zealand operation is significantly higher than that of the same operation when carried out by the overseas supplier industry.

It thus seems that the small difference between the wholesale selling prices of overseas and locally assembled cars conceals marked divergence in duty, transport costs, and assembly and manufacturing costs. This can be seen from Table 23.

Table 23:
SUMMARY COMPARISON OF COST OF OVERSEAS AND LOCALLY ASSEMBLED VEHICLES

| | Original data | | | Adjusted data | | |
	Overseas assembled	N.Z. assembled	Differ- ence	Overseas assembled	N.Z. assembled	Differ- ence
Manufacturing costs*	662	819	157	662	844	182
Freight and handling	182	59	—123	182	63	—119
Wholesale margin	86	81	— 5	—	—	—
Sub-total:	930	959	29	844	907	63
Duty	154	41	—113	154	52	—102
Total:	1084	1000	— 84	998	959	— 39

* Manufacturing costs comprise c.d.v. value of pack or assembled vehicle, local assembly and component parts, depreciation, manufacturing margin.

Source: Derived from average company data.

Inevitably the figures presented in Table 23 and preceding tables are approximate and are subject to limitations, some of which are discussed subsequently. Nevertheless, the results presented in Table 23 carry three important implications:—

1. The level of total costs, exclusive of duty, suggests that in national economic terms the industry's performance is better than many of its critics might suppose.
2. The cost comparison suggests that the existing tariff structure provides sufficient incentive to local assembly.
3. The comparison of manufacturing costs alone suggests that the marginal cost of incorporating local content is likely to be high.

Import licensing, the tariff and other measures currently in use provide a pattern of protection which varies between industries. In assessing the economic worth of any one industry it is of interest to compare the cost of saving exchange in it with that in others. As we have seen, it has not been easy to measure this cost in motor car assembly, and similar difficulties would no doubt be encountered elsewhere. For this reason comparisons of the cost of New Zealand and overseas produced goods are rare, but there are three relevant studies. Hampton has compared the factory door and import prices of comparable items produced in New Zealand and overseas, using evidence submitted at Tariff and Development Board inquiries. Candler and Hampton have made a similar comparison of prices for tradeable items represented in the regimen of the consumers' price index, on information from New Zealand and overseas suppliers. The empirical evidence in both studies is limited to estimation of the nominal tariff that would be necessary to equalise prices, but the analysis is extended on various assumptions to yield an estimate of the effective rate of protection. More recently, Elkan has estimated the effective rate of protection enjoyed by the main manufacturing industries in 1964-67. His estimates will be published in a forthcoming Institute research paper.

Unfortunately all these comparisons relate to the period prior to the 1967 devaluation. It is not possible to make any simple adjustment for this. The accompanying British devaluation meant that the change in New Zealand exchange rates varied between countries, so that different commodities will have been affected differently. Furthermore, variations in import content between the goods or industries concerned will have influenced the effect of devaluation upon the level of effective protection. So also will variations in the existing tariff structure. In neither case do we know how important this influence will have been. All that can be said is that devaluation will have reduced the nominal levels of protection required, by something like the $17\frac{1}{2}$ per cent average change in exchange rates (relative to our major trading partners). The effective rate of protection will usually have been reduced by a greater amount.

The three sets of estimates are presented in Table 24 along with those developed in this chapter. Of the three, Elkan's forthcoming set is by far the most comprehensive and detailed yet attempted and while the statistical problems of applying a uniform method over a vast array of data mean that any one of his single estimates may be in error, his overall average figures may be assumed to be fairly reliable. It, and the estimates advanced by earlier researchers, suggest that the typical average level of effective protection required by New Zealand industry in the years prior to devaluation was well above the 31 per cent average for local motor car assembly derived earlier in this chapter. Adjustment to allow for devaluation would reduce the difference but would not eliminate it. We may thus conclude that compared with other manufacturing industries, the economic performance of the New Zealand motor car assembly and component industries is relatively good.

Table 24:
LEVELS OF PROTECTION IN MANUFACTURING INDUSTRY

	Nominal Level of Protection %	Effective Level of Protection %
PRE-DEVALUATION DATA		
Hampton		
Infants' wear—group 1	64	123
Infants' wear—group 2	96	280
Infants' wear—group 3	56	98
Yarn samples	33	not calculated
Fabric samples	29	,,
Crockery (earthenware)	30	,,
Candler/Hampton		
38 items from C.P.I. regimen (weighted)	59	163
Elkan		
All manufacturing industries	47	73
Vehicle assembly	25	102 ⎱
Other transport products	35	33 ⎰ 44*
POST DEVALUATION		
Motor cars (adjusted estimates)		
3 large Australian cars	15	83
3 small English cars	7	30
Company data—average of 12 examples	7	31

* See note (8)

Source: Hampton (1965), pages 6 and 17. Candler/Hampton (1966), page 54. Elkan (forthcoming publication). Motor cars, Table 21, above.

5. POLICY INSTRUMENTS AFFECTING THE MOTOR INDUSTRY

The motor assembly industry, like any other, operates in a commercial environment substantially modified by government intervention designed to change the shape of the industry consistently with public policy. The following sections describe the form and effect of the major policy instruments. At present these are the customs tariff and determinations, import licensing, price control, and most recently, arrangements made under the New Zealand-Australia Free Trade Agreement.

5.1 The Tariff

Since 1907 the New Zealand tariff has provided explicit protection for the local body-building and assembly industries. Except for the period 1915-1921 the tariff has differentiated the body and chassis of motor cars and more recently unassembled and assembled cars. The various tariffs have been described in Chapter 2 and appear in Appendix 2. The current tariff is a modified version of that introduced by Coates in 1934 and has two main features. It provides a lesser tariff for unassembled vehicles, and it gives the Minister of Customs power to define such vehicles. Vehicles conforming to the Ministerial definition of unassembled cars are admitted at concessional rates whereas those which do

Table 25:

TARIFFS ON MOTOR CARS 1970
Per Cent

	Assembled	Unassembled in accordance with determination of Minister of Customs
British Preferential	20	$6\frac{1}{4}$
Most Favoured Nation	55	45
General	75	65
Canada, where final work is done in Canada, and where Canadian and Commonwealth content is		
not less than 75%	$33\frac{1}{3}$	$13\frac{3}{4}$
less than 75% but not less than 65%	55	$16\frac{2}{3}$
less than 65%	55	45

Source: Customs Tariff of New Zealand, Chapter 87.

not pay a higher rate of duty. Imposed on top of this pattern is the general preferential system.

The present tariff rates are shown in Table 25. In practice only the first two lines are important. In 1968-69, for example, 89 per cent by value of unassembled, and 73 per cent of assembled cars, were sourced from British Preferential countries, and 11 per cent of unassembled, and 27 per cent of assembled, from Most Favoured Nation countries. Imports from Canada were negligible, and there were no imports that would have been dutiable at general tariff rates.

As was seen in the previous chapter the level of protection effectively provided by a tariff on a product depends also on the tariff levied on imported materials used in its manufacture and on the level of domestic content. Because domestic content is relatively low and because the tariff on the assembled car is greater than that on the c.k.d. pack the effective level of protection offered to the motor car assembler is much higher, particularly at low levels of content, than the 20 per cent British Preferential rate might at first sight seem to imply. Table 26 sets out a schedule of the levels of effective protection implicit in the tariff. The levels shown are the maximum that can be gained under the tariff and assume that the output of the domestic industry is priced up to the full extent permitted by it. As the previous chapter has shown this is not the case in practice. The Most Favoured Nation Tariff generally offers higher levels of effective protection than does the British Preferential Tariff, although this is not so at very low levels of domestic content. It will be noted that whereas the effective protection offered by the Most Favoured Nation Tariff falls slowly over the range shown, that offered by the British Preferential Tariff falls rapidly. This reflects the large difference between the rates of duty on c.k.d. packs. These duties are the main factor determining the marginal rate of protection accorded by the tariff to local component manufacture. In the case of the British Preferential Tariff this is very low so that the average level of protection accorded to the whole operation falls rapidly as domestic content increases.

In summary the British Preferential Tariff offers a very high level of protection to assembly (as defined in the tariff) but offers very little incentive for additional use of New Zealand components. The Most Favoured Nation Tariff offers more uniform protection to all stages of manufacture.

To benefit from the lower rate of duty c.k.d. packs must conform with determinations made by the Minister of Customs. The first, made in August 1935 by J. G. Coates, defined a c.k.d. car as one in which the chassis frame could be assembled and the engine and gear box, but no other parts, attached. Other elements, such as the scuttle and windscreen assembly, and the body shell, could be assembled and primed, and upholstery materials could be cut to shape but not sewn. There was at this stage no restriction on the components which could be included; the whole purpose of the determination being to limit the degree of assembly.

Table 26:

EFFECTIVE PROTECTION PROVIDED BY THE TARIFF

	Average Level of Effective Protection	
Domestic Content	British Preferential	Most Favoured Nation
per cent	per cent	per cent
20	98	67
30	53	57
40	37	52
50	29	49
60	25	47
70	21	46

NOTES: Domestic content is measured as the percentage of New Zealand added value (exclusive of duty) to the New Zealand wholesale price (exclusive of duty). It is assumed that the local product is priced up to the full extent permitted by the tariff.

Duties are imposed on the c.d.v. rather than the c.i.f. value of imports. In the above table it is assumed on the basis of the earlier company examples that for assembled cars the c.d.v./c.i.f. ratio is 0·8 and that for unassembled cars it is 0·9.

A description of the underlying formulae appears in Appendix C.

A new determination was made by W. Nash in April 1939. This reduced the permitted degree of assembly by excluding soldering, filling, and trimming of welded panels, by requiring body shells to be unpainted, and bumper bars to be imported as rough stampings (this last requirement was never enforced). More importantly the new determinations stated that some materials and components could no longer be imported as part of a c.k.d. pack.

These first exclusions comprised: electric batteries, hide leathers, upholstery textiles, and flock and other kinds of upholsterer's padding. Over the years the items listed in Table 30 have been excluded from the tariff definition of a c.k.d. pack.

Because the determinations are concerned to demarcate precisely what may and may not be done they are detailed documents, often phrased negatively, and all in all complex and hard to follow. A brief positive statement of the purport of the determinations to date appears in Table 28. Basically the current definition of a c.k.d. motor vehicle stems from the 1930's and the terminology is

Table 27:
ITEMS EXCLUDED BY CUSTOMS DETERMINATIONS FROM DEFINITION OF C.K.D. PACKS FOR MOTOR CARS

Year	Items excluded
April 1939	Electric batteries
	Hide leathers
	Upholstery textiles
	Flock and other kinds of upholsterer's padding
October 1948	Pneumatic rubber tyres and tubes
April 1949	Wireless sets for use in motor vehicles
June 1958	Radiator assemblies
July 1958	Laminated undercarriage springs
June 1964	Exterior rear-vision mirrors

Source: N.Z. Gazette, various dates. A full reference is printed in Tariff circular No. 1964/30.

anachronistic. Today's cars are constructed from welded panels and for most models, terms such as chassis and windshield assemblies have no direct reference.

In practice the definition of a c.k.d. pack is not that specified in the determination, although that provides the legal sanction, but is that agreed between the importer and the Customs Department examiner policing c.k.d. packs. When a new model is introduced the first shipment will be inspected in detail and, after negotiation of any contentious points, instructions will be issued

Table 28:
TARIFF DEFINITION OF A C.K.D. MOTOR CAR

The motor car is defined as a passenger motor vehicle other than an omnibus and *is seen as comprising*
1. Chassis
    a. members, brackets, engine and gear box.
    b. scuttle and windshield assemblies, undercarriage springs.
2. Body
    a. metal panels and framework.
    b. seat springs.
    These can be imported in the following condition:
1a. frame can be assembled and engine and gear box attached.
1b. windscreen assembly can be fully assembled but not fitted to the frame.
2a. body may be built up to a shell and doors attached; a protective coating may be applied; the seams shall not be soldered, filled or smoothed.
2b. seat springs may be built up and assembled in the frame.
    The items specified in Table 27 cannot be included in the c.k.d. pack, neither can they, if imported separately, be used in vehicle assembly.

Source: Based on Customs determinations as presented in tariff circular 1964/30 and information from Customs Department on customary dispensations.

for changes to be made in future shipments. So far as items excluded from the pack by determination are concerned the determination provides for some exercise of discretionary powers. In practice, these will be exercised only in instances where the local supplier is not prepared to supply or where the cost of the locally-supplied component is thought to be "totally uneconomic".

The exclusion of a particular item by Customs determination is an extraordinarily strong weapon. For example, placing a strict interpretation on the law, the effect of importing a radiator would be to transform the pack from a c.k.d. to an assembled vehicle with a consequent increase in duty from $6\frac{1}{2}$ to 20 per cent British Preferential. Thus including a radiator, which might cost $10-20 in a c.k.d. pack costing $1200 could render the pack liable to duty amounting to $240 instead of the normal $75. Such an increase resulting solely from the inclusion of a radiator could be said to represent a nominal tariff of the order of 1000 per cent.

In actual practice, where such determined goods have been imported in c.k.d. packs, the Customs Department has readily granted dispensations for individual shipments, both in respect of new models and in the case of genuine packing errors on the part of the exporter. Should deliberate infringement of the determinations be suspected, the department would probably do no more than charge the higher duty on the value of the offending components, a stricter application of the law being likely only if such infringements recurred.

Nevertheless, the degree of "overkill' inherent in the Customs determination procedure is strong enough to restrict its use. In practice the number of exclusions has been small and no doubt the Customs Department is reluctant to recommend new exclusions unless it is satisfied that all assemblers will be able to source locally at reasonably comparable prices. Other items have been proposed for exclusion, usually by an interested component manufacturer, but it appears that lack of general acceptance by assemblers has so far prevented the making of further general exclusions. The mechanism appears too overwhelming for greatly extended operation.

Items other than those excluded by c.k.d. determinations may be imported separately from c.k.d. packs, and if so are dutiable at the rate for the particular material or component. (Tariff rates for selected materials and components are shown in Appendix B.) In general the tariff provides little incentive to separate importation which is thought to be rare. Any tariff gain would have to be weighed against the considerable cost of separating the component out from the c.k.d. pack and freighting it separately.

Items such as springs which are protected by the c.k.d. determinations are also usually subject to a moderate, 20-30 per cent British Preferential nominal tariff if imported separately. The determination decrees that such separate imports cannot be used in assembly and the tariff protects the domestic producer in the replacement market and in any manufacturing operations not covered by the c.k.d. determinations.

The tariff on c.k.d. components from British Preferential sources provides little incentive to domestic production of components. A local manufacturer incorporating 70 per cent New Zealand content in a component would, assuming that his imports were duty-free, gain effective protection of only 9 per cent from the British Preferential tariff. This is a maximum and the rate of effective protection could well be zero or even negative in some cases. In contrast the Most Favoured Nation tariff, by imposing a 45 per cent tariff on c.k.d. packs, provides a considerable incentive to the use of local components. For a component with 70 per cent New Zealand content, and duty-free materials, the effective rate of protection would be 64 per cent. This difference has induced a rather higher local content in the case of M.F.N. sourced vehicles.

The differential British Preferential and Most Favoured Nation tariff rates are intended to favour Commonwealth manufacture and the present margin of preference has existed, with some minor variations, since 1934. Historically the tariff led to a dramatic diversion of trade from the United States to Britain. The present relevance of the preference is less clear. Both the Australian and Japanese motor industries are post-war developments. One benefits from the British preference whilst the other does not. It is by no means clear that New Zealand would, if she had not been bound by past concessions, have wanted to discriminate in this way between these increasingly important trading partners.

The extent of the preference granted to British-sourced c.k.d. packs is measured directly by the difference between British Preferential and Most Favoured Nation rates. A c.k.d. pack sourced in Britain and having a c.d.v. value of $1200 will attract a duty of $75 whilst a similar pack from Japan will attract a duty of $540. The duty paid price of the Japanese c.k.d. pack would be $1740 and this is the amount to which the English supplier could competitively raise the price of his product above that in the absence of the Most Favoured Nation tariff. A duty paid price of $1740 implies a c.d.v. of $1638 at British Preferential rates. The tariff thus grants nominal protection to the United Kingdom car manufacturer of $36\frac{1}{2}$ per cent (i.e. $\frac{\$438}{\$1200}$).

On the basis of 1968-69 trade flows it appears that customs duty collected on imports of assembled and unassembled motor cars would have totalled $5.8 million. The detail of this is displayed in Table 29, the most notable features being the high relative share of duty paid in respect of Most Favoured Nation imports. These accounted for only $12\frac{1}{2}$ per cent of the total but bore 47 per cent of the duty.

Table 29:
IMPORTS AND DUTY, MOTOR CARS 1968-69 $m

	Imports c.d.v.			Customs Duty		
Source of Imports	Unassembled	Assembled	Total	Unassembled	Assembled	Total
British Preferential	37·1	3·9	41·0	2·3	0·8	3·1
Most Favoured Nation	4·4	1·4	5·8	2·0	0·8	2·7
Total:	41·5	5·3	46·8	4·3	1·6	5·8

5.2 Import Licensing

Motor vehicles have been subject to import licensing in most years since 1939 and imports have varied according to the changing balance of payments situation. The licensing system has also been used to encourage a greater depth of local assembly. The course of imports and the various incentive schemes have already been described in Sections 2.3 and 2.4. The present section discusses the more permanent features of the import licensing regime as it affects motor vehicles.

During the 1960's successive import licensing schedules classified c.k.d. and assembled cars in category "C". Importers' applications were thus treated individually and importers were not entitled automatically (as with "basic items") to licences equal to some set percentage of imports in a base year. In practice however, and with the exception of the various incentive and bonus schemes, licences issued to the various companies moved in parallel by percentages which varied according to the exchange situation. There is however, no public record of import licences issued for motor cars (nor of course is there for other commodities).

Import licensing depends upon a working relationship involving the Departments of Customs and of Industries and Commerce, their Ministers, and the assembly companies and franchise holders.

Each licensing period the Ministers of Customs, and of Industries and Commerce, in consultation with their colleagues, decide the total allocation of funds for motor vehicles, and whether there is to be any variation in the method of distributing these between franchise holders, as for example under the production incentive scheme. They also decide whether to exempt any categories of vehicles from control. The day-to-day administration of import licensing is the function of the Customs Department which issues the licences (these are specific as to marque) and ensures that agreements as to degree of local content are honoured.

The import licensing system establishes restrictions on import content approximately conforming to but in some instances over-lapping those set by the tariff determinations. Over the years, each company will, under the various production and incentive schemes, have reached an understanding with the Department as to parts which will be sourced locally. These understandings are continued under each new licence. The only available description of such understandings is that contained in a letter widely circulated in March 1965 from the Comptroller of Customs to the trade setting out the terms of the "revised special motor vehicles manufacturing scheme". Although new entrants are no longer admitted under the scheme, standards set by it can be assumed to apply still. They are illustrative of the extent to which protection provided to component suppliers by import licensing extends beyond that established by Customs' determinations. The components specified in the letter are set out in Table 30. In practice the requirements applying to production runs of 450 and 600 units proved unrealistic and companies generally found it preferable to produce additional runs of 300 rather than to aim for higher local content.

Quite apart from the incentive and other schemes, import licensing provides an inducement to increase local content. Any reduction in the cost of imported components per vehicle enables an increase in the number of vehicles imported within a licence entitlement. As the market is undersupplied additional vehicles can be sold profitably. In practice the companies have to arrive at some balance between increased local costs per unit as a result of incorporating more expensive local components, and increased turnover. In practice the trade has a well-developed formula for assessing the economics of local sourcing. This compares the price of the local component with the deletion allowance, plus freight and duty savings, plus a margin. One component manufacturer suggested that the margin was of the order of 20 to 40 per cent. Import licensing stretch (as it is referred to by the trade) is thus quite a powerful protective device. Although the margin applied can be expected to vary between companies it is likely to have been a considerably stronger inducement to local sourcing than has the British Preferential tariff.

Table 30:
REVISED SPECIAL MOTOR VEHICLES MANUFACTURING
SCHEME 1965

Volume of Production	Items to be included
300 units	Battery
	Radiator
	Tyres and tubes
	Front coil and rear leaf springs
	Trim
	Glass, curved or flat
	Exhaust system
	Ignition coils
	Rubber mats, carpets, or alternative floor coverings
	Internal door trim and interior panels
	Internal sun visors
	Battery and earth straps
	Rear view mirrors
	Air filters
	Brake hoses and cables
	Speedometer cables
	Seat springs, frames and pads
	Hose clips
450 units	Wiring looms
	Hub caps
	Spark plugs
	Exhaust manifolds
	Rubber bushes and mountings
	Rubber weatherstrips
	Horns
	Driveshafts
	Petrol caps
600 units	Pistons
	Valves
	Shell type engine bearings
	Brake drums and disc brakes
	Shock absorbers
	Wheels
	Bumper bars
	Carburettors
	Fans
	V-belts Inlet manifolds U bolts

Where a particular component could not be included, "alternative worthwhile components" could be considered.

Projects would not be approved unless the price structure was not in excess of that of a vehicle imported in built-up condition.

Source: Letter from Comptroller of Customs to the trade, 9 March 1965.

The incentive implicit in import licensing stretch was augmented by the various production incentive schemes which typically (see section 2.4) offered a $2\frac{1}{2}$ per cent increase in import entitlement for a $2\frac{1}{2}$ per cent increase in local content. These schemes did not as noted have any pronounced effect upon content and the reason for this is clear. An assembler incorporating 65 per cent imported parts would upon reducing this to $62\frac{1}{2}$ per cent "stretch" his licence entitlement by 3·8 per cent. The additional $2\frac{1}{2}$ per cent entitlement proposed under the scheme was thus smaller than that inherent in licensing stretch. Although the gains were additive they were small.

In practice the incentive schemes were soon swamped by changes in policy envisaging substantial increases in licences quite unrelated to content, and an officially declared expectation that the new schemes "would satisfy the existing demand for motor cars and within a reasonable space of time allow prospective buyers to obtain the car of their choice."[1] Although this hope was forlorn the statement must be presumed to have raised in the assembly companies' minds a question as to the wisdom of committing themselves to local content which could be justified in cost terms only because of import licensing stretch.

A continuing problem under import licensing is that licences issued on the basis of past importing tend to inhibit change within the industries and trades affected. This is particularly so in motor vehicle importing which is unique in that import licences can only be used for vehicles for which the importer holds the franchise. Section 2.4 discussed in detail the bonus and production incentive schemes which were introduced in the 1962-63 import licensing year in an attempt to overcome this rigidity.

5.3 Price Control

Ever since the war the retail price of new motor vehicles has been controlled, maximum prices being set by the Price Tribunal for each shipment of each model. Conceived as a war time measure, price control originally operated on a cost plus basis allowing a fixed margin on top of established costs. Because there were no new cars during the war, price control became effective only in the post-war period, and for a decade followed the general pattern in allowing a fixed percentage margin. A major change occurred in 1956 when two companies, others followed later, were allowed to calculate the New Zealand retail price in a fixed relationship to the United Kingdom retail price.

At present there are three price control formulas, two relating to unassembled cars, and one to assembled. Some cars are priced by a formula based on the original cost plus method. For such vehicles a 25 per cent mark-up is allowed on the assembled factory door cost of the car. Except in some few cases where assembly is sub-contracted, this cost includes no assembler's margin. A 10 per cent margin is however allowed on sub-contracted work. Motor cars are subject to sales tax on their wholesale value, at rates which have varied frequently, but which stood at 40 per cent at the time of writing. The pricing formula allows the 25 per cent mark-up to be applied to the first 20 per cent of sales tax, the remainder being added as a "plusage" without mark-up. In summary, the formula can be expressed as in the following equation where: R = approved retail price; W = wholesale price; and M = manufactured cost;

$$R = 1 \cdot 25M + (0 \cdot 25)(0 \cdot 2)W + 0 \cdot 4W$$

| (Factory cost plus mark-up) | (Mark-up on half of sales tax) | (Sales tax) |

or $R = 1 \cdot 25M + 0 \cdot 45W$

The formula does not fix the wholesale price which is determined between the assembler and retailer. So long as the Customs Department, which collects sales tax, is satisfied that the relationship is at arms length, it will accept this price, so that the amount of sales tax and mark-up are determined.[2]

In 1956 a new price formula for cars assembled by General Motors and Ford was introduced and several other companies have since followed suit. The new formula set the allowed New Zealand retail price with reference to the United Kingdom retail price, and was intended to translate existing margins approximately. The New Zealand retail price was set at 1·6 times the United Kingdom retail price, exclusive of purchase tax. The sixty per cent increase above the United Kingdom price allowed for elements such as higher local assembly costs, freight, duty, and New Zealand sales tax.

At the time, sales tax on new motor cars was 20 per cent. Since then it has been changed several times, necessitating changes in the pricing formula. The usual procedure is to make an adjustment by way of "plusage" calculated with reference to the wholesale price. For example the 1958 increase in sales tax from 20 to 40 per cent had the effect of modifying the formula from

$$R \text{ (N.Z.)} = 1 \cdot 6 \text{ (R U.K.} - T \text{ U.K.)}$$

where R = retail price and
T = purchase tax

to $R \text{ (N.Z.)} = 1 \cdot 6 \text{ (R U.K.} - T \text{ U.K.)} + 0 \cdot 2 \text{ (W N.Z.)}$

where R and T as above and
W = wholesale price.

In 1962 the existing 33⅓ per cent sales tax and the new tariffs were incorporated into a modified formula setting the New Zealand retail price at 1·76 times the United Kingdom retail price, exclusive of purchase tax.

In 1967 sales tax was increased and New Zealand devalued. These changes plus the adoption of decimal currency led to the formula

$$\$R_{N.Z.} = 3.78 \,£(R_{U.K.} - T_{U.K.})$$

For cars imported fully assembled a percentage margin on landed cost plus 20 per cent sales tax is allowed. For cars having a unit value of up to $2000 the percentage is 25 per cent on pre-devaluation cost and for values $2500 and above, the percentage is 20 per cent on pre-devaluation costs. A flat margin applies in the range $2000—2500. For a small group of importers whose main sales are direct to the public and who are classified as "importing retailers" the procedure is to apply sales tax to the duty paid value plus 25 per cent.

All new cars are subject to sales tax assessed on the wholesale price. The rates applicable in the post-war period have fluctuated between 20 and 40 per cent. No statistics are published of the total sales tax yield on motor cars but on the basis of an average wholesale price of about $1600 the 1967 level of registrations would have entailed sales tax of about $35 million. As noted earlier in this chapter, customs duty on imports of c.k.d. packs and fully-assembled cars was about $5 million, so that the total indirect tax generated by the industry was about $40 million in 1966-67. This is a substantial amount both in total and relative to the untaxed value of the product. The fact that the market has in general been able to bear this, and that low-mileage, second-hand vehicles generally command a premium above list price, points to the shortfall of supply below demand under conditions of import control. It is this shortfall which has justified the continuation of price control on motor cars. It is however beyond the scope of this study to judge its success.

The high level of sales tax relative to customs duty means that little of the indirect tax load imposed on the industry is protective. This is particularly so in respect of materials and components included in c.k.d. packs from British Preferential sources. This means that it would be possible to vary the protective incidence of indirect taxes by shifting the emphasis from sales tax to customs duty, without affecting the total tax yield or the final price of the vehicle.

5.4 N.A.F.T.A.

The 1965 New Zealand—Australia Free Trade Agreement did not include any items of importance to the motor assembly industry in the schedule of goods which are subject to a phasing out of duties.

The agreement did however include a clause, Article 3.7, which has proved to be of considerable importance to the industry. This provided for special measures which "may include the remission or reduction of duties on agreed goods or classes of goods in part or in whole". Following subsequent negotiations the two governments introduced a system by which New Zealand grants import licence concessions in exchange for tariff concessions granted by Australia, in respect of mutually agreed trade deals. The official booklet outlining the scheme, "NAFTA, Article 3:7", envisages a wide range of possible arrangements but in the motor industry a fairly typical package has emerged. This is that exports of components or related products to Australia by a New Zealand firm are admitted at a preferential or zero duty and in exchange import licences are granted by New Zealand for motor vehicles to a value equal to 90 per cent of the domestic content of the f.o.b. value of the exports to Australia. In addition no import duty is payable on imports admitted to New Zealand under such licenses. Each agreement requires the consent of the two Governments. The scheme has attracted considerable interest and a large number of agreements has been approved.

In cases where the agreement is effectively between an international automotive grouping and a component supplier, the main incentive offered by the scheme is analogous to that implicit in import licensing stretch. The New Zealand assembly company supplying a starved market is given a strong incentive to encourage automotive exports to Australia. In addition the component company can expect to benefit from tax incentives for increased exports and to secure replacement import licenses on account of imports used in producing the exported component.

The tax exemptions, together with the duty remission gained by the assembly companies, suggest that some of the links established under the scheme would continue even in a more fully supplied New Zealand market. It is also clear that the two governments are firmly committed to increasing cooperation between the two national motor industries, and further moves to stimulate this can be expected. Article 3:7 is also applicable within firms and provides a framework within which specialization in production between associated companies can be promoted. In all the article would seem to have a large potential.

6. MOTOR CAR ASSEMBLY

6.1 The Assembly Operation

Car assembly comprises five main activities, body assembly, painting, hard trim, assembly and fitting of engine and transmission, and soft trim. These are supported by factory functions such as stores handling, inspection, and administration. Although the techniques of assembly vary dramatically between plants, particularly those of different size, the main processes are the same.

The first stage in assembly is cleansing of the imported body panels, usually by immersion in a solvent. The cleansed panels are then fitted together by means of hand clamps to form a number of sub-assemblies which are then welded, and in turn joined by a further series of clamps to form the body shell. The process of clamping is performed around the jigs, static frameworks which position the clamps so that the separate body panels fitted to them will form the car body. The jig is a precision item, specific in design to each particular model. The main jig commonly comprises a base plate or framework with several standing members incorporating clamps.

Welding is effected by electric spot or seam welding guns directed at the flange or overlapping seams of the panels. Within limits the rate of production off a jig can be varied by changing the number of operators and welding guns working around it.

From the jigs the body shell is passed on to the metal finishing section. Here the welded seams are soldered and ground and the entire surface inspected and corrected for any irregularities.

In preparation for painting the shell undergoes a series of operations, the number of which varies between plants. They include washing in acid, and the application of pre-primer, primer and sealing compound. Between each stage the vehicle is dried either by letting it stand or by passing it through an oven. At various stages the surface is sanded and rubbed down. In the more sophisticated plants air cleansing, by keeping dust from the shell, removes the need for rubbing down at some stages.

The body shell then moves to the painting booth which is usually the most expensive item in the plant. In this, under controlled air conditions, paint is hand sprayed. In the larger plants duplication of pipelines enables variation in colour with each unit, whereas in the smaller plants painting is carried out in runs of one colour at a time. Up to three coats are applied and after final drying the shell is inspected.

If this is satisfactory the shell proceeds along the hard trim line on which glass, hardware, exterior mouldings, panel instruments, heaters, windshields and similar items are fitted.

At the next stage, conventionally called body drop, the main assembly line merges with those delivering the engine, transmission and wheels. Engine and transmission are imported fully assembled and require little more than unpacking before being fitted to the vehicle but for other items there will commonly be some small side operation preparing the part for assembly to the vehicle.

Next the vehicle proceeds to soft trim for fitting of seats, upholstery, door and head linings, and other items. The soft trim line is usually supplied by a soft trim department which cuts materials to shape, sews, welds plastics, and generally prepares the upholstery.

At this point the car is virtually complete subject to testing on points such as waterproofing and a general check on completeness and performance.

Such are the functions of an assembly plant. There is some variation. One plant for example approaches body drop after soft trim has been completed but in general the pattern conforms to the schematic presentation in Chart 4.

All plants in New Zealand handle more than one model and there is little equipment along the line that is specific to model. The main exception is the jig set. Plants commonly have two or three jig lines feeding different models to metal finish, but the smallest plants may concentrate on one model at a time. In some instances a further line assembling truck cabs also feeds in to the metal finish section. A common line, sometimes with duplication, operates through metal finishing, painting and body drop, following which some companies split the line to provide two trim lines each handling a different model. Truck cabs will at this point move away to the main truck chassis line.

The degree of mechanical handling of the body shell varies considerably. In the smallest plants hand trolleys are used on an open floor, whilst somewhat larger plants have fixed channels for the trolleys to run in. In the largest plants various sections of the line are mechanized, the vehicle under assembly slowly moving on from stage to stage.

Apart from the equipment directly involved on the line the assembly factory has the usual back up facilities of tool room,

CHART 4. THE STAGES OF ASSEMBLY

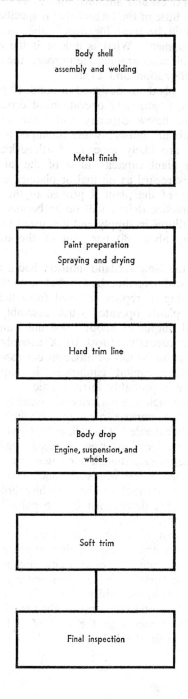

Body shell
assembly and welding

Metal finish

Paint preparation
Spraying and drying

Hard trim line

Body drop
Engine, suspension, and
wheels

Soft trim

Final inspection

stores, supply services, and administration. As in many industrial processes there is little of the factory that is specific to the industry. The building could be used for many other activities, as could much of the equipment. What is unique is the organisation and design of that equipment around one purpose, the assembly of cars.

6.2 Capacity Utilization and Costs

An assembly plant is designed around a planned level of production and will generally operate most economically at that level. Production below capacity will leave some capital and perhaps some labour unused, while attempts to push the plant beyond capacity are likely to cause bottlenecks.

In discussing plant capacity most of the larger firms distinguished what they regard as normal or planned capacity from the technical capacity of the plant if pushed to the limits and if all went well. In practice delays will occur because of breakdowns, stoppages, and failures in supply and it is usual to think of normal capacity as being about 80 per cent of the ultimate technical capacity.

In mid 1967 the New Zealand industry had a normal capacity, on a single shift with overtime basis, of close to 90,000 motor cars and vans, according to replies received from the companies. In addition several plants operated truck assembly lines having a combined annual output of about 5,000 units and presumably a somewhat higher capacity. Most truck assembly lines use the metal finish and paint booths of adjacent car assembly plants and because little other capital equipment is required for truck assembly capacity is probably fairly elastic.

At time of interview the majority of assembly companies were working well below normal capacity, although one large firm claimed to be fully extended. Overall, output (which was declining as import licence allocations were reduced) had been at about 70 per cent of capacity although for some few, and mainly very small firms, the percentage was very much less. Typically these latter assemble on contract to the franchise holder and have a plant whose capacity, determined by the paint booth, is well in excess of actual production.

As the main cost of a car arises from imported and locally purchased materials, and as capital charges are low, there is little reason to expect changing use of capacity to cause large variation in total costs. The variation which does occur is however significant, particularly to the assembler who tends to view the variation in relation to factory operating, rather than total, costs. Table 31 records the main elements in the cost of a locally assembled vehicle as recorded in the industrial production statistics.

Table 31:
COST COMPOSITION OF A LOCALLY ASSEMBLED VEHICLE

		parts per 000
Imported components		629
Other components		136
Other expenses		
Electricity and fuel	7	
Insurance	2	
Repairs and maintenance	6	
Management and office expenses	19	
Interest	1	
Rent	2	
Depreciation	15	
	—	52
Salaries and wages		
Wage earning employees	84	
Other	22	
	—	106
Surplus		77
Value of Production		1,000

Source: Industrial Production Statistics 1967-68, full detail is given in
Appendix 1, Table 2.

It is reasonable, even if arbitrary, to divide these costs into
three. First there are those which can be expected to increase
proportionately with output, these are the so-called variable costs
comprising purchases of components and direct wage payments.
Second some costs can be regarded as more or less fixed and
unaffected by variations in plant operation. The classic items are
interest, rent, and depreciation, but it is also reasonable to so
classify all the items of "other expenses" and the "other" salary
and wage payments. In practice some of these will vary with use
of capacity so that our categorization will exaggerate the extent
of such fixed costs, and thus the effect upon unit costs of varying
use of capacity. Thirdly we have the manufacturing surplus. This
of course is a residual between selling price and production costs.
If the selling price is held constant then unit surplus will increase
if fuller use of capacity leads to lower unit production costs. In an
undersupplied market subject to price control selling prices are
unlikely to fall and even in more fully supplied markets overseas
variation in selling price is infrequent. It is however of interest
to examine the effect of assuming that the unit margin does not
change with varying use of capacity.

Table 32 sets out the cost implications of varying use of
capacity. Movement from 60 to 100 per cent use of capacity

would entail movement in total variable and fixed costs from 935 to 901, i.e. a reduction of 4 per cent. On the assumption that the selling price was unchanged this would imply an increase in surplus from 65 to 99; by 52 per cent. On the alternative assumption that the surplus is constant the ex factory price could be expected to fall by 3 per cent, from 1012 to 978.

Table 32:
UNIT COSTS OF VARIOUS LEVELS OF PRODUCTION

	Single shift plus overtime				
% *use of capacity*	*60*	*70*	*80*	*90*	*100*
Variable costs; c.k.d. components	629	629	629	629	629
other	220	220	220	220	220
Fixed costs	86	74	65	58	52
Total variable and fixed costs	935	923	914	907	901
Assumption A. final price fixed					
Surplus	65	77	86	93	99
Ex factory price	1000	1000	1000	1000	1000
Assumption B. surplus fixed					
Surplus	77	77	77	77	77
Ex factory price	1012	1000	991	984	978
NOTE: Fixed and variable costs excluding c.k.d. components	306	294	285	278	272
Fixed and variable costs excluding all components	170	158	149	142	136

NOTE: Because the table is expressed in unit costs the usage of variable and fixed costs, which usually refer to total rather than unit costs, appears a little incongruous. Fixed total costs imply that costs per unit will vary with production, whilst variable total costs imply constant unit costs.

Source: Derived from data in Table 34 on the assumption that 1967-68 production was at an average capacity of 70 per cent.

Narrowing our focus somewhat we can observe that total costs exclusive of imported components would fall by 11 per cent, and exclusive of all components, by 20 per cent. In practice most people interviewed saw the relevant area of costs as exclusive of c.k.d. components, the cost of which is felt to be beyond their control. The locally incurred costs on the other hand arise either in areas of direct management responsibility or, as in the case of locally purchased materials, where local decision is required.

The spreading of fixed costs is only one of several factors operating to reduce unit costs as capacity is more fully used. Advantages also flow from the employment of more people. A larger labour force permits finer division of jobs with less waste of time in changing from one task to another. It also enhances the skill of the person on the job. A larger labour force will also usually enable a better balance of labour along the line so there is less waste time.

During the course of the study the assembly companies were asked to what extent unit costs of production would vary as the percentage use of capacity moved from 60, to 80, to 100 per cent. Answers were expressed in relation to various totals, usually to labour costs plus overhead, but in some cases also including locally purchased materials, and were of varying exactness and reliability. One result was judged so extreme as to be unreliable but the others, several of which were derived from detailed costings, showed a broadly similar pattern and have been used to derive Table 33. On this evidence we could expect that the consequence of operating an assembly plant at 60 per cent of capacity, rather than full capacity, would be to increase the unit costs, by and large exclusive of materials, by 20 per cent.

Table 33:

VARIATION IN UNIT COSTS, EXCLUSIVE OF MATERIALS,
WITH CHANGING USE OF CAPACITY
Unit cost at capacity = 100

| Percentage use of capacity | Range | Unit Costs | |
		Mean, unweighted	Mean, weighted*
60	111–125	116	120
80	104–110	107	108
100	100	100	100

* Weighted according to volume of output.
Source: Derived from estimates supplied by assembly companies.

This estimate compares reasonably with that derived from factory production data. Over the same range, i.e. from 100 to 60 per cent use of capacity, that data showed increases of 25 per cent in unit costs exclusive of materials, and of $12\frac{1}{2}$ per cent in unit costs inclusive of New Zealand materials.

This similarity is a little surprising in that discussion with the companies revealed divergent assessments of the relative importance of fixed and variable costs. Although practice varies the most common costing convention is to apply an overhead rate to the direct wage cost. The overhead rate is of course derived from past experience and most establishments have a clear view of the proportion of this which is fixed. Rates of total overhead ranged from 40 to 200 per unit whilst the proportion seen as fixed ranged from one quarter to more than one third.

In general the larger companies stand to gain more as production moves to capacity. This, which is reflected in the higher savings shown on weighted data in Table 33, was to be expected, as the larger plants are generally more heavily capitalized and thus likely to have a higher proportion of fixed overheads.

Proportionately, the cost saving is greater as the plant moves from 60 to 80 per cent of capacity than when moving from 80 to 100 per cent, the main reason being that for most plants movement to full capacity requires a more than proportionate increase in overtime working so that the average hourly wage rate tends to rise.

All in all the industry has a clear interest in operating at close to capacity. However the long run demand for motor vehicles is far from static, and given the prospect that it will increase there is no permanent optimum for the firm. Inevitably capacity has to be increased by discreet stages, particularly as far as paint plants and conveyor mechanisms are concerned, so that each particular investment must be assessed with an eye to longer term requirements, as well as to the shorter term costs incurred in operating below capacity.

Variation in unit costs with capacity is also of significance in that the industry is particularly susceptible to short term fluctuations in economic activity. The level of production is frequently affected by import licensing and the demand for cars by changes in economic conditions and more directly by changes in the rate of sales tax. Although the justification for fiscal and import licensing measures derives from considerations much wider than those of a particular industry it is worth noting that the loss in output per unit of labour and of capital, implicit in the increase in unit costs associated with falling output, is a real cost to the industry, and to the nation, which must be weighed against the more general and diffuse benefit presumed to flow from government action.

The New Zealand assembly industry customarily operates on a single shift, with overtime, basis. In this it conforms to practice in most of the smaller scale motor industries including that in Australia. Although there is fairly general agreement amongst New Zealand companies that double shifting would yield some economies most think that these would be small, and in the range of a 5 to 10 per cent reduction in unit operating costs. One firm however did suggest the possibility of a significantly higher gain but advanced no direct evidence in support of this.

The main objection to the introduction of shift working is the problem of staffing. Staff turnover is already a major worry for most plants and the general feeling is that staff attracted to shift work would probably be less satisfactory and less stable. At the same time double shifting would require doubling of supervisory and other staff, which might well prove impossible even assuming that they could be given the assurance of continued employment. It is also of interest to note that one of the elements contributing to the anticipated reduction in unit costs was that the average hourly rate would be less under shiftworking than under ordinary time plus overtime working. Given that assembly work is generally held to be relatively unattractive and that the industry, more than most, depends upon high wages, including those yielded by overtime,[1] to attract labour it is probable that plants would experience great difficulty at present shift rates in attracting sufficient staff to operate a second shift, and would face a higher rate of labour turnover on the main shift if overtime was dropped. An attempt to overcome these problems by increasing shift rates would reduce the prospective saving.

These considerations would weigh less heavily in a more capital intensive industry. The absence of shiftwork reflects the particular circumstances of the New Zealand industry rather than universal considerations. At some point the increasing capital investment per worker involved in increased capacity would tip the scales in favour of more intensive use of existing plant even if that entailed significant changes in staffing policies and re-thinking of wage scales. It has not proved possible to quantify this point but it is probably well in excess of the present maximum size of unit in New Zealand.

6.3 Mixing of Models

Nearly all companies assemble a range of models. The market is usually seen as comprising several sub-markets for different sizes of car, and firms anxious to maximise sales will aim to supply each of these if the production pattern of the overseas parent or associate permits. In the undersupplied postwar market the incentive to supply all sub-markets has been reduced. For some of the smaller companies which have sought the path of least resistance in the difficult task of acquiring licences under the "300 club" the explanation of their present product mix is simpler. Import licensing and franchise considerations have outweighed market strategy.

In general it costs more to assemble several models rather than one. Increasing the range of models assembled requires an increase, in the range of materials required, in the amount of specialised equipment, and in the knowledge of the labour force. If production economies were paramount the modern motor assembler would no doubt follow Henry Ford's precept and produce cars of any colour, so long as they were black. In practice most firms lay emphasis on marketing considerations and hold that the benefits derived from supplying a range of models outweigh the extra cost of producing them. One company executive put it this way:

"the paramount consideration in deciding product mix is market and selling requirements. It is not really related to the economies of factory production. The market is undersupplied and one wants to supply each of the main price brackets and to obtain as large a proportion as possible of no-remittance and other business."

Nevertheless it is important to assess the extra cost incurred in producing an array of models. One of the most common criticisms made by advocates of industry rationalization is the cost assumed to flow from such diverse production. Even although the companies consider their production pattern to be determined by marketing considerations, from a broader viewpoint it is obvious that the market is affected by government regulation and fiscal action. A change in these could well lead to a situation in which the assembly companies would place more emphasis on production economies and price as elements in market strategy.

The degree of fragmentation seen in motor vehicle assembly depends in part upon what is held to constitute a separate model. One of the prouder claims of some of the major United States Corporations is that the range of options offered the consumer means that one basic model supports a million or more distinctive vehicles. Narrowing the focus to exclude minor variations such as colour, the tuning band on the car radio, and variation in soft or hard trim we can note that in January 1969 an Automobile Association survey listed 88 distinct price control approvals for motor cars assembled in New Zealand. Narrowed still further, to exclude such options as automatic transmission, and saloon or station wagon versions of the same basic body shell, the AA list reduced to 40 models but even this included some duplication in the case of Austin, Morris, Riley and Wolseley cars.

The official production statistics provide no indication of the number of models produced but it is possible to build such a picture from the statistics of motor vehicle registrations interpreted in the light of information from the assembly companies.

Of the 53,300 motor cars registered in 1969, 52,100 were new registrations of marques assembled in New Zealand and in which there were more than 100 registrations in each engine size category. Some few of these will have been assembled overseas but the figure will serve as a basis for analysis.

The 52,100 registrations can be broken down as in Table 34 and 35, and as displayed in Chart 5. In all 33 basic car models are distinguished, a basic model being used to describe the family of cars which can be built around a standard set of body panels, and are assembled on a common set of jigs. Thus the Holden appears as a single model because the front end and main body panels were common to all Holdens assembled in New Zealand even although variation in rear end panelling (as in station wagon versions), in engine, internal and external trim, and finish, supported a variety of models. The list duplicates the B.M.C. Mini, 1100, and 1800, cars which were assembled by both Austin and Dominion Motors in 1969.

Eight of the 33 models had annual volumes greater than 2,000 and these accounted for 60 per cent of total production in New Zealand. These 8 models were assembled within the five largest plants whose output, including production of a further seven models having annual volumes of less than 2,000, comprised 82 per cent of the national total.

For the eight leading models the average annual volume was 3,900 whilst for the remaining 25 production averaged 800 units. Overall the average annual level of production per model was 1,600.

The assembly company producing several models has to decide two major issues. First, the extent to which different models should be assembled on a common production line and secondly whether different models should be freely mixed along the line. There is considerable variation in practice.

Because assembly jigs are specific to a model the first stages of assembly are inevitably separate. The usual practice is to pass the welded shells from the jigs onto a common line for metal finishing and preparation for painting, although two of the middle range of companies operate two lines at this stage. For at least one of these this results from space limitations which forced expansion of capacity away from the main plant. Painting, the most capital intensive operation in the assembly plant, is almost invariably done in a common paint booth and oven. In two plants however there is duplication of painting booths. In the larger plants an array of spray guns enables full variation of colour between successive vehicles whilst in most of the smaller plants colour is varied less frequently. Practice is more diverse at the trim stage. The largest and smallest companies generally operate a single trim line whilst most of the middle range of companies have duplicate trim facilities, using one line for the main production model, and the other for other models. There was fairly

CHART 5. VEHICLE REGISTRATIONS BY COMPANY 1969

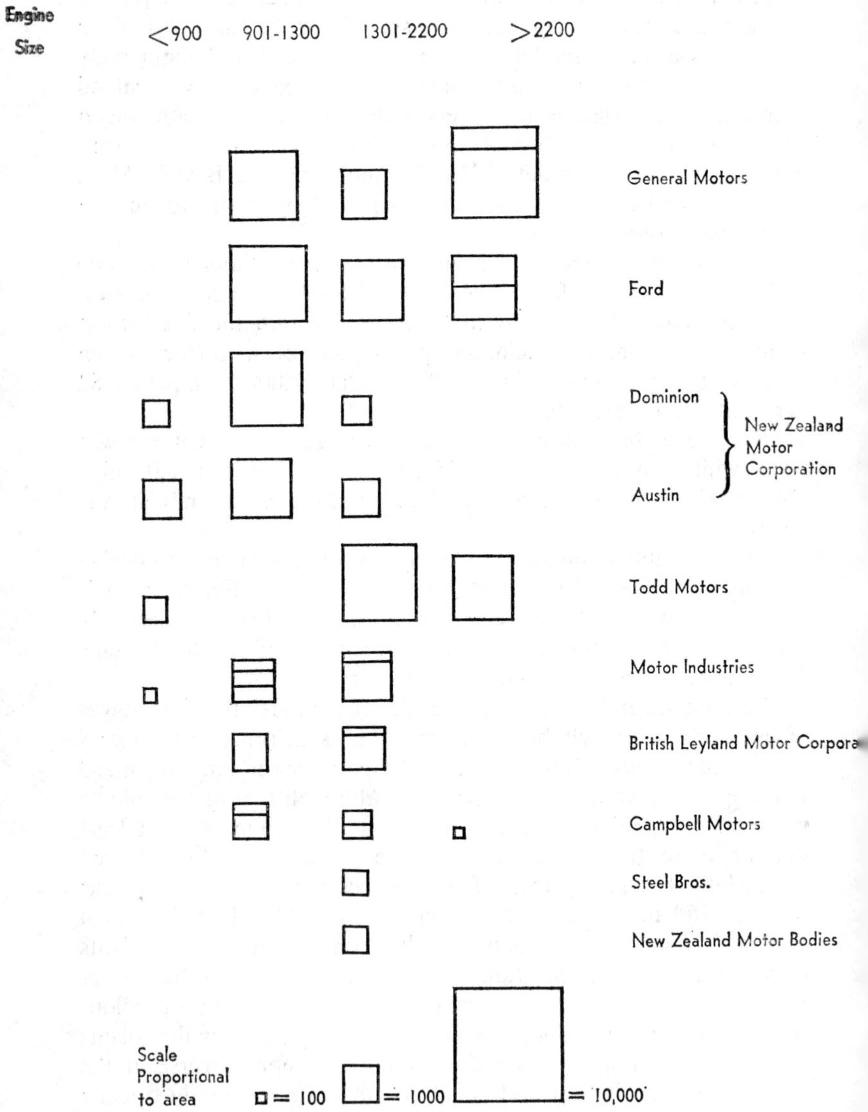

Engine Size

<900   901-1300   1301-2200   >2200

General Motors

Ford

Dominion } New Zealand Motor Corporation

Austin

Todd Motors

Motor Industries

British Leyland Motor Corpora

Campbell Motors

Steel Bros.

New Zealand Motor Bodies

Scale Proportional to area   □ = 100   ☐ = 1000   ☐ = 10,000

NOTE: Where a firm produces more than one model in a size range the box is sub-divided horizontally.

Source: Table 34.

REGISTRATIONS CLASSIFIED BY ASSEMBLER AND ENGINE SIZE 1969

	Engine size c.c.				Number of Models	Total Registrations (000)
	< 900	900—1300	1301—2200	> 2200		
General Motors		Vauxhall Viva 3·7	Vauxhall Victor 1·8	Vauxhall Cresta 1·6 / Holden 4·8		
		3·7	1·8	6·4	4	11·8
Ford		Escort 4·8	Cortina 3·3	Zephyr and Zodiac 1·7 / Falcon 1·8		
		4·8	3·3	3·5	4	11·5
New Zealand Motor Corporation						
Dominion Motors Plant	Morris mini 0·6	Morris and Wolseley and Riley 1100 4·2	Morris 1800 0·8			
	0·6	4·2	0·8		3	5·6
Austin Plant	Austin mini 1·3	Austin and Wolseley 1100 and 1300 2·7	Austin, B.M.C. and Wolseley 1800 1·3			
	1·3	2·7	1·3		3	5·3
Todd Motors	Sunbeam Imp 0·5		Hillman Hunter and Singer 4·8	Chrysler Valiant 3·2		
	0·5		4·8	3·2	3	8·5

Table 34 (continued) :

REGISTRATIONS CLASSIFIED BY ASSEMBLER AND ENGINE SIZE 1969

	Engine size c.c.				Number of Models	Total Registrations (000)
	< 900	900—1300	1301—2200	> 2200		
Motor Industries	Fiat Bambina 0·2	Fiat 850 0·5 Simca 0·4 Skoda 0·6	Fiat 125 0·5 Volkswagen 1·5			
	0·2	1·5	2·0		6	3·8
British Leyland Motor Corporation		Triumph 13/60 1·0	Triumph 2000 1·2 Rover 0·3		3	2·5
Campbell Industries		Renault 0·3 Toyota Corolla 0·7 1·0	Isuzu 0·4 Peugeot 0·4 0·8	Rambler 0·1	5	1·9
Steel Bros.		1·0	Toyota Corona 0·8	0·1	5	1·9
New Zealand Motor Bodies			Datsun 0·6 0·6		1	0·6
			0·6		1	0·6
Total Registrations					33	52·1

92

Table 35:
ANNUAL REGISTRATIONS—IN ORDER OF SIZE—1969

Annual Level of Production	Model	Registrations 000	
Less than 500	Rambler	0·1	
	Fiat Bambina	0·2	
	Rover	0·3	
	Renault	0·3	
	Isuzu	0·4	
	Peugeot	0·4	
	Simca	0·4	
	Sunbeam Imp	0·5	2·6
500—1000	Fiat 125	0·5	
	Fiat 850	0·5	
	Datsun	0·6	
	Morris Mini	0·6	
	Toyota Corona	0·6	
	Skoda	0·6	
	Toyota Corolla	0·7	
	Morris 1800	0·8	4·9
1000—1500	Triumph 13/60	1·0	
	Triumph 2000	1·2	
	Austin, B.M.C. and Wolseley 1800	1·3	
	Austin Mini	1·3	4·8
1500—2000	Volkswagen	1·5	
	Vauxhall Cresta	1·6	
	Ford Zephyr and Zodiac	1·7	
	Vauxhall Victor	1·8	
	Ford Falcon	1·8	8·4
2000—3000	Austin and Wolseley 1100 and 1300	2·7	2·7
3000—4000	Chrysler Valiant	3·2	
	Ford Cortina	3·3	
	Vauxhall Victor	3·7	10·1
4000 and higher	Morris, Riley and Wolseley 1100	4·2	
	Ford Escort	4·8	
	Holden	4·8	
	Hilman Hunter and Singer	4·8	18·7
Total Registrations:			52·1

general agreement amongst the middle and small size companies that there is little to choose in cost terms between single line and duplicate trim facilities. Most car companies were not prepared to essay firm opinions on this point, their comments being limited to explaining present practice, or in one case, in a company operating twin lines to a judgement that the decision to operate two lines might have been a mistake. In large part this hesitancy of judgement arises because soft trim is the most labour intensive and one of the most varied activities in the assembly factory so that its cost is difficult to measure.

In summary, in all New Zealand plants there are at least some sections of the line which are common to all vehicles but there is considerable variation. In the smallest and largest plants there is a tendency to perform all assembly operations on the one line. The daily output of the smaller plants is so low, up to 4 units, and their capital equipment so sparse that it is somewhat artificial to speak of them as having a production line except in the sense that assembly involves a sequence of operations. At the other extreme the largest plants make the most use of automatic conveyor systems so that there are obvious cost advantages in placing all units on the one line. Duplication of lines is concentrated in the middle sized units and is common in labour intensive sections where there is a considerable volume of production but not sufficient to justify the installation of conveyors.

Most assembly companies mix models on the assembly line but some of the smaller companies and one of the middle grouping produce in separate runs. As we have noted the mixture of models in production is usually explained in terms of supplying the full array of vehicles produced. This justification was commonly buttressed with other elements including the maintenance of balance on the line and of labour familiarity. Neither of these amount to a separate justification for producing a variety of vehicles but reflect issues which are important once it has been decided to do so.

The amount of time spent on a vehicle in the main stages of assembly varies between models. This being so a policy of batch production would randomly cause an uneven workload between various stages of the line. As most assembly labour is specialised, even if unskilled, the transfer of labour from one point to another, in an attempt to balance production requirements and labour supply, is not attractive. In practice the majority of companies have found it preferable to mix their production runs so as to maintain an even workload along the line.

Mixing of models in production also has the advantage of maintaining labour familiarity with the assembly problems of each model. It takes time for a worker to learn the techniques best suited to assembly of a particular model and all companies, whether freely mixing models or assembling in batches, agree that using the latter method in an industry with a high rate of labour turnover means that many workers will be faced by an unfamiliar vehicle with each new production run. Free mixing of vehicles ensures that at any time the majority of employees are familiar with all models under construction so that the production line can more easily carry the new employee whilst he learns his job in relation to all models. Intuitively it seems probable that the average learning time per vehicle will be shorter under mixing because of the instruction and example of others familiar with the job. Mixing is also likely to reduce the possibility of major bottle-necks occurring at particular stages of production.

Nevertheless while mixing perhaps lessens, and certainly spreads and makes less obvious, the cost of producing several models it cannot eliminate it.

Production of a variety of models is likely to increase capital costs, to make the organization of production more complex, and to increase the total learning time for each worker. As we have seen the only capital cost specific to a model is that of the jig. A jig set will normally outlast the production life of the vehicle and as is discussed in section 6.4, the design and cost of the jig is varied according to the output expected to be required from it. The additional capital cost consequent on assembling a range of models is thus reduced.

The productive effort of the assembly plant is made more complex by the admixture of models. As the car proceeds along the line parts are fitted and the smooth functioning of the plant depends upon their ready supply. More models makes parts supply more complex, and so more costly. Similarly soft trim machinists have to cope with wider variety. It has not proved possible to estimate the cost of such elements as these. There can however be no doubt that the costs are real.

The major additional costs resulting from the production of several models are probably those associated with management and worker learning. Although most jobs in an assembly plant can be picked up within a few hours or days it is generally agreed that the employee's performance will improve noticeably during the first 2 or 3 months and that some further improvement can be expected beyond then. What is true of the individual is also, in this instance, true of the group. Experience suggests modifications in technique and organization. Application of these will usually reduce costs.

This pattern, which is typical of most assembly type operations, has been examined extensively overseas, particularly by Cole, and is embodied in a general rule, characterized as the "learning curve". The learning curve, which is now commonly reflected in costing procedures, suggests that

"as the total quantity of a product or model manufactured for the first time doubles, the direct labour cost of the 2nth unit will be less than the direct labour cost of the nth unit by the same fixed proportion of the nth unit."[2]

This formulation suggests for example, that if the direct labour cost of the 10th unit in a production run is $1000, and that of the 20th unit is $800, then the direct labour cost of the 40th unit will be $640. Although originally derived from experience in large size operations such as airframe construction, similar patterns have been found to exist in many industries. More surprisingly it appears that the percentage change in unit costs is approximately the same for a wide range of products, a reduction of 20 per cent for each doubling of output.

During the course of this study several New Zealand assembly companies made estimates which relate to the learning effect. One company for example suggested that three months after the beginning of a run the average hours spent per vehicle would have fallen by about 25 per cent. Other companies which were prepared to contemplate longer production runs of fewer vehicles suggested that reductions of 5-10 per cent in labour costs and overheads could result from a doubling of the average length of run.

One company, which undertakes batch production and so could identify with precision the assembly times required for various vehicles, supplied information on vehicles assembled in the early stages of production runs. Statistically this fitted closely to the function suggested by Cole.

Although the supporting information is sketchy, it is reasonable to assume that assembly benefits from the learning effect, and that unit labour costs will reduce with increasing volume in such a way that each doubling of volume lowers the marginal unit cost by the same percentage. In assessing the learning effect two other factors must be taken into account. First, as noted previously the industry has a high rate of labour turnover (typically annual male terminations of employment exceed the average level of employment) so that the direct labour cost cannot be expected to reduce indefinitely. Second, as we are interested in comparing production of one model with production of several we should not ignore the fact that much that is learnt in assembly of one applies to others. These factors suggest that the rate of reduction in unit labour costs could well be less than in the diverse large size assembly type operations examined overseas, an inference which is however at variance with the company example instanced earlier.

How important is the learning effect likely to be in practice? In 1966 New Zealand assembled 34 models at an average production run of 1700 units. For purposes of comparison the relative total labour cost has been calculated (see Table 36) for an industry having the same total output but

(a) producing 34 models in equal volume

and (b) producing 15 models in ten plants of the present size, the largest 5 producing two models each, and the remainder one.

Although these calculations can support no more that tentative inferences they are of interest. First, the table shows that it would be more expensive to produce the present range of models in equal volume rather than according to the present pattern.

Table 36:

DIRECT LABOUR COST AND RANGE OF MODELS,
INDEX PRESENT LEVEL = 100

	Assumed percentage reduction in marginal direct labour cost with each doubling of output	
	20 per cent	10 per cent
34 models produced on 1966 pattern of output	100	100
34 models produced in equal runs	111	106
15 basic models	81	91

NOTE: Appendix C describes the method of these estimates and details Cole's formula.

Given the nature of the cost function this would be true for any number of models and reflects the fact that in an uneven pattern of production greater weight attaches to those models having the lowest direct labour cost.

More interest attaches to the last line of the table which suggests that a reduction in the number of models from 34 to 15 would cause direct labour costs to fall by 9 or 19 per cent depending on the percentage reduction, in marginal direct labour cost, that was assumed to flow from each doubling of output. A more thorough-going rationalization could be expected to have a more marked effect.

The combination of high labour turnover and multiplicity of models means that a significant proportion of labour time involves learning so that productivity is lower than it would be if the range of models was reduced. Wage costs comprised 8·4 per cent of the factory value of motor vehicles produced in 1967-68 and 22·6 per cent of New Zealand costs. Reductions of 9 and 19 per cent in direct labour costs would thus imply reductions of 0·8 and 1·6 per cent respectively, in the ex-factory price, and of 2·0 and 4·3 per cent respectively, in total New Zealand costs.

Although this assessment is arbitrary it seems clear that the cost of producing a wide range of models is considerable. A reduction of 0·8-1·6 per cent in the factory price of a motor car would have equalled about $12-25 in 1968-69. It may be that the New Zealand consumer is happy to pay this loading as a means of ensuring a wider choice of vehicles. But, in the undersupplied market of the post-war period, where the choice has often been between taking what is offered or joining somebody else's waiting list this is surely doubtful.

7. THE EFFECT OF SCALE IN ASSEMBLY

7.1 Plant Size and Cost of Production

One of the commonest phenomena in production economics is that of economies of scale. Most goods can be produced more cheaply in large numbers, and in popular imagination this tendency is perhaps most clearly seen in motor vehicle manufacture and assembly. Many of the techniques of modern mass production were pioneered here. In particular the development of the automotive production line from Ford's first efforts in a street alongside his plant has provided one of the strongest symbols of mass production. On a wryer note Chaplin in Modern Times commented on the division of labour integral to Ford's new mode of production.

We have noted in the previous section that average production costs can be expected to reduce with increased production of particular models. In addition, it is to be expected that average production costs will vary between plants of different size. There are many reasons why this should be so in motor assembly.

1. Most equipment is designed to a particular capacity. The smaller plant often finds itself using an item below its capabilities and must recover capital costs against a lower volume of output so that unit costs rise. For many processes this tendency can be reduced, or even offset, by using equipment designed to lower capacity but there are usually limits to this. For example one of the smaller assemblers uses a paint shop, the smallest which it could acquire, at less than half of its single shift capacity.

2. For many items of equipment a simple increase in capacity with no change in function or technique, will reduce the capital cost per unit of capacity. The classic example of this is the storage tank in which the material cost increases approximately in proportion to the surface area whilst capacity increases with the volume of the tank. The labour cost of manufacturing such capital goods also often increases less than proportionately. In a recent United States study[1] of engineering data for capital equipment it was shown that, for the more than 600 items studied, capital cost per unit of capacity fell on average by $22\frac{1}{2}$ per cent with a doubling of capacity.

3. One of the main elements contributing to economies of scale is that different techniques can be employed at higher outputs.

As already noted much capital equipment is essentially indivisible. This is commonly the case with new and improved techniques. In New Zealand plants metal body panels are hand fitted to the assembly jigs for welding. At higher volumes of production automatic placing of panels and automatic welding would be employed. Such automatic jigging plant is designed to handle annual volumes of 60,000 units or more, at which level unit costs will be less than with non-automatic techniques. At lower volumes the high capital cost makes use of the technique uneconomic.

4. Higher volume permits a finer division of assembly. Such specialization will often facilitate use of different techniques and open up possibilities of using more specialized capital equipment. Finer division of work will usually enhance employee performance.

5. At higher outputs a better balance of both labour and capital along the line is usually possible so that waste of resources is less likely. A plant uses many items of equipment from hand tools to welding and spray guns, to jigs, paint ovens, and conveyor and transfer systems. Each has its optimum capacity and when the plants output exceeds this the item is duplicated. Increased plant size tends to reduce the imbalance inherent in this situation. Similarly a larger work force enables more exact matching to the requirements of the line.

For these and other reasons unit production costs will usually be less in larger plants. Once established the capital cost of a plant is of course fixed and along with it a significant proportion of operating costs. Given informed design each plant will embody those techniques appropriate to its planned level of production. If however it operates significantly below this then it may well operate more expensively than a plant designed to a lower level.

It is important not to judge the magnitude of economies of scale solely in relation to the experience of the largest plants. A backward extrapolation of their average cost curve may offer a poor guide to the experience of smaller plants. In Chart 6 for example where we sketch the average cost curves for two factories, T_1 and T_2, designed to different capacities, it is apparent that for volumes of production below OA the technology of firm T_1 is more appropriate. This is so even although T_2 offers significantly lower costs at higher volumes. Even although T_2 is a firm that we would normally think of as technically superior to T_1 it is, for low volumes of production, economically inferior. In looking at economies of scale for the industry as a whole we are more interested in the underlying envelope curve T^*, which links the succession of curves, (T_i), for all techniques which offer minimum average costs at some particular volume.

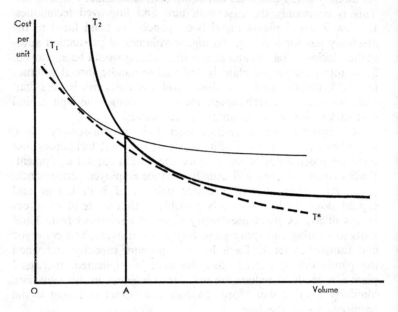

CHART 6. ECONOMIES OF SCALE

In the following pages four main approaches are made in assessing economies of scale in motor car assembly. First, the international literature is reviewed; second, international practice is surveyed; third, New Zealand statistical data is examined; and fourth, estimates are given based upon information supplied by the New Zealand companies.

7.2 The International Literature

The literature on automobile manufacture and assembly is not extensive[2]. There have been some academic studies of automobile manufacture in the western metropolitan economies. Although their main emphasis has been on economies of scale in manufacture all have contained estimates of the optimum level for assembly. In addition there have been official, usually tariff authority, studies of the industry in Canada, Ireland, South Africa and Australia. In the last three assembly developed under a regime broadly similar to that in New Zealand. In Canada and Australia, and more recently and to a lesser degree in South Africa, the industry has been encouraged into fuller manufacture. Studies relating to these four countries have laid emphasis on the disability of small scale and estimates of optimum scale quoted in them usually derive from experience in the United States and the United

100

Kingdom. Despite this they are of interest in that they are made from within a frame of reference broadly similar to that of this study.

Chronologically the four main studies relating to the metropolitan powers are those of Bain, 1956 (the United States); Maxcy and Silberston, 1959 (the United Kingdom); Edwards, 1965 (the United States); and Jurgensen and Berg, 1968 (Europe) Bain's estimates were made from information supplied by the major manufacturers, in the course of a wider study of factors limiting the entry of new firms to American industries. He was concerned to analyse the extent to which economies of scale, by encouraging large productive units, militated against competition. In surveying the automobile industry he noted, as have all subsequent investigators, that economies of scale are most noticeably present in manufacture, particularly in body panel pressing, and that the optimum scale for assembly is well below that for full manufacture. Together with transport and related costs this lower optimum had induced a dispersal of assembly points in the United States. Bain recorded that for assembly alone a volume of from 60,000 to 180,000 units per annum was considered optimal.

The study of the United Kingdom industry by Maxcy and Silberston is the most detailed to date. They estimated that:—

"the efficient use of the best assembly techniques calls for a volume of roughly 60,000 units per annum, which need not be all of one model. There are probably further smaller gains at higher volumes, but the significant economies in car assembly appear to be exhausted at a volume of 100,000 units. This relatively low figure stems from the complexity of the product, the importance of direct labour, and the non-specific nature of most of the equipment, the use of which is normally limited solely by the length of its physical life."[2]

This judgement was based primarily on observation of the size of United States assembly plants and of the duplication of equipment evident in the largest of those in the United Kingdom. Whereas in the United States distance prompted dispersal, in the United Kingdom facilities were duplicated as the optimum scale was reached.

Maxcy and Silberston saw the progressive application of flow production techniques to more stages of production as the most important element relating to economies of scale. As they noted the term flow production is a little misleading in that even the smallest plant in a sense uses it. As volume is raised however it becomes economic to adopt mechanical conveyor, transfer, and work processes for the various assembly operations and, in their judgement, an annual volume of around 60,000 units was required to make the extensive use of flow production techniques that was necessary to secure most of the economies of scale.

Edward's study of the United States industry had as its focus the problems faced by the independent motor companies, that is the companies other than the big three, General Motors, Ford and Chrysler. The main sources of information were statements made by corporation executives to various Senate committees, including principally the 1958 submission of George Romney, then president of American Motors, to the Kefauver Antitrust and Monopoly Subcommittee. Romney suggested that optimum manufacturing conditions were achieved with production of 62·5 cars per hour on each of two assembly lines.

"A company that can build between 180,000 and 220,000 cars a year on a one shift basis can make a very good profit and not take a back seat to anyone in the industry in production efficiency. On a two shift basis, annual production of 360,000 to 440,000 cars will achieve additional small economies."[2]

Romney was however envisaging an optimum manufacturing unit, the scale of which would be set by the press and machine lines rather than the assembly line. It is quite possible that the two assembly lines would operate at levels beyond that necessary to achieve minimum costs—all that Romney's statement implies with certainty is that he judged the quoted scale too small to justify three assembly lines. His estimate thus implies that all important economies in assembly will have been exhausted at a single shift annual volume of at or below 90,000 to 110,000 units. At the hearing Romney disagreed with evidence given to an earlier Senate Committee hearing by a General Motors executive who suggested that optimum scale for manufacture was only about half that suggested by him. He felt that the G.M. estimate would have been appropriate to pre-war conditions but not to the late 1950's.

As Edwards notes, Romney's estimates are broadly compatible with those of Bain, and Maxcy and Silberston. All three overlap and suggest that all major economies are exhausted somewhere below 100,000 units per annum but that further small economies will be realised beyond that point.

A significantly different picture is suggested by Jurgensen and Berg on the basis of their study of the European automotive industry. They state:—

"Assembly plants reach their optimal size, under present day conditions, already at a relatively low unit output—of between 25,000 and 50,000 units per annum."[2]

Although the basis of this estimate is not given in their article (which summarizes a forthcoming book) it can be assumed to be informed by examination of European company practice and by discussion with those companies. The estimate is important in that it suggests an optimum size less than half that indicated by any of the earlier three studies. It was made a decade later than any of them and may reflect changes in assembly techniques. If so it is surprising because the main changes in techniques during the period have been towards automatic jigging and electrostatic painting. The former at least has generally been associated with very large scale. It is also likely that the estimate to some extent reflects the existence in Europe of a considerable number of independent producers of quality cars which command a selling price premium, which to some extent would enable absorption of higher costs resulting from sub-optimal production.

In Australia, Canada, Ireland and South Africa, production was encouraged in the pre-war period by tariff and other arrangements. By the end of the 1950's all had for one reason or another come to the fore in policy discussions, Australia and South Africa were pressing ahead with increasing local content, the Canadians were anxious about the fate of their industry in the face of American competition and the Irish were examining the possible consequences of entry to the European Economic Community.

The main issue facing the South African Board of Trade and Industries in 1960 was the extent to which official policy should encourage local manufacture. Local assembly was long established and although the Board commented in detail on many aspects of assembly it did not attempt to specify its optimum scale. It did however comment on economies of scale as they affected manufacture and the levels of production suggested are so low as to make them interesting in the present context. The Board stated:

"a volume of 20,000 units per annum must be considered as the minimum output that can be produced on an economic basis, but that production can be considered to attain a really profitable basis when a yearly output of 30,000 vehicles is attained. On a production basis of 50,000 units all the most important economies are effected and further economies after that output is on a much reduced scale."[2]

Although the Board was discussing production economies implicitly it must have seen the economies of assembly in terms of the stated or lower volumes.

The references to "economic" and "really profitable" make it clear that the Board's reference is not to production costs alone but presumably reflects in addition considerations such as the transport cost of competing vehicles from England and Europe. Only one estimate, that of 50,000, seems to relate primarily to production. In this case the point nominated is one at which all the important economies are exhausted, but beyond which further economies can be expected. Conceptually it is equivalent to the lower point of the ranges quoted from other sources. In summary we can observe that the South African Board concluded that the major economies in assembly were realized at a point equal to, or more probably below, 50,000 units a year.

In 1961 V. W. Bladen, an academic, presented his one man royal commission report on the Canadian industry. Assisted by a staff of eight and informed by detailed public and confidential material supplied by the motor vehicle manufacturers, and on the basis of discussions with executives of all major manufacturers in Canada, the United States, the United Kingdom, France, Germany and Sweden, Bladen was in many ways uniquely equipped to judge on the issue of optimum size. He concluded that maximum efficiency could be achieved around 100,000 units per annum noting that this size of assembly plant was common in the United States and that where bigger plants existed in Europe they usually contained duplicated assembly lines.

In 1961 the Irish Government, disturbed by the possible consequences of British entry to the European Economic Community established a Committee on Industrial Organization. This examined the prospects for a number of industries, including motor assembly. If Ireland entered the E.E.C., the industry would soon lose its quota and tariff protection and face duty free entry of assembled cars from within the Community. In this situation the committee was particularly interested in assessing any disability inherent in the small scale of the Irish industry, which produced only 27,000 cars in 1961.

The Committee based its judgement of optimum scale in assembly on three considerations; first, the Maxcy and Silberston estimate already noted, second, the predominance in America of assembly plants having an annual capacity of 100,000 units, and third, an estimate from the Belgian counterpart of an Irish assembler that in order to survive in the new situation it would be necessary to increase output to "say, 125,000 a year". The Committee concluded that the small scale of the Irish industry meant that in the absence of quota and tariff protection it would disappear.

Neither the 1957 nor the 1965 Australian Tariff Board reports attempted to state an optimum size for production units. On both occasions the Board was considering means of encouraging the further development of the Australian manufacturing industry and was less interested in assembly. It was primarily interested in getting on with the job and not in judging the economic efficiency of the industry. In the period between the two studies Maxcy, joint author of the English study quoted earlier, spent a period at the University of Melbourne studying the Australian industry. He suggested

"In assembly, estimates obtained from Australian sources point to an optimum in the range of 85,000 to 115,000 units per annum for one shift. The key figure here is the number of units assembled per hour, and something like 45 to 60 units per hour is considered to be ideal. Beyond this too much stock area is involved, and it becomes increasingly difficult to co-ordinate and cope with the necessarily huge quantities of incoming supplies. Assembly at the rate of 90 units per hour has been achieved in the United States, but breakdowns are very costly at such levels of output, and the industry there appears to have had second thoughts concerning the desirability of such high hourly rates."[2]

The estimate is interesting in that it is slightly higher than his earlier one relating to the United Kingdom and also in the suggestion of increasing disabilities at high scale. The latter observation is suggestive of decreasing returns to scale beyond a volume of 115,000 units on a single shift.

The estimates discussed in the last few pages are summarized in Table 37. With two exceptions they are compatible, and suggest that the major economies of scale in assembly are realized in a range of production reaching from somewhere below, to somewhere above 100,000 units per annum. Jurgensen and Berg and the South African Board of Trade suggest that the main economies are realized at much lower outputs. This conflict is however somewhat less than appears at first sight.

Optimum scale is not determined by production economies alone but is affected by transport and marketing costs. In practice a series of optima have to be resolved and to some extent the differing assessments reflect different judgements on the relative importance of these factors. The main group of estimates is clearly production oriented, although references to the United States usually note the effect of internal transport costs. The South African estimate seems in part to have been influenced by questions of what is "economic" and not only the parameters of the production cost curve. Jurgensen and Berg's estimate on the

Table 37:
ESTIMATES OF POINT AT WHICH MAJOR ECONOMIES OF SCALE ARE REALIZED IN ASSEMBLY

Source	Country or Region	Date of estimate	Annual level of production at which major economies are realized
A. Major producers			
Bain	U.S.A.	1956	60,000—180,000
Maxcy and Silberston	U.K.	1959	60,000—100,000
Edwards	U.S.A.	1964	100,000
Jurgensen and Berg	Europe	1968	25,000—50,000
B. Smaller producers and assemblers			
Tariff Board	South Africa	1960	50,000
Bladen	Canada	1961	100,000
Committee on Industrial organization	Ireland	1962	60,000—125,000
Maxcy	Australia	1962	85,000—115,000

References: See note 6.

other hand appears to have been influenced by marketing considerations relating to quality cars assembled by the smaller European assemblers, who can command a price sufficient to offset some of the disabilities of small scale.

Further, although most of the estimates quoted specify volume figures none quantify the magnitude of the cost reduction envisaged over that range. It is thus possible that the differences are only semantic and revolve around the definition of the point at which "major economies are realized." This is however unlikely and the differences can be assumed to reflect different assessments of the extent to which volume affects production costs. More importantly for our present purpose, the absence of estimates of cost reduction is unfortunate in that it precludes any inference as to the likely cost of assembly at lower levels of production.

7.3 The Size of Assembly Plants Overseas

Our primary concern in this chapter is to assess the effect of plant size upon production costs. In planning assembly facilities an automobile company must also consider transport and wholesaling costs, and tariffs. A survey of assembly plants will therefore reflect many influences additional to that of production costs. Nevertheless overseas practice does provide some guidance on this question and the diversity of practice is itself of interest.

In the United States during the 1950's the typical plant assembled something in the vicinity of 100,000 vehicles per annum. Bain noted that in 1951 General Motors operated ten assembly plants for Chevrolet, with an average annual output of about

105,000 cars, and a further ten for Oldsmobile and Buicks, with an average of about 85,000 units. Fords assembled cars in 17 plants having an average output of 70,000 units. Similar figures were quoted in other studies and were generally seen as reflecting the resolution of the conflicting economies of production and transport. Edwards suggested that changes in methods of transport seemed likely to reduce the relative importance of transport costs so that assembly plant sizes were likely to increase. It seems that this has happened. In California the General Motors Freemont plant, completed in 1963, has a capacity of about 1000 cars a day, or 250,000-300,000 units a year. The plant makes extensive use of conveyor systems but it is in no sense an automatic factory—in particular it produces several models off the same line and makes use of off-shift and shift changeover time to change jig side gates for parts such as doors. The plant functions around one basic assembly line and this suggests that plant economies continue to a higher level of production than envisaged in the earlier sources quoted.

The extreme example of large scale assembly lies in Europe however, not North America. The main Volkswagen assembly plant at Wolfsburg has been developed, over the years to become perhaps the world's most highly automated assembly plant. It embodies an extraordinarily high degree of automatic jigging, welding, and transfer of panels from stage to stage. The front end body panels, for example, are automatically fitted together and welded on a giant turntable which carries the workpiece from stage to stage and operates, at a capacity of 240 front sections per hour, under the supervision of only five men. A further five men operate the rear section assembly, and another five control roof assembly. The three main body sections are then brought together automatically.

Despite the high level of automation in the body section and the high level of production (the "beetle" line handles about one million cars a year), other sections involve high labour usage, as is evident in the following:

"the trim lines. These are almost devoid of automation, since everything is done by hand. . . . . The sound-absorbing material is fixed inside the body, then cables, headlights, turning signals and other electrical equipment is installed. By degrees the body comes to resemble a proper motor car. Fuel gauge, speedometer, door handle, window winders and bumpers are attached with careful dexterity by skilled hands and then the windows are fitted."[3]

Volkswagen has of course been exceptional in holding the

basic body design of the "beetle" stable throughout the post-war period and this has encouraged development of capital intensive assembly techniques. The underlying marketing assumptions have often been criticized but there is a clear presumption that in terms of production costs alone the vast and sustained throughput of the Wolfsburg plant has enabled a progressive reduction in costs. Unfortunately the extent of this has not been made public.

Wolfsburg apart, little relating to the optimum scale of assembly plants can be inferred from European practice. As both Maxcy and Silberston, and Jurgensen and Berg have noted, British and European manufacturers usually assemble in one plant. Geographic considerations give less incentive to dispersal of assembly facilities than in the United States so that the scale of assembly reflects the scale of the firms total output and implies little about the economics of assembly.

One of the more spectacular of recent developments has been the rapid growth in Japanese car production and assembly from only 50,000 units in 1958 to more than one million in 1968. In addition production of commercial vehicles increased at a similar rate to about two million units. To handle this remarkable expansion the industry has created an assembly capacity of rather more than 5 million units. According to one source[4] the Japanese industry in late 1968 operated 30 major assembly plants having a size distribution as in Table 38. It is likely that the size of most Japanese plants reflects manufacturing rather than assembly considerations. As in Britain and Europe, even if the major economies were exhausted at a low level of output, geographic compactness would provide little incentive to dispersal. Nevertheless the Japanese experience is suggestive of an optimum scale for assembly at least as high, and probably higher than 100,000 units, particularly as the thirty plants were operated by only eleven companies.

Contemporary practice in the major manufacturing economies

Table 38:

ANNUAL CAPACITY OF JAPANESE ASSEMBLY FACTORIES—
ALL VEHICLES—1968

Annual Capacity	No. of Factories
0 — 25,000	1
25 — 50,000	4
50 — 75,000	6
75 — 150,000	7
150 — 300,000	5
300,000+	7

is thus suggestive of an optimum level for assembly rather higher than indicated in the quoted theoretical sources. Once again none of the examples enable assessment of how much costs reduce as capacity increases. In each country however, there are numerous instances of plants assembling less than 100,000 units and surviving, which suggests that the disabilities of smaller scale are not so great as to be insurmountable.

Away from the metropolitan powers there are many examples of small scale assembly. In most instances these have been fostered by national protective policies and imply little about the economics of assembly. A few instances are however of interest.

Australia has, in the post-war period, developed her industry from simple assembly to one in which the majority of cars are manufactured. At the time of the 1965 Tariff Board report the industry comprised eleven companies, five of which used Australian made body panels. Historically the major companies had dispersed assembly plants because of internal freight costs. Plants were built in Western Australia, South Australia, Victoria, New South Wales, and Queensland. The development of local manufacture has led to some measure of concentration, principally in Victoria, and to a lesser degree in New South Wales.

"It is noteworthy too that G.M.-Holden's with their relatively large volume, have restricted body assembly of the Holden to Sydney, Dandenong (Melbourne), and Woodville (Adelaide), each with a volume of over 40,000 units. The Brisbane plant with some 20,000 units and the Perth plant with half that, are restricted to final assembly, that is adding the front end and chassis parts to the assembled body, plus paint and trim."[5]

The total number of vehicles assembled by G.M.-Holden was thus 150,000, in five plants having an average output of 30,000 units. Maxcy notes that the weighted average freight saving, between the internal shipping of assembled and unassembled cars, was about $25 compared with an average ex-factory value of about $1,000.

The decision to disperse assembly in this situation suggests that the additional costs incurred in assembly at an average output of 30,000, rather than 150,000 units was less than $2\frac{1}{2}$ per cent of ex-factory costs. Unfortunately there are no Australian statistics which enable assembly costs to be isolated from total ex-factory costs but it is reasonable to assume that these represented approximately 15 per cent of ex-factory cost as in New Zealand.[6] If this is so the Australian example would imply that the increase in unit assembly costs between assembly at 150,000 units and at an average of 30,000 units was less than 17 per cent.

109

The New Zealand assembly industry originated contemporaneously with similar industries in Australia, South Africa and Ireland. The experience in each was similar in that local assembly was protected, so that local assemblers could discount the disadvantage inherent in small scale production. By its nature simple fiscal intervention tends to neutrality between firms and as a rule encouragement of local assembly led to the establishment of numerous plants as each of the major manufacturers sought to safeguard its position in the newly protected market.

Since the second world war this practice has been followed by an increasing number of countries including many of the newly independent. The pattern is everywhere the same. Faced with pervasive and strong inducements to local assembly most of the corporations have opted to preserve their position in the market. As a result there were, in 1967, sixty-eight countries in which at least some, and on average five, of the fourteen largest international corporations had their vehicles assembled. One of the more spectacular responses came from the French Renault Corporation whose 1966 operations are summarized in Table 39.

Obviously these last examples give no indication of the optimum size of assembly plant. The appearance of small scale

Table 39:
RENAULT CORPORATION—PRINCIPAL ASSEMBLY OPERATIONS OUTSIDE FRANCE, 1966

Latin America		North America	
Mexico	7,600	Canada	4,100
Peru	3,700	*Oceania*	
Venezuela	2,200	Australia	1,300
Brazil	7,400	New Zealand	300
Argentina	27,400	Philippines	300
Chile	300	*Asia*	
Uruguay	100	South Korea	8,000
Costa Rica	300	Vietnam	not stated
Africa		Cambodia	not stated
Algeria	8,000	*Europe*	
Ivory Coast	1,900	Belgium	64,600
Madagascar	800	Spain	71,200
Morocco	2,500	Ireland	1,100
Tunisia	1,000	Portugal	2,800
South Africa	3,500		
Eastern Europe			
Rumania	50,000		
Bulgaria	10,200		
Hungary	10,000		

Source: International Metalworkers Federation, World Automotive Companies, IX Renault, 1968, pp. 11-17.

plants in country after country might at first sight seem to imply that the cost disability imposed by small scale assembly cannot be massive. Experience in other areas is however sufficient to remind us that policy makers are frequently prepared to tolerate uneconomic operations. It would be as unwise to infer the economic size of assembly plants from this incredible diversity as it would to judge the optimum size of a dairy farm from the smallest units that survive under the protection of the common agricultural policy of the European Economic Community.

7.4 The Influence of Size in the New Zealand Assembly Industry

The literature on economies of scale contains frequent suggestions that little can be inferred about the scale effect from cross-sectional examination of an industry's cost data. The major problem is that in comparing the performance of individual firms many variables other than scale are in play. An observed difference in performance may reflect superior management, better product design, more favourable location, happier labour relations, or any of a number of factors.

This and other objections have led several researchers to attempt to measure economies of scale through an engineering approach. Comparisons are made, on the basis of engineering data for particular items of plant, or for whole plants, of the comparative capital and labour costs inherent in plants designed to different capacities. This approach has yielded useful results for some industries but it has not proved practicable to apply it within the scope of this study to the assembly operation. The diversity of activities involved in assembly would entail a far greater expenditure of time than has been available. It seems that similar difficulties have also precluded application of the technique to the assembly industry overseas.

During the present study the Government Statistician supplied an analysis, of the 1964-65 factory production schedules for the industry, which split the industry into three groups. The first comprised the four largest companies, the second the fifth to seventh largest companies, and the third the remainder. Because only a few establishments in the third group assembled cars it is excluded from subsequent analysis. Table 40 displays a number of estimates derived from this data.

The first entries in the table identify the average scale of operations, the largest four companies having an average output more than three times that of the smaller. The two groups concentrate to a similar extent on car production so that product mix is unlikely to seriously distort comparisons.

111

Table 40:
1965-66 PRODUCTION DATA ANALYSED ACCORDING TO COMPANY SIZE

	The four largest Companies	*The 5th to 7th largest Companies*	*Total for seven largest Companies*
Average number of vehicles produced per company	13,500	4,100	9,400
Value of cars produced as per cent of total value of production	79·5	82·3	80·1
Costs as parts per 1000 of factory value of vehicle			
Imported and local materials	757	781	761
Salaries and wages and other expenses	140	166	145
Manufacturing surplus	103	52	95
Wage rate per ordinary time hour $	1·08	0·98	1·06
Total plant labour hours per vehicle produced	130	157	140
Fixed assets per person employed $	8,300	7,600	8,100
Annual electricity purchases per person $	62·6	37·7	57·4

Source: Special analysis of factory production schedules, and information from companies.

There are noticeable differences between the two groups in the composition of costs. First the proportion of material to total costs is higher in the smaller group of companies (the difference is greater for imported components alone). As noted in a previous chapter it is likely that this reflects a tendency by the two largest companies, which are subsidiary companies, to stretch licensing entitlements, with a prospect of recoupment on English sourced cars through a higher margin. This possibility removes significance in the present context from the difference in material costs and also from that in surplus.

The difference in salary and wage and other non-material expenses is more significant. The sixteen per cent fall in such expenses between the smaller and the larger companies is almost certainly due to economies associated with scale.

The remaining four variables also behave in the manner which we would expect with increasing scale. The higher average ordinary time earnings in the larger plants is perhaps surprising in view of the similar labour demands of the companies and the high mobility of labour. It does however repeat the experience of manufacturing industries as a whole, so far as that can be judged from factory production data, and is consistent with increasing returns to scale. It is reasonable to suppose that in such a situation employees in the larger plants would be more successful in wage negotiations than their colleagues in smaller plants.

The number of hours required to produce a vehicle in the larger plants is 17 per cent less than in the smaller plants, and because the average factory door value of cars produced in the larger plants is higher (by about 14 per cent), the saving in labour time is probably greater than this. The counterpart of this higher labour productivity is a higher level of capital investment, evident both in capital and electricity usage per employee.

During the study the companies were asked to estimate the extent to which lower unit costs could be achieved if they were today planning plants of, (a) about the same capacity as at present, and (b) about double the present capacity. Implicit in the answers to these questions is a judgement as to the likely reduction in costs associated with a doubling of plant size between plants designed to use the appropriate contemporary techniques. As with other questions answers varied from off the cuff judgements to the results of more detailed examination (the companies were sent the questions ahead of the interview). Seven usable results were obtained and suggested an average reduction in unit operating costs of $12\frac{1}{2}$ per cent, with a doubling of output. If the results are weighted according to company size the envisaged reduction increases to $14\frac{1}{2}$ per cent reflecting a very high estimate from one large company. The other results were much more uniform, as well as including some of the more detailed estimates, so that the $12\frac{1}{2}$ per cent estimate seems preferable.

In a recent study Haldi and Whitcomb used engineering data to investigate economies of scale in a wide range of industries. They concluded

"in many basic industries such as petroleum refining, primary metals, and electric power, economies of scale are found up to very large plant sizes. . . . These economies occur mainly in the initial investment cost and in operating labour cost, with no significant economies observed in raw material cost. Scale economies can also result from learning curve effects, spreading of set up costs, and certain stochastic processes associated with inventories."[7]

In their analysis, which covered capital costs of particular capital goods, the capital costs of complete plants, and plant operating costs, Haldi and Whitcomb fitted an exponential function of the type $C = ax^b$ (where C = cost, x = output capacity, and a and b are parameters), to a range of data relating to plant operating costs. The 32 examples given by Haldi and Whitcomb show considerable variation but on average yield an estimate of b =

0·678 which implies that each doubling of plant size will reduce average and marginal operating costs by 20 per cent.

The function has the same form as the learning curve discussed in section 6.3, and like it has the principal characteristic of implying that proportionate increases in output will yield equal percentage reductions in average costs, regardless of the base level of production. That is to say, if average operating costs can be expected to fall by 10 per cent between plants having a capacity of 5,000 units and those having a capacity of 10,000 units, then a further 10 per cent reduction can be expected in moving to a plant having a capacity of 20,000 units.

Although this assumption is clearly arbitrary it is useful to consider its implications. It suggests that the answers given by New Zealand assemblers to the question "to what extent would you expect unit costs to fall given a doubling of capacity" should have been similar regardless of the size of assembly plants. They were. Although the small number of responses removes the possibility of statistical significance it is of interest that five of the seven replies fell within $2\frac{1}{2}$ per cent either way of the mean value, $12\frac{1}{2}$ per cent. Further, the answers were given by firms representative of the full range of the New Zealand industry.

This response lends some support to use of the exponential function in describing the relationship between operating costs and capacity in plants up to twice the size of the largest operating in New Zealand today. Table 41 works on this assumption to compare the likely effect on operating costs of moving from an industry shaped as that today to one in which there were only two plants of equal size. It does this for various values of "b" and

Table 41:
OPERATING COSTS UNDER THE EXPONENTIAL FUNCTION

	Assumed values of coefficient "b" together with implicit percentage fall in costs with each doubling of output.			
"b"	0·926	0·848	0·807	0·766
% fall	5	10	$12\frac{1}{2}$	15
	(Indices of average operating costs 1966 = 100)			
Ten plants as in 1966 (see Table 36)	100	100	100	100
Two equal plants producing 1966 industry volume	91	83	78	74
	(Indices of average operating costs· four largest = 100)			
The four largest plants	100	100	100	100
The fifth to seventh largest plants	107	115	120	125

NOTE: The method of calculation is described in Appendix C.

also displays the implicit fall between the average operating costs of the four largest and fifth to seventh largest companies. This last figure is of interest because it enables comparison with the stratified official production statistics quoted earlier. Those data showed (see Table 40) that the proportion of salary, wage and other non material costs to total value at factory door increased by 16 per cent between these two groups of companies. This compares closely with the increase derived in Table 45 on the assumption that operating costs fall by 10 per cent with each doubling of output, compared with the $12\frac{1}{2}$ per cent suggested by the individual company estimates.

The stratified production data and the company estimates thus appear reasonably consistent and lend support to each other and to the use of the exponential function in this context. It is important not to overstate this consistency between three uncertain elements; first an approximate comparison of costs between plants, second a set of informed guesses and estimates of varying quality, and third a theoretical construction of uncertain relevance. Moreover as we have noted the stratified production data makes no allowance for changes in unit capital costs, whilst the company estimates generally do. The results are thus rather more divergent than appears at first sight.

Despite these shortcomings the estimates suggest that an industry comprising two plants of equal size, and assembling in total the same number of cars as the whole industry does today, might well achieve average unit operating costs as much as 20 per cent below those of the industry today. It is useful to compare this estimate with two others.

First as noted earlier, figures quoted by Maxcy, for the Australian spread of G.M. plants, imply that the increase in unit assembly costs, between assembly in one plant at 150,000 units and in five plants at an average of 30,000 units, was less than 17 per cent. Given the nature of the data the actual saving could well be much less. A 17 per cent or less reduction in operating costs over the range instanced would imply a value of "b" of 0·9 or greater. This is much higher than that suggested by New Zealand data and thus implies a smaller rate of decline in operating costs as capacity increases. However, the Australian comparison is drawn over a span which reaches well beyond the optimum level of assembly. There is little likelihood of significant reductions in costs beyond the 100,000 level and even before then the rate of reduction in costs will have fallen.

Placed alongside each other the New Zealand estimate and the Australian example span the more relevant part of industry experience and suggest that unit operating costs might fall by as much as 37 per cent between the average size of New Zealand plant and optimum production levels.

The second estimate is an extreme comparison between assembly of one model in one of New Zealand's smaller sized units, and overseas assembly at a level well above that at which the major economies of scale are likely to have been realized. This suggested that direct man hours per unit are about 55 per cent lower in the larger plant. Overheads are however much higher and when these are taken into account the fall in costs is reduced to 20 per cent. This measure is wider than the previously used concept of unit operating costs in that it includes all manufacturing surplus and not only that part which could be regarded as a capital cost. It is not possible to assess the importance of this limitation but it suggests that unit operating costs would fall by considerably more than 20 per cent, perhaps by as much as 30 per cent.

How then do these three estimates stand together? The first two suggested falls in unit operating costs of 20 per cent between an average plant size of 5,000-6,000 units, and one of 30,000, and of less than 17 per cent between 30,000 and 150,000 units. The third estimate which spans beyond these suggests a fall of about 30 per cent. This wider span is probably not significant in the area beyond 150,000 units where unit costs are unlikely to fall much. It is more likely to be important in the lower reaches in that the plant from which the example was drawn had a capacity of less than 5,000-6,000 units, and so must be presumed to have had higher costs.

There is thus some conflict between the estimates and implicitly the New Zealand based estimate is if anything too high when it suggests that unit operating costs would fall by about 20 per cent between an industry shaped as at present and one in which two plants produced the same total output. Because operating costs comprise only about 15 per cent of the ex-factory price this latter price would fall by only about 3 per cent and retail prices by less than 2 per cent if the outlined savings in operating costs were achieved. As a measure of the possible saving that could be achieved by a more efficient allocation of resources within the industry this estimate supports the argument of those who advocate industry rationalization but it does perhaps imply a saving rather less than commonly imagined. Nevertheless although the saving to the consumer may seem small it is necessary to note that in terms of the allocation of domestic factors of production it is the 20 per cent saving that is relevant. A reduction of one fifth or more in the labour required to produce the present output would constitute a significant saving.

How would this saving be achieved in practice? The assembly companies see three main areas in which larger size would yield significant economies; materials handling, painting and jigging. For the larger companies a doubling of output would permit more use of conveyors on the main line. For the smaller companies conveyors would become economic for some sections. It is generally claimed that increased volume would enable important economies in the handling of components and materials to the line but is is difficult to assess how important this is. To some extent the frequency with which this subject was mentioned seemed to reflect the fact that scheduling of parts to the line, which is a problem for any assembler, is particularly so in car assembly.

The larger companies suggested that a doubling of capacity would enable some use of automatic jigging, in which the various body panels are automatically positioned. At present, jigs vary from simply designed, low capacity, locally manufactured sets costing between $10,000-$20,000 and complex overseas manufactured, high capacity, jig sets costing as much as $250,000. The cost of an automatic jig set would be several times this. Although several examples were quoted to me it has not been possible to attempt measurement of the variation, in capital or labour costs per unit, which are associated with various jigging techniques. This would require detailed study of the operation of different jigs on similar models, and knowledge of capital costs.

Painting is the other area in which many companies see potential economies of scale. The smallest assembly plants are frequently forced to use paint shops with a capacity considerably higher than their normal output. As size increases, facilities and techniques change, with the introduction of multicolour booths, automatic conveyor movement, immersion baths and so on. In large degree these changes are justifiable in terms of quality but they are also associated with reductions in cost. One equipment manufacturer supplied capital data which suggested that the per unit capital costs of booths and conveyors fell substantially between annual capacities of 2,000 to 10,000 units but fluctuated beyond that. At the same time labour costs could be expected to reduce.

Materials handling, jigging, and painting are the most capital intensive operations in assembly and the major part of plant investment is involved here. As size increases management is able to use the more sophisticated techniques embodied in capital equipment designed around the requirements of the overseas base industry. More and more operations are assisted or taken over by machine and opportunities are taken to improve quality. In some cases the capital cost of particular operations can be reduced.

However in one important area, hard and soft trim, which occupies perhaps 30 per cent of the industry's labour force, there is little likelihood of major economies of scale.

New Zealand plants are small and perform the last stages in the complex chain of car manufacture. Although the industry is popularly seen as one in which economies of scale are of great importance a major part of activity in the New Zealand industry is in areas such as trim and administration that are labour intensive and offer little prospect of automation. One of the main areas of local assembly in which economies of scale are felt is body assembly and welding and the freight savings resulting from this provide the main explanation of past decisions to assemble in New Zealand. The transport saving is however reduced by the extent to which local costs at this and subsequent stages of assembly are higher than those overseas. It is generally agreed that in two of these, body assembly and painting, economies of scale are important. The natural protection of transport costs supplemented by the tariff and import licensing has ensured local assembly, but the encouragement has been effective across the board with the result that New Zealand has a variety of plants operating well below what is generally agreed to be the technical optimum. There is no doubt that this has meant additional costs of production and higher prices to the consumer. The problem that faces the policy maker in this situation essentially revolves around choice. The motivation for local assembly is clear as is that for maintaining a wide array of vehicles. The wider that array however, the higher the average cost of local assembly is likely to be. And the higher that cost the smaller will be the economic advantage derived from local assembly. This dilemma is taken up again in the final chapter.

8. MANUFACTURE

8.1 Component Manufacture

The high import content of motor assembly has, over the years, motivated government to encourage increased use of local materials. The tariff determinations were altered in 1939 to ensure use of local upholstery and batteries, in 1948 to add tyres and tubes, and in 1958 to add radiators and undercarriage springs. Throughout the period import licensing has provided a general incentive to use local parts and this has been augmented on occasion by special schemes. All this has had some effect upon the proportion of materials sourced locally but this is still small. In the three years ended 1950-51 12·3 per cent of all materials were purchased separately from the c.k.d. pack. This percentage increased, only slightly, to 14·0 in the three years ended 1959-60 and then more rapidly to 18·4 in those ended 1968-69.

Today New Zealand assembled cars include a large number of local components and materials, the more important of which are tyres and tubes, hard and soft trim, radiators and batteries. Other items include springs, seat frames, exhaust systems and spark plugs. However, none of the major areas of car manufacture are undertaken in New Zealand. Body panels, engine, transmission and steering are all imported although body panels of fairly simple design are pressed locally for the Trekka utility.

It is not possible to provide any statistical summary of the component industry. Motor car components flow from a wide range of industries, and for many items no production statistics are published (usually because of the need to preserve confidentiality in instances where production is concentrated in one or a few establishments). For the few items for which data is available only a proportion of national output is used in the assembly industry either because, as in the case of tyres, there is a large replacement market, or because, as with industrial paints and glass the product is used in other industries. Similar conditions will exist for many other items including most soft trim, which is drawn from the textiles and plastics industries.

In general local components are fairly simple hang-on elements. Because major items such as engines are imported fully assembled, there is no opportunity to use locally manufactured components such as gaskets or pistons. The raw materials incorporated in

Table 42:
NATIONAL PRODUCTION OF MAJOR ITEMS USED IN CAR ASSEMBLY

Component	National Production Quantity Million	Value $m	Assembly Industry Usage[1] per cent
Batteries	0·4	3·0	14
Tyres	1·1	12·3	24
Tubes	0·9	1·2	8
Industrial paints and Lacquers (gal.)	1·6	4·0[2]	26
Glass	—	15·0[3]	8
Transport equipment (industry 479)[4]	—	12·4	n.a.

Source: Industrial Production Statistics 1967-68.

[1] Percentages relate to quantity except for glass where it relates to value.
[2] Industrial paints, and lacquers comprises about ¼ of the output of the paint and varnish industry.
[3] The value of all glass and glass products.
[4] This industry produces items such as pistons, piston rings, mufflers, springs, radiator cores, gaskets, rear-vision mirrors as well as non-automotive items such as pram wheels and hoists.

local components are by and large easily worked items such as textiles, plastics and rubber. Where the components are of metal they are in the main limited to elementary items for which tooling[1] and capital investment required are fairly low, at least by the standards of a fully developed industry. Nevertheless, by New Zealand standards tooling and investment costs can be very high, a problem which is compounded by the wide range of models for which components must be produced. Most of the metal components come from engineering shops which could produce a wide range of products. Similarly, motor components are, for many plants producing trim, only one of a range of products. Many items do however require specialized equipment and some, such as tyres, require a highly specialized production line. Even where the equipment is universal in type, the planning of the production line around particular components, and the orientation of management and marketing to the automotive industries' requirements establishes many of the factories as basically automotive component manufacturers.

The small size of the New Zealand market and the wide array of vehicles means that most components are produced in small volume. The exceptions are those where there is a large replacement market or where there is some standardization. Such factors have permitted a higher volume of production of tyres, batteries and mufflers, although this tendency is to some extent offset by a multiplicity of producers. This higher volume together with protection of the local market has encouraged the considerable investment required in special tooling and equipment.

Tooling costs are at the centre of most firms' thinking when contemplating production of a new item. Their established plant gives them a general capability, but to produce a particular item, specific tooling, such as embossing rollers, moulds or jigs, will be required. The cost of these will have to be recovered against the expected level of production, although in some instances the component manufacturer is able to protect himself by charging the assembly company a separate tooling charge. In the case of one metal component quoted, the proposed basis of charge was a tooling cost 1,500 times greater than the unit charge which would cover material, direct labour, and overhead charges. The implications of this costing in terms of average total cost per unit, to the assembly company, are drawn in Chart 7 on the assumption that production would be undertaken for three years (the contemplated annual output of 3,000 units thus implies a total production of 9,000). In this instance, tooling costs represented an additional unit cost, at the contemplated level of output, equal to one sixth of other unit costs. At smaller annual volumes, the disability would be greater. At 500 units per annum, for example, unit tooling costs would equal other unit costs.

Tooling costs are usually more important in metal working stages of motor car manufacture than in operations involving more pliable materials. In soft trim, they are often of minor importance and to some extent manufacturers use this opportunity

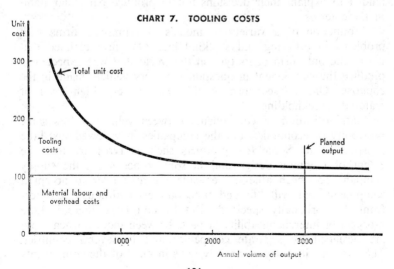

CHART 7. TOOLING COSTS

to introduce minor elements of product differentiation. Even in such areas, tooling costs can still be critical, and there are many instances where items similar in type to, but technically more complex than those produced, are ruled out because of tooling.

The spreading of tooling costs is only one element contributing to the fall in unit costs. The price quote instanced in Chart 7 makes no allowance for the effect of longer runs upon elements such as labour time per unit and reduction in downtime.

The wide variety of products and models produced in most plants implies frequent changeovers in tooling and materials. Downtime is consequently high and for one process where two main characteristics of the final product could be varied fairly readily, one month's production schedule implied a total downtime of almost 40 per cent. In another instance set up time for making 100 units of a metal product was equal to 31 per cent of total labour time. At production of 1000 units, this fell to $6\frac{1}{2}$ per cent. Together, reduced downtime and the learning effect can bring important reductions in cost, as was illustrated in one example where production of each unit of a commodity took 1·75 man hours to produce in runs of 200 units; 1·50 hours in runs of 500 units; and 1 hour in runs of 1000 units. In this instance the saving was probably exaggerated slightly in that there was some suggestion of quality increase between items produced in smaller as compared with larger runs.

All component manufacturers interviewed saw the conflict between high fixed costs and small runs as a major problem and tended to explain their decisions not to produce particular items in these terms.

Production of a variety of models also presents firms with problems in ordering and stockholding. One firm claimed that it was the only firm of its type in the world that was expected to produce the component in question for every vehicle made in the country. One consequence of this was a very high level of materials stockholding.

Standardization of components between vehicles offers some possibility of economies, but the companies interviewed saw little prospect of it. Some few products such as tyres are to some extent of common design and in some other areas the supply company has been able to persuade the assembler to accept a component that will "fit and function" even although it differs from that originally specified. But by and large there is little prospect of interchangeability of parts between models when those are designed by separate companies and in several countries. The overseas industry commonly buys in most of the components incorporated in the car and is thus influenced by design standards adopted by manufacturers of components such as bearings, electrical items and automatic transmissions. Such instances usually however, reflect a bargaining position given to the supplier company by the existence of major economies of scale. It follows that such items are unlikely to be manufactured in New Zealand. For the rest, the separate design of each model rules out all but elementary steps to standardization. Even for items such as rear-vision mirrors, where the mirror head itself can be standardized, separately designed and formed brackets are necessary to enable it to be fitted to the different profiles of different cars.

Standardization could be expected to reduce component costs but it seems that a precondition of extensive gains is a reduction in the number of models produced. This course is strongly advocated by some component manufacturers.

One of the factors leading to reduced production costs with larger volumes is that these permit the adoption of different techniques. As volume increases, manually-operated machines are replaced by automatic machines, and then by automatic transfer of the workpiece between machines. In most instances, the component manufacturers interviewed saw little prospect of major change in techniques over any forseeable level of production. One rubber company, for example, felt that it would need an annual volume of output 20 times greater than at present, before this could be justified. One metalworking firm with a heavy machining programme for a large number of small runs ruefully noted that in the United Kingdom an automatic transfer line producing one component for one model was turning out a quarter of a million units a year. In the New Zealand plant, all but two machines were hand loaded and there was no automatic transfer between machines. Several of the companies interviewed had capacity well in excess of potential demand because they had bought in to more sophisticated techniques, the technical optimum of which lay well beyond present production.

The implication of small production runs is increased costs, and although no comprehensive study of comparative component costs has been undertaken in this survey, some impression can be derived from the information given by assembly and component companies. Generally price comparisons are more favourable for items such as batteries where there is a substantial replacement market, and for the more easily worked upholstery materials. Prices compare less favourably for metal products, particularly for those requiring more complex machining. New Zealand prices generally compare most favourably with those of competing pro-

123

ducts from Australia, less favourably with those from the United Kingdom, and least favourably with those from Japan.

A major difficulty arises in comparing component and assembly companies' estimates of the comparative cost of New Zealand components because the two groups make their comparisons at different pricing points. On the one hand the component manufacturer tends to view the ex-factory cost of his products relative to those of the f.o.b. or imported cost of the same items as supplied by the overseas component manufacturer. On the other hand the local assembler tends to compare the cost of the local component with the "deletion allowance"; the amount allowed as a credit by the supplier when an item is excluded from the c.k.d. pack.

Deletion allowances are one of the more contentious items within the industry, local assemblers, component manufacturers and public officials were at best sceptical of their adequacy, whilst subsidiary companies tended to uphold them. Deletion allowances have been examined by official boards in Australia, South Africa, and Ireland, and commented on by independent authorities. All have agreed that the deletion allowance for a component is justifiably lower than the price at which the overseas supplier offers it for general sale. First, it is to be expected that the cost of producing for the large and certain original equipment market will be less than that involved in producing for the replacement market. Second, component manufacturers regard use of their product as an important form of advertising, which helps direct replacement sales to their product. They are consequently prepared to price down to gain original equipment orders. Third, the manufacturer may well incur some special costs in deleting items from the c.k.d. pack. This is particularly likely in instances where the deleted item comprises an integral part of a sub-assembly, such as an engine. Fourth, the manufacturer loses the opportunity to recoup research and development costs associated with the component, specifications for which are usually passed on to the local component supplier without payment of royalties. Finally, the cost of deletion is also influenced by the extent to which production has been planned around the c.k.d. pack.

Although it is accepted that deletion allowances are justifiably lower than prices quoted for general sale, there is little agreement as to the extent of the difference that can be justified. The Australian Tariff Board for example, concluded that in some cases deletion allowances were inadequate, but that there was no evidence that this practice was a continuing one, or that it was a "vicious" attempt to interfere with the local market. The South

African Board, after concluding that the practice justified special protection, added a back-handed and qualified rider, "This does not necessarily mean of course, that all the complaints that have been made of the inadequacy of deletion allowances are necessarily justified."[2]

In New Zealand, Mr H. C. Holden, a senior Industries and Commerce Department official, queried[3] the adequacy of deletion allowances on the grounds that some overseas manufacturers, who were unable to enter the market because of import licensing, were offering more favourable allowances in respect of new assembly proposals. He conceded that this might be seen as the price of entry but suggested that a more competitive situation could hold worthwhile advantages.

It is commonly asserted that deletion allowances are based on marginal production costs for the component and that the manufacturing company does not alter the packing and other overheads, nor the total level of profit on the c.k.d. pack. Needless to say, marginal production costs for the component are likely to be well below average total ex-factory costs. Baranson illustrated this point by suggesting:

"For example, for a complete kit priced at $2,000, if 40 per cent value normally priced at $800 were deleted, only $500 might be credited as a deletion allowance. Thus the residual price of a 60 per cent kit would be $1,500 (in place of the $1,200 one would normally expect)."[4]

The illustration is hypothetical but is presumably informed by the author's discussions with some of the major automotive manufacturers.

In short there are many reasons why the deletion allowance for a component should differ from the cost of importing it from the overseas component manufacturer. To what extent do these prices diverge in practice?

Generally, component manufacturers admit to some price disability relative to the imported (but duty free) cost of a comparable component. Several claimed "reasonable" comparability whilst several suggested that the average disability was about 25 per cent. This figure can be taken as reasonably representative of the range of examples quoted to me.

In contrast the assembly companies, measuring local prices against the value of the deletion allowance, suggested that the local component was at a substantial disadvantage. Data supplied by two companies is displayed in Table 43. Examples quoted by other companies ranged from a figure of 250 down to an exceptional 30 (the latter implying a local supply price only one third

Table 43:

COST OF LOCALLY-PURCHASED COMPONENTS RELATED
TO THE DELETION ALLOWANCE
Index Deletion Allowance = 100

Company A	United Kingdom	Australia	Company B	United Kingdom
Leaf springs	201	198	Tyre sets (a)	244
Radiators	222	113	(b)	197
Trim panels	186	109	Windscreen	203
Hub caps	153	118	Foam seating set	183
Coil springs	144	110	Battery	128
			Exhaust system	116
			Radiator	178
			Miscellaneous	214

Source: Two assembly companies.

of the deletion allowance). So far as can be judged from limited information, the average ratio of local component costs to deletion allowance would be in the vicinity of 1·60—2·00.

If, as Baranson suggests, deletion allowances are approximately 60 to 70 per cent of the average cost of the item, then the above ratios imply that the average cost ratio of New Zealand components (as compared with the imported cost of an overseas component) would be in the range 0·96—1·40. This compares well with the estimates made by component manufacturers so that the three sets of data appear reasonably consistent.

Despite their use of different reference points when commenting on the comparative cost of local components, assemblers and component manufacturers are forced to come together when assessing the economics of incorporating a particular component. As was seen in section 5.2, the industry conventionally uses a formula in which the supply price of the local component is compared with its deletion allowance, plus freight and duty savings, plus a margin. Taken together these do not imply a very strong incentive to incorporate local content. The transport saving is unlikely to be more than about 10 per cent of the f.o.b. value of the c.k.d. component, the tariff saving is only 6¼ per cent British Preferential (but 45 per cent Most Favoured Nations), and the margin allowed by assembly companies on overseas funds saved was claimed by one component manufacturer to be in the range 20 to 40 per cent. In aggregate these suggest that the acceptable difference between the deletion allowance and local supply price will be about 45 per cent British Preferential and 85 per cent

Most Favoured Nation. This difference would fall in the absence of import controls.

Assembly companies, and those component manufacturers interviewed, were in agreement that there is little prospect of further incorporation of local components, at least as long as the tariff incentive remains as at present. Several component manufacturers felt that there could be minor extensions and one held that a considerable increase was possible, but the items proposed were not consistent with the suggested increase in content. A further significant increase in local content would involve local manufacture of some of the more complex metal components, or engine assembly. Such activity is most unlikely to prove attractive unless the tariff or customs determinations are altered to make it so. Whatever the merits of the counter arguments about deletion allowances, the fact remains that these are the point against which the local company assesses the commercial attractiveness of local components. If as has been concluded in South Africa and Australia, the practice of deletion allowances justifies some additional margin of protection, then the tariff is the means by which this must be provided. There is little prospect of the assembly companies moving to a higher local content without that inducement.

In this context it is worth noting that there are reasons for expecting some divergence between short and long term deletion allowances.

When an assembler requests deletion of an item during the lifetime of a car model, he interrupts the production pattern of the base industry. In this situation, the typical response of allowing only the marginal cost of the item as a deletion allowance is quite natural. Not only does it approximate the cost of the change, it may also discourage it. It is less likely that the overseas manufacturer will marginally cost deletions, when planning a production profile for a new model and having knowledge of likely c.k.d. requirements. This will be particularly so for companies which attach importance to the c.k.d. market and which are exposed to competitive pressures.

We have already noted the suggestion by an Industries and Commerce official that the deletion allowances offered by proponents of new assembly operations were more competitive than those offered by established suppliers. During this study two instances of reduced pricing within New Zealand appeared. In one instance a company referred to concessions of 9 and 11 per cent in the f.o.b. value of the c.k.d. pack. The correspondent continued, "by concession I mean a reduction in the price which would normally be established by taking the usual ex-works price and making standard allowance for non assembly and deletions".

Moreover in a situation in which a progressive increase in local content is undertaken, the process of marginal costing of excluded components must be finite. The practice raises the cost of the remaining items above their true average and at some point this differential must enable negotiation of a more realistic supply price.

It is thus probable that the deletion allowance initially offered by an overseas manufacturer understates the long-term supply price of the component. Deletion allowances do not therefore provide a sufficient base from which the national policy maker can draw cost comparisons. It is difficult to suggest the appropriate size of adjustment that should be made on this account but the preceding observations underline the shortcomings of the present New Zealand tariff on c.k.d. packs.

The British Preferential tariff of $6\frac{1}{4}$ on c.k.d. components is quite inadequate as a means of protection. Because of this, the main burden of protection has fallen on import licensing and on the system of exclusion of items by customs determination The final chapter of this report returns to this question and outlines changes which would make the tariff the main instrument of protection.

8.2 Economies of Scale in Manufacture

The optimum scale for manufacture of major motor components such as engines and body panels is several times that for assembly. Casting, machining, and stamping of metal, all require high fixed investment and high tooling costs, particularly the latter. Each car model needs a host of special moulds, dies, jigs and fixtures, the cost of which must be written off over its production. In the first half of the 1960s tooling for a single model in the United States cost about $US20—40 million. As some of the more expensive tools, including those for the complexly contoured body panels, have a production life of about one million stampings, there are potential economies of scale up to at least that level.

As was noted in discussing the nature of economies of scale in assembly, there are few independent studies of the automotive industry. The following paragraphs review the assessments made in them.

From his discussions with major American motor manufacturers Bain concluded that 300,000 units per annum was a low estimate of what was needed for productive efficiency and that there were probable added advantages to 600,000 units. He continued:

"As regards the shape of the plant scale curve at smaller outputs, the trend of the estimates is that costs would be 'moderately' higher at 150,000 units, . . . substantially higher at 60,000 units and uneconomical at smaller scales. But it has been impossible to obtain quantitative estimates of what a 'moderate' cost advantage is; the firms of the automobile industry seem generally uninterested in publicizing their plant and firm scale curves."[5]

He also noted that the major manufacturers usually operate only one engine plant per brand of car and that they appeared to "have made some efforts to concentrate all possible body production (at least function by function or part by part) in single plants".

Maxcy and Silberston have provided the most detailed and fully sourced estimates published to date. They concluded that optimum productive levels were very different for the various stages of production. Foundry operations, despite the high original investment requirement, involve relatively little in the way of special tooling and, mainly because of this, had an optimum of about 100,000 units, the same as assembly. Machining of the main foundry product, the cylinder block, on the other hand had a very much higher technical optimum of about 500,000 units, this being set by the capacity of a fully automated transfer machine line. The optimum scale for body pressing was estimated as being even higher, mainly because of the need to spread "the tremendous cost of the two or three thousand dies needed for each model", but also because of the need to operate press facilities to full capacity. They concluded that savings in cost probably tapered off at an annual volume of one million, a volume far beyond that achieved by any English firm in the 1950's.

In the light of these estimates, and also on the basis of unit cost estimates supplied by one company for the 100,000 to 400,000 unit range, Maxcy and Silberston attempted to picture the long-period average total cost curve of the firm.

". . . economies for the firm appear to be very great in the early stages of expansion. Something like a 40 per cent reduction in costs can be expected as production increases from 1,000 to 50,000 units per annum. Doubling volume to 100,000 units should lower costs by 15 per cent; while a further doubling to 200,000 should achieve another 10 per cent in savings. The jumps to 400,000 yields an additional 5 per cent, and expansion beyond this point results in progressively smaller savings for each 100,000, the gains tapering off at a level of about 1,000,000."[6]

This specification of the average unit cost referred to all costs, including materials, labour, and overheads. It is of interest to note that between annual production of 100,000 and 400,000 units average material costs were expected to fall by 8 per cent, direct labour costs by 24 per cent, fixed overhead by 40 per cent and total unit cost by 13 per cent.

In practice no English firm produced at anything like the level of a million units at the time of the study and the authors concluded that none was likely to be in a position to realize the main economies of scale for many years. In a subsequent study Silberston, in co-operation with Pratten,[7] suggested that it was this sub-optimal level of output in Britain and in the other West European producing countries, which was the main explanation of the more than two fold difference between the number of vehicles produced per worker in Europe and in the United States of America. This data is discussed more extensively in Section 8.3.

Edwards[8] was interested primarily in the fate of the smaller automotive companies alongside the big three. In the post-war period the combined passenger car production of the independents fluctuated about the half million mark, it rose to 750,000 in 1948, fell to less than 200,000 in 1957 and then recovered to more than half a million. In the same period passenger car production by the big three increased from two to seven million. Despite post-war successes, all four of the main independents, Hudson, Kaiser-Frazer, Packard and Studebaker, ran into crisis in the early 1950's and from these emerged the American Motors Corporation and the Studebaker-Packard Corporation. Edward's question was to what extent were the difficulties a result of small scale?

In examining this, Edwards reviewed the Bain, and Maxcy and Silberston estimates and supplemented these with statements made by industry officials at various U.S. Senate Committee hearings. The most important were the submissions made by Romney, then president of American Motors, to the Kefauver committee (the subcommittee on Antitrust and Monopoly of the Senate Committee on the Judiciary). Romney's statements were consistent with those made by Kaiser, the president of Kaiser Motors, and Nance, then president of Studebaker-Packard.

Romney suggested as we have already seen that optimum manufacturing conditions were achieved between 180,000 and 220,000 cars a year on a one shift basis, that two shift production of 360,000 to 440,000 cars would achieve additional small economies but that beyond that volume only theoretical and insignificant reductions in manufacturing costs are possible.

Edwards observed that these levels seemed consistent with aspects of the experience of the big three. The "actual physical capacities resulting from automation of engine machine lines, in which automation perhaps had its greatest refinement, ranged up to outputs of approximately 500,000 or more units per year on a two-shift basis." Further it was of interest that initial production levels set for the ill-fated Edsel, and also for the Corvair, Falcon and Valiant were all about 200,000 units.

The gap between Romney's and Maxcy and Silberston's estimates could perhaps be covered by Romney's reference to theoretical and insignificant reductions in manufacturing costs beyond the 360,000 to 440,000 level. Further, in moving from technical to practical optimum levels account has to be taken of factors such as the increased maintenance costs and differential labour costs necessary to maintain a third shift. Edwards believed that these might well outweigh the gains resulting from full use of capacity and so concluded that in practical terms optimum production was close to the levels suggested by Romney "and that 200,000 units per year were about the absolute minimum requirement for reasonable unit cost and that 400,000 units were somewhat better to permit two-shift function and some further unit cost savings." This judgement was however weakened to some extent by his observation that in the years around 1960 the level of tooling costs incurred per vehicle produced by American Motors was about half that of the big three. The fact that the big three could competitively afford to expend about $50 extra in tooling costs per vehicle suggests that they enjoyed greater economies in other areas, either in production or in subsequent distribution and marketing costs.

In 1968 Jurgensen and Berg[9] suggested:

"that a high degree of utilization of the economies of mass production, based on present-day advances in technology, can only be secured at an annual output of between 200,000 and 300,000 cars of one basic model and its adaptations to various purposes."

They noted however, that there were still companies which were able to produce with a lower unit capital input and to remain competitive. These included the Dutch firm DAF, which produced 52,000 cars in 1967, and the German NSU Moterenwerke AG, with a 1967 car output of about 100,000 units. In the longer run however, it seemed likely that to survive these firms would either have to achieve above average growth rates, which would enable them to realize economies of scale, or move into production of expensive cars so as to avoid direct confrontation with the big European suppliers.

Jurgensen and Berg also considered the possible implications of radical changes in car technology.

"Estimates which have been presented to the authors show that the range of 'low mass production unit costs' (for car bodies made of plastic materials) will be reached already at an annual output of only about 60,000 car bodies, should the new construction material prove a full equivalent or even technically superior to steel. Replacing the combustion engine as the prime mover of the modern car, perhaps by fuel cells, might also be very likely to cut down optimal output numbers in this field of manufacture."

The question of the possible consequences of changing technology has also been discussed by two Indiana University economists, Farmer and Orr,[10] who examined the implications for developing economies in an article published in 1968. Noting that conventional steel bodied cars, powered by internal combustion engines, required production of up to 500,000 units per year to gain maximum efficiency, they went on to suggest optimum levels of production for the main components. These were based on information from the relevant manufacturers. Production data suggested that electric motor costs would not fall significantly beyond 50,000 vehicles, whilst in battery production optimum output required only 20,000 vehicles. For maximum efficiency in fibreglass body construction about 80,000 units were required whilst new developments in thermoformed plastics suggested that bodies could be economically manufactured in lots of 10,000 or less.

Both Jurgensen and Berg, and Farmer and Orr, were careful to inject a note of caution into their comments but considered that there was a very real possibility of a major break-through in the technologies of body and engine building.

The overseas motor car industry is actively exploring the potential of plastics. For example,

"In the United Kingdom both Rootes and Rolls-Royce are conducting extensive research into plastic car bodies. British Leyland are planning cars with bodies made from structural urethane foam and rotationally-moulded plastics: I.C.I. have rebuilt a Rover 2000 body in polypropylene: Honda are all set to mass produce large body panels: stimulated by her deal with Fiat, Russia is making a huge investment in vehicle plastics technology; and Marbon, Bayer and Citreon are all confidently predicting ABS car bodies for 1972. Another

132

stimulus will be the long awaited electric car, which will incorporate plastics for lightness in both its structure and its batteries."[11]

A recent article by Rowbotham, an English Ford Motor Company engineer, discusses the major design problems raised by plastics and their very considerable qualities. He concluded,

"Certainly the potential for plastics in the motor industry is very high indeed. The all plastic car is inevitable; what is difficult to predict is the time. There have been numerous cars produced on a low production basis compared to the mass production manufacturers' output, so we know it can be done, but it all comes back to the question of economics. The break-even points, that is the point where it is as cheap to lay down metal press tools and manufacture with mild steel sheet, as it is to utilize another material and manufacturing technique, have been estimated. For glass reinforced polyester using matched metal dies and hot pressing, the break-even point is 20,000-30,000 units per annum. Using A.B.S. part vacuum formed, part pressed it is 80,000-90,000 units per annum. Pressed phenolic fibre board is between 75,000 and 85,000 units per annum. These figures may be compared with a current high production vehicle of 400,000-500,000 units per annum."[12]

Rowbotham sees the extended use of plastics as something that will be carried out in stages. "No mass production motor manufacturer is going to gamble with the all plastic car in one go; areas such as hoods, boot lids, and doors are the most probable items to be considered for plastic initially, followed by a gradual progression for the remainder of the body."

It seems likely that the next few years will see a major change in motor car construction and on present indications the optimum scale of production seems likely to be much lower than that for pressed steel. Production techniques are however still in their infancy and it is quite possible that if plastic bodies prove acceptable there will be a radical development of techniques. For example in injection moulding a 1000 tons lock machine was considered large a few years ago but there are now 3000 ton machines operating and the industry may move to 5000 or 10,000 ton machines with a production cycle of 1 to 2 minutes. At the slower rate such a machine would be capable of moulding one million units a year on a three shift basis. Already Citreon are vacuum forming from ABS plastic, in a production cycle of ten minutes, the main chassis component for the Mehari utility.

The investment required to support such large capacity machines is likely to be very large but unit costs are likely to be less than in lower capacity plants. The introduction of plastics may in fact lead to a lowering of the long run production schedule as a whole with economies of scale continuing to high levels. If so then the advantage seen by some authors as accruing to smaller scale industries may well prove transient.

We must now return to a consideration of economies of scale in conventional production techniques in the light of the four studies relating to South Africa, Canada, Ireland and Australia. Only the first two and last are of interest. The Irish study did not seriously consider the possibility of local manufacture. As already noted, the South African Board of Trade concluded, in 1960, that:

> "a volume of 20,000 units per annum must be considered as the minimum output that can be produced on an economic basis, but that production can be considered to attain a really profitable basis when a yearly output of 30,000 units is attained. On a production basis of 50,000 units per annum all the most important economies are effected and further economies after that output is on a much reduced scale."

This estimate is very much at variance with that advanced by the authorities quoted earlier. It is not in any way substantiated in the Board's report and must be regarded as being influenced to some extent by the strongly protective feeling of the Board. This influence is supported by the proposed doubling, to £293, in protective duty on built up imports and the Board's proposal that the content required for concessional entry of the c.k.d. pack should be increased "progressively over a period of years to, say, first 40 per cent, then 50 per cent, and so on until, say, at least 75 per cent content is attained." At this point a still significant proportion of parts would be imported, and implicitly the Board accepted that economies of scale were the main element dictating this slow progress. In this context it is of interest to note that to qualify for the status of manufacturer for duty purposes under present rules, South African companies had to achieve a minimum content, by weight, of 50 per cent by the end of 1969 and 70 per cent by the 1st of January, 1971.

In his report on the Canadian industry, Bladen suggested optimum levels of output similar to those estimated by Maxcy and Silberston. For machining of items such as engine blocks, the optimum was likely to be as high as 500,000 whilst body stampings would require about one million units. Impressed as Bladen was by economies of scale and having a duty to report on the measures required "to improve the ability (of the automotive industry) to provide increased employment in the economic production of vehicles for the Canadian and export markets", he advanced two main proposals. Both modified the existing Canadian tariff practice of rebating entry on imported car parts in a manner related to domestic content and value of production. The first proposal was that the value of exports of Canadian automotive parts should be counted as if they were domestic content. This proposal led, after unilateral Canadian action, to the 1965 United States—Canadian Automotive Agreement. Second, Bladen proposed a major amalgamation of the schedule relating domestic content and the volume of production, to take account of the production economies of the industry as he saw them. For volumes up to 5,000 units an average content of 30 per cent should be required rising progressively, as described in Table 44, to a 65 per cent requirement for a production volume of 200,000.

Table 44:

THE BLADEN SCHEDULE

Number of passenger cars produced or imported by manufacturer	Average Canadian content required for duty free entry—per cent
5,000	30
20,000	45
50,000	54
100,000	60
200,000	65

Source: Report, Royal Commission on the Automotive Industry. pp. 59 and 72.

Australian experience provides little direct evidence relating to economies of scale in manufacture. Maxcy's paper on the Australian industry suggests optimum levels similar to those stated in his study with Silberston, and concludes that Australian manufacture is generally well below the technical optimum and that future expansion should bring appreciable cost reductions. The Australian Tariff Board in its 1957 and 1965 reports was called upon to comment on particular policy matters and was not required to assess the likely nature of production economies. It did note in its 1965 report, however, that "according to vehicle builders, local content as high as 95 per cent is not economically attainable unless the annual production of a vehicle exceeds 30,000 units". This refers not to a technical optimum but to an economically attainable position in a situation where an Australian manufacturer had to compete with imported fully assembled motor cars (for which the Board proposed duties of 35 per cent British preferential and 45 per cent most-favoured-nation), as well as with locally assembled vehicles. The Board's judgement has since been supported by the 1968 decision of Volkswagen, whose sales had fallen from 35,000 vehicles in 1964 to 19,000 in 1967, to withdraw from the tariff status of plan A (which offered duty free entry for imports of remaining parts to all firms agreeing to move to an Australian content of 95 per cent according to a specified timetable), and to dispose of their foundry and engine assembly plant. At the time ten vehicles had been entered under Plan A and the Board felt it doubtful if all could survive.

Table 45:
THE AUSTRALIAN TARIFF BOARD SCHEDULE

Production volume of basic model and derivatives	Minimum local content for concessional entry—per cent
up to 2,500	45
2,501 — 5,000	50
5,001 — 10,000	60
10,001 — 20,000	70
20,001 — 30,000	80
30,001 — 40,000	90
over 40,000	95

Source: Australian Tariff Board. Report on Motor Vehicles, p. 15.

The Australian Tariff Board also proposed tying eligibility for duty free entry to a sliding scale relating domestic content to the volume of production. Whereas present Australian practice is to require companies to achieve agreed levels of local content by set dates, the Board's proposal (which is similar to one put forward by Renault at the hearing) would have tied the required local content to the volume of production achieved. The Board's proposal is basically of the same form as that advanced by Bladen but relates to the volume of model production rather than to the firm's total output. The proposed schedules are displayed in Chart 8. Quite apart from the difference just mentioned it is uncertain whether the two schedules reflect different assessments of the underlying technical economies of scale because the rates of protection proposed by the two official authorities varied considerably. Bladen phrased his report in terms of a proposed British Preferential rate of 10 per cent and a general rate of $17\frac{1}{2}$ per cent. The Australian Board proposed rates of 35 and 45 per cent, respectively. Further, the Australian Board was contemplating a market thousands of miles away from the nearest competitor and could rely on a much higher level of natural protection than that accorded to the Canadian industry by the simple act of driving a car across the border. In the case of fully built-up imports to Australia freight costs approximate 20 to 25 per cent[13] of landed value. Together these differences in duty and freight imply a

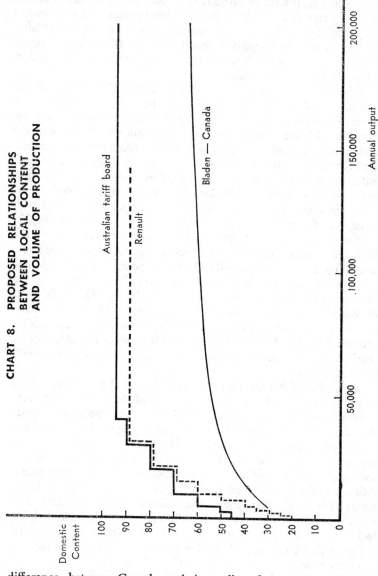

CHART 8. PROPOSED RELATIONSHIPS BETWEEN LOCAL CONTENT AND VOLUME OF PRODUCTION

difference, between Canada and Australia, of some 40 to 50 per cent in the tolerable margin above optimal production costs. For Bladen the low Canadian tariff and minimal transport costs dictated a schedule closely related to his assessment of production economies. For the Australian Tariff Board distance and the

137

established high level of protection enabled adoption of a schedule requiring significantly higher levels of local content for any volume of production. Although the Australian schedule is at a higher level, it is not significantly different in shape from that proposed by Bladen and may well reflect a similar assessment of the underlying production economies.

The Australian market provides another illustration of the interaction of market environment and production economies. A domestic manufacturer must be competitive not only with imports but also with the output of other manufacturers. Whereas in the early post-war years an output of 20,000 Holdens proved economic their expansion to an output of 150,000 vehicles in 1968 had radically changed the market situation facing potential new entrants. In February 1969 Agnelli, head of international operations for Fiat, stated at a press conference in Sydney that with three manufacturers operating within a total car market of 500,000 a year it would certainly prove uneconomic for Fiat to enter the field. He claimed that to make such an operation economic Fiat would have to produce 300,000 cars a year.[14] The developing competitive situation in Australia is strongly suggestive of the existence of production economies to high levels. The withdrawal of Volkswagen from manufacture, the decision of Ford to incorporate only 60 per cent content in its Capri model, and the market problems facing other manufacturers, all confirm the existence of significant economies up to at least the present production levels of G.M.-Holden.

It is also of interest that G.M.-Holden, unlike its competitors, was able to reduce its prices during much of the 1950's; a development which Maxcy suggested probably resulted from the production economies brought about by rapidly expanding operations.

Of the estimates discussed in this section all but two, those for South Africa and Australia, are basically estimates of the technical economies of scale. It is noticeable that the more recent estimates of Edwards, and of Jurgensen and Berg, suggest lower production levels than the earlier classic studies of Bain, and Maxcy and Silberston. This may reflect some change in underlying technical considerations but more probably a fuller recognition of the offsetting costs, both in and beyond the factory, that arise as production increases to the full technical capacity.

It is possible that successful development of electric powered plastic bodied vehicles will lead to a substantial reduction in the technical optimum for motor car manufacture. This possibility is revolutionary in its implications. As the examples of Australia and South Africa have shown, and is evidenced in the next section the developing economies have been prepared to incur a substantial cost disability as the price of establishing a domestic manufacturing industry. The new technology holds out the hope that that price may well be reduced in future.

Table 46:
ESTIMATES OF POINT AT WHICH MAJOR ECONOMIES OF
SCALE ARE REALIZED IN MANUFACTURE

Source	Country or region	Date of estimate	Annual level of production at which major economies are realized
A. Steel bodied car powered by internal combustion engine			
Bain	U.S.A.	1956	300,000 — 600,000
Maxcy and Silberston	U.K.	1959	up to one million
Bladen	Canada	1961	up to one million
Edwards	U.S.A.	1964	200,000 — 400,000
Jurgensen and Berg	Europe	1968	200,000 — 300,000
B. Fibre glass or plastic bodied car with electric engine			
Jurgensen and Berg	Europe	1968	60,000
Farmer and Orr	U.S.A.	1968	50,000

Sources: See notes and references.

8.3 International Experience

The spread of motor assembly and manufacturing around the world means that many models are produced in more than one country. As the scale of manufacture varies between countries, it is possible to compare the economic performance of plants of different size producing the same kind of car. In practice many difficulties arise.

A major problem inherent in economic comparisons between countries is that of exchange rates. Such comparisons depend upon the conversion of costs expressed in the currency of one country into the currency of another, and although official exchange rates are normally used, these may be over- or under- valued. The magnitude of this problem will become apparent later.

Countries differ in economic structure, size, wealth, and state of technology, all of which can affect comparisons between them. In particular such factors are likely to affect the relative valuation of capital and labour inputs (e.g. an underdeveloped economy may find itself buying investment goods at full international price whereas labour rates reflect local market conditions only) and in turn this is likely to affect the relative capital intensity of similar operations in different countries.

In practice cars produced in different countries are rarely identical. Even in New Zealand where production is limited to late stage assembly, variation in local parts precludes exact comparisons with overseas assembled vehicles. This problem becomes more difficult as local content increases and more parts become subject to local variation in design.

Finally international price comparisons are affected by the pricing policies of the companies. As we have seen the pricing of c.k.d. packs has frequently been criticized and there is commonly wide variation in pricing policies between companies and between markets.

Despite these severe limitations, international comparisons can be expected to illuminate two broad issues. The first of these is the extent to which production costs vary between plants of different size in different countries. Second, a comparison of the landed cost of an overseas manufactured vehicle with that of one manufactured locally provides a simple measure of the economic efficiency of local manufacture. This latter comparison is also affected by freight and other non-manufacturing costs but is less affected by the previously stated shortcomings. A government judging the utility of local manufacture can, at least in the short run, take prices offered by overseas producers as data regardless of whether or not they accurately reflect the cost of production.

In the following pages three main data sources are drawn on, first, international comparisons of labour productivity in the major automobile producing countries, drawn by Pratten and Silberston,[15] second, comparison drawn from data supplied to the U.S. Senate during hearings on the United States—Canadian Automobile Agreement,[16] and third, a series of comparisons drawn between major producers and less-developed economies by Baranson, a World Bank economist.[17]

In 1967 Pratten and Silberston published estimates of the number of vehicles produced per person employed in the motor industry for each of six major automobile manufacturing countries. Their main problem was to derive reasonably comparable estimates of the number of vehicles produced and of the total labour force engaged. Their output measure was standardized by weighting the different types and sizes of vehicle roughly according to their labour content. Their employment estimates were drawn to include all persons employed in the automobile industry, taking into account those employed in firms making parts and accessories as well as in vehicle manufacturing firms. On this basis they derived the figures shown in Table 47.

The authors suggested:

"One of the chief explanations for the difference between the U.S. and the European countries must be that greater econo-

Table 47:
OUTPUT PER EMPLOYEE AND SIZE OF INDUSTRY 1965

	Number of vehicles produced per employee	Annual output of industry* (million vehicles)
Japan	4·4	1·6
United Kingdom	5·8	2·3
France	6·1	1·6
Germany	7·1	3·1
Italy	7·4	1·2
United States	13·9	12·4

* Estimates derived from Tables 2, 4, and 9 of source.
Source: Pratten and Silberston (1967).

mies of scale are achieved in the U.S.A. . . . Among the European countries, themselves, however, there is at present no clear relationship between the scale of vehicle output and productivity per head."[18]

On this latter point it was likely that the high ranking of Italy, Germany, and to a lesser extent France, reflected the high degree of concentration within the industry.

Another factor which the authors felt might be important was the degree of capital intensity general in the countries studied. But, from the limited information which they could gather on this point, Pratten and Silberston concluded that the gap between the United States and Europe was not great. They consequently concluded that the major explanation of differences in productivity lay in the scale of production.

Perhaps the major deficiency in the comparison drawn by Pratten and Silberston is the use of national production as the measure of scale. A more relevant measure of scale as it affects production economies is the typical size of car-producing firms in the various countries. The effective economies are those relating to body panel pressing and engine manufacture, which relate to the individual firm rather than to the automobile industry as a whole. In measuring typical firm size, a simple average is of little use as it is affected by varying numbers of small producers. This can however be overcome by considering only the dominant firms within the industry and for this purpose it is possible to use estimates, also relating to 1965, produced by Baranson. Baranson calculated the average annual production of those firms which accounted for 80-90 per cent of the total. These estimates are displayed in Table 48, alongside a measure of the number of man years required to produce 1000 vehicles (this being derived directly from the estimates of Pratten and Silberston).

Table 48:
LABOUR REQUIREMENTS PER UNIT OF OUTPUT AND AVERAGE SIZE OF DOMINANT FIRMS 1965

	Man Years per 000 cars	*Average size of dominant firms* (000 vehicles p.a.)
Japan	227	211
United Kingdom	172	498
France	164	383
Germany	141	649
Italy	135	988
United States	72	3477

Source: Derived from Pratten and Silberston (1967), Table 9, and Baranson (1969), Table 1 and Appendix Table 5.

CHART 9. LABOUR INPUT AND SCALE OF OUTPUT 1965

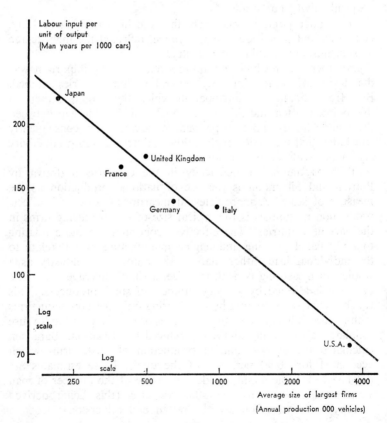

142

The relationship between these two variables is clearly much closer than that in the previous comparison and when plotted on logarithmic scales as in Chart 9, this relationship is seen to be very close indeed. This suggests use of an exponential scale function $y = ax^b$ (where x equals the volume of production and y the unit cost) of the type used previously. The data fits closely to one such function,[19] which suggests that the man years required to produce 1000 vehicles will fall by 24 per cent for every doubling in production.

The most surprising feature of this result is that the function fits closely over the full range (250,000—4,000,000 approximately) and thus suggests the continuance of significant economies well beyond the levels suggested as typical in each of the studies summarized in Table 46.

From the point of view of this study however, more interest attaches to the behaviour of the relationship at lower volumes than those spanned. An attempt has been made to draw together reasonably comparable data for six further countries. In practice the major difficulty encountered was in measuring the total labour force engaged in automotive manufacture consistently with the methods adopted by Pratten and Silberston. The additional results presented in Table 49 and sketched in Chart 10 can only be regarded as approximately comparable.

Table 49:
LABOUR REQUIREMENTS PER UNIT OF OUTPUT AND AVERAGE SIZE OF DOMINANT FIRMS 1965-67

	Man Years per 000 cars	Average size of dominant firms (000 vehicles p.a.)
Yugoslavia	963	14
India	840	15
Brazil	625	49
Argentina	473	28
Spain	294	78
Australia	207	78

Source: Author estimates based on data specified in note 20.

The additional estimates fit surprisingly well with those given earlier. Two qualifications are necessary however. In each of the six smaller economies the local car industry uses some imported components. Although import content varies, the estimated man years per thousand vehicles will in each case be less than it would if the local industry produced the complete car. Second, it is unlikely that the ratio of capital to labour inputs is as stable

CHART 10. LABOUR INPUT AND SCALE OF OUTPUT 1965

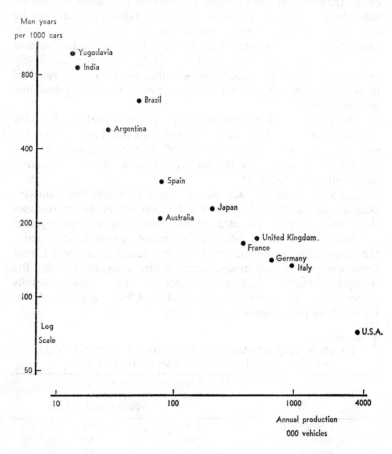

amongst the six smaller economies as it appeared to be amongst the six metropolitan industries. Together these factors could be expected to lower and steepen the function relating man years per vehicle to the volume of production. The first factor tends to lower the man year estimates below those applicable to a fully integrated industry whilst the second, the relative labour intensity of small scale production, could be expected to bias the lowest scale estimates upwards. There is some suggestion of this in the data. In this light the relationship between labour input per unit of output, and the volume of output of the average dominant firm appears remarkably consistent over a wide range, from 15,000 to 4 million units.

These estimates relate to the volume of output per unit of labour input, and not directly to the cost of that output. While they are instructive as to the relationship between scale and labour productivity in physical terms, they offer no guidance as to the economic rationality of vehicle manufacture in the countries concerned. As we have noted the relative importance of capital and labour inputs can be expected to vary. Probably of more importance is the wide variation in wage rates between the countries concerned (see Table 50), and if account is taken of these it appears that variation in wage costs per vehicle between countries is much less than that in labour productivity. Thus for a country such as India a labour productivity (in the industry) of less than one-tenth that in the United States is more than offset by the difference in wage rates. If factor rewards are low, relative to those in competing economies, the disability of small scale may well be outweighed. If however, as in Australia, factor rewards are relatively high, the problems of small scale can be compounded.

The effect of scale upon production costs was discussed extensively during the 1965 U.S. Senate hearings on the United States—Canadian Automobile Industry.[22] Essentially this agreement revolved around the production policies of the big three American

Table 50:
LABOUR REQUIREMENTS AND WAGE COSTS

	Man years per 000 cars	Wages per employee per annum	Wage cost per vehicle produced
		$US	
Yugoslavia	1230	491.5	604.5
India	1061	462.1	490.3
Brazil	754	793.9	598.6
Argentina	489	—	—
Spain	329	949.3	312.3
Japan	227	1455.7	330.4
Australia	221	3012.0	665.7
United Kingdom	172	2586.0	444.8
France	164	2019.6	331.2
Germany	141	2334.0	329.1
Italy	135	1506.0	203.3
United States	72	7180.8	517.0

NOTE: Wage data drawn from ILO Yearbook. Converted to $US at 1965 rates. In this respect it is worth noting that subsequent devaluations in the case of India, Brazil, Spain, and the United Kingdom suggest that the exchange rates embodied above were overvalued for these four countries. At mid 1968 exchange rates, the country figures would be India (306.9), Brazil (412.4), Spain (268.7), United Kingdom (378.1).

For details of method see note 21.

corporations and the concern of the Canadian government to secure from them a higher level of production in their Canadian subsidiaries. The effect of scale was commented on by many witnesses and the following points emerged:

1. The average level of model production was 15·4 times higher in the United States (491,000) than in Canada (31,900).[23]
2. The average hourly wage in motor vehicle manufacture was 29 per cent higher in the United States than in Canada.[24] (From official data it seems that the difference in added value per person engaged was about 26 per cent.)[25]
3. The factory retail price of Canadian-built cars was on average 14 per cent higher than that of the same models produced in the United States.

The Canadian industry thus operated at significantly lower volumes than its United States counterpart, its rate of factor earnings was significantly less, and its prices were significantly higher. The last two elements suggest a much poorer economic performance by the Canadian industry. Taken together with a local content of only 60 per cent, they imply that output per unit of factor input, both in volume terms, was about 32 per cent higher (or alternatively that the factor input per unit of output was 24 per cent lower) . . . in the United States than in Canada.[26] The main explanation of this difference was probably scale, and indeed this was the explanation advanced by most witnesses.

The Canada-United States comparison thus suggests a 24 per cent fall in volume terms in factor input per unit of output as the average volume of model production increases fifteen fold over the range 30,000 to 500,000 units per annum. This is in marked contrast to the previously quoted data of Pratten and Silberston which suggested a 24 per cent fall with every doubling in the average size of the dominant firms. It is however reasonably consistent with the estimate of Maxcy and Silberston that "doubling volume (from 50,000) to 100,000 units should lower costs by 15 per cent; while a further doubling to 200,000 should achieve another 10 per cent. The jump to 400,000 yields an additional 5 per cent."[27] Taken together, these imply a 30 per cent fall over the full range.

The comparison between the Canadian and United States industries is however one between a fully-fledged industry and a dependent one producing only 60 per cent local content. In this situation the corporations could be expected to limit Canadian production to those areas in which economies of scale were least important. The comparison is thus likely to understate substantially the effect of scale upon production costs.

146

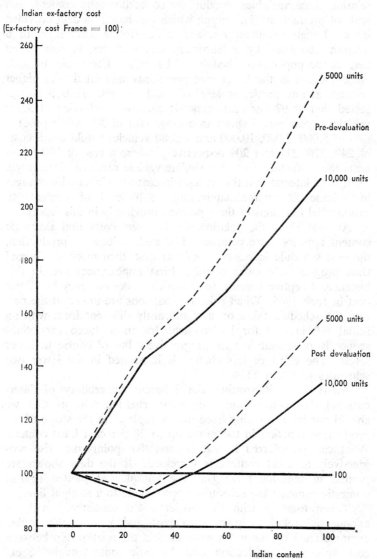

CHART 11. INDIAN PRODUCTION COSTS

Indian ex-factory cost
(Ex-factory cost France = 100)

260

240

220

200

180

160

140

120

100

80

0   20   40   60   80   100

Indian content

5000 units

Pre-devaluation

10,000 units

5000 units

Post devaluation

10,000 units

100

The impact of depth of local manufacture upon costs was perhaps the most important area studied by Baranson in his report prepared for the International Bank for Reconstruction and Development.[28] His concern with this problem was also reflected

147

in a section of the World Bank Report on the New Zealand Economy.[29] In the former report, Baranson presented a graph, relating three variables, production costs, domestic content, and scale of production. This graph which was based on data provided by an Indian manufacturer, and which follows the form of a diagram suggested by a European manufacturer, is reproduced here as the upper two schedules of Chart 11. Economies of scale are embodied in the lower cost premiums associated with higher volume, at any particular level of local content. Thus it is suggested that at 97 per cent domestic content, production of 3,000 vehicles a year would entail an average cost of 300, while production of 5,000, 8,000, 10,000 and 12,000 vehicles would entail costs of 249, 220, 211 and 204 respectively, where a cost of 100 represents the ex-factory cost of a similar vehicle produced in Europe.

It is of interest that the changes in cost associated with changes in volume fit approximately, for each level of content, to exponential functions of the type used previously in this report.

At first sight the relationship between costs and domestic content appears more complex. For each volume of production, the cost schedule increases steeply at first, then more slowly and then progressively more steeply. First appearances are, in this instance, deceptive because India devalued her currency by 37 per cent in June 1966. When price comparisons are drawn at the new rate the schedule takes on a significantly different form with an initial fall in cost for low content Indian-produced cars. Subsequently the schedule rises progressively but of course to lower levels. The effect of this change is illustrated in the lower two schedules of Chart 11.

Apart from illustrating the inherent uncertainty of international cost comparisons this transformation tells us that we should not infer anything from the example as to the shape of the production function in the range up to 28 per cent local content. What can be inferred is that beyond that point costs rise progressively as local content is increased. If the data shown are plotted in semi-log form (i.e. the log of cost plotted against domestic content) the schedules approximate to a straight line.

Taken together with the earlier noted consistency with an exponential relationship between cost and volume the Indian example cited by Baranson suggests that the relationship between cost, volume of production, and domestic content might be expected to be of the following form.

$$LC = a + bD + cLQ$$

or $$C = e^{a\ +\ bD}Q^c$$

where C = average unit cost

$$D = \text{domestic content}$$
$$Q = \text{volume of production}$$
$$LC \ \& \ LQ = \text{log values of C and Q}$$
$$a, b, \text{ and } c = \text{parameters}$$

(NOTE: In subsequent discussion of associated functions the same symbols are used. The values taken are not necessarily the same.)

A function of this form has two main features. It implies that any proportional increases in volume will have the same percentage effect on costs, and also that the percentage increase in costs that results from a percentage increase in content is the same regardless of volume. It is not to be expected that relationships between variables are in fact so uniform. The best that can be hoped is that the form of the equation reasonably approximates the typical reaction between the variables.

In the nature of things, data for sufficient observations to test a relationship of this type will be rare. Fortunately Baranson has published a schedule, supplied by a French manufacturer (Renault), which shows relevant data for production in fifteen countries. This data, which is reproduced in Table 51, refers to the ex-factory cost of vehicles produced.

This yields the following result:[30]
$$LC = 0.309 + 0.00318D - 0.248LQ$$
$$(0.035) \quad (0.00082) \quad (0.0413)$$
$$(R^2 \text{ (corrected)} = 0.69)$$

(NOTE: D specified as per cent, Q in 000 units)

Although it would be unwise to lean too heavily on this, the statistical fit is sufficiently good to justify exploration of the implicit relationships. The exponent to Q, (-0.248), implies that each doubling of output will lead to a fall of 16 per cent in both the average and marginal cost of production. It is of interest to compare this rate of change with those noted in some earlier instances. On the basis of New Zealand data for example, we concluded that a doubling in output might well be associated with a $12\frac{1}{2}$ per cent reduction in operating costs and that local component costs could be expected to fall as local production increased. It seemed unlikely however that the price of the c.k.d. pack would fall significantly so that the fall in total ex-factory costs was likely to be small. Earlier in this section we noted that Pratten and Silberston's estimates implied a 24 per cent fall in man hours required with each doubling of output. In this instance however, differences in the rate of factor reward would do much to offset this influence upon costs per unit.

149

Table 51:
PRICE PREMIUM IN OVERSEAS PRODUCTION,
FRANCE AND ABROAD

Country	Firm's Annual Output	Domestic Content per cent	Price Index France $= 1 \cdot 0$
Belgium	70,000	18—19	1·0
Spain	66,000	90—94	1·3
Algeria	8,000	19—23	1·3
Canada	5,500	22—23	1·5
Venezuela	2,600	30	1·6
Portugal	2,500	28—32	1·6
Ireland	2,000	15—20	1·6
South Africa	3,500	22—40	1·7
Argentina	24,000	97—99	2·0
Ivory Coast	2,500	16—18	2·0
Morocco	2,500	17—19	2·0
Madagascar	1,200	13—15	2·0
Brazil	15,000	100	2·3
Peru	1,200	10—14	3·0
Chile	600	45	4·0

Source: Baranson (1968), p. 17.

Again on the basis of Canadian-United States data we noted that the fall in cost between production at 100 per cent local content of 500,000 units, and production at 60 per cent local content of 30,000 units, was 24 per cent in terms of standardized factor rewards and 12 per cent in actual prices. The above equation applied to this data suggests that the price could be expected to fall by 19 per cent. Each of these examples thus suggests a lesser fall in costs than that implicit in the Renault data.

If the Renault derived function is fitted to the profile of the New Zealand industry (as described in Table 6) it yields an estimate of 1·70 for the ex-factory cost of vehicles produced in New Zealand, as compared with the ex-factory cost of a completed vehicle in the original country of manufacture. The company examples discussed in Chapter 4 show a rather lower ratio, 1·45, between the ex-factory cost (adjusted) of a New Zealand assembled car and the c.d.v. value of an overseas assembled car.

Each example thus suggests that the function derived above tends to overstate the combined effect of scale and domestic content upon costs. Despite this two other features of the equation deserve comment. First, it quantifies (albeit arbitrarily) the approximate shape of the relationship between domestic content and price. Table 52 displays schedules of average cost for vehicles produced at successive levels of local content, and also of average cost of production in the intervals between them. The average

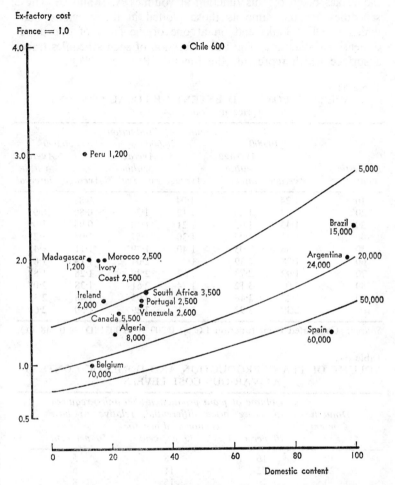

CHART 12.   RENAULT DATA AND DERIVED FUNCTIONS

Ex-factory cost
France = 1.0

cost schedules are also displayed in Chart 12, along with the individual observations to which the function was fitted.

Secondly the function relates three variables, and can be visualized in three dimensions as in Chart 13. In this, the relationship between volume of production and price is displayed on the plane PZQ and that between domestic content and price on the plane PZD. The functions $P = e^{a + bD}$ and $P = aQ^b$ are drawn in two limiting cases. In respect of each, however, a succession of parallel functions can be drawn. In the case of the function $P = e^{a + bD}$ there will be a different schedule for each value of Q. In the chart dotted lines P^I, P^{II} and P^{III}, illustrate the values taken by this function at volumes A. B and C. These schedules are the same as those plotted in the previous chart which in effect looks end on at one of the faces of our three-dimensional diagram. The full succession of such schedules traces a surface which represents the function P $=$ e$^{a + bD}$Q^c.

Table 52:
AVERAGE COST AND EXTENT OF LOCAL CONTENT
(price in France $= 1\cdot0$)

| | Volume of Production | | | | | |
| | 10,000 | | 20,000 | | 50,000 | |
Domestic content	Average	Average within interval	Average	Average within interval	Average	Average within interval
10	1·24	—	1·04	—	0·83	—
20	1·33	1·43	1·12	1·20	0·89	0·95
30	1·43	1·63	1·21	1·38	0·96	1·09
40	1·56	1·95	1·30	1·57	1·03	1·25
50	1·66	2·05	1·40	1·79	1·11	1·42
60	1·78	2·39	1·50	2·04	1·19	1·61
70	1·92	2·73	1·62	2·29	1·28	1·82
80	2·07	3·12	1·74	2·61	1·38	2·07
90	2·22	3·48	1·87	2·93	1·48	2·32
100	2·39	3·92	2·01	3·29	1·60	2·60

Source: Calculated from function LC $=$ 0·309 $+$ 0·00318D $-$ 0·248 LQ.

Table 53:
VOLUME OF PLANT PRODUCTION AND DOMESTIC CONTENT AT VARIOUS COST LEVELS

| Domestic Content | Volume of plant production (000 units) required to bring price differential, relative to base economy, down to | | |
	10 per cent	30 per cent	50 per cent
10	16	8	5
20	22	11	6
30	29	15	8
40	39	20	11
50	52	27	15
60	70	36	20
70	95	48	27
80	127	65	36
90	171	87	49
100	230	117	68

Source: Derived from function $LQ = \dfrac{0 \cdot 309 - LC + 0 \cdot 00318D}{0 \cdot 248}$

which implies that for any level of C, LQ is a function of D.

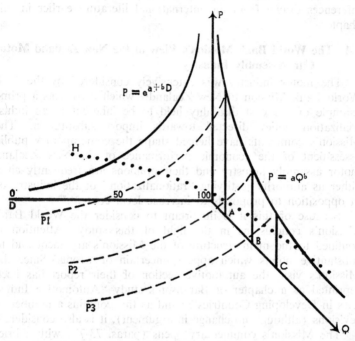

Implicit within this relationship is another, describing the interaction of domestic content and volume. This can be visualized as a series of horizontal contours (H) describing the various combinations of volume and domestic content consistent with production to a particular price level. This schedule is important to the policy maker. If he is prepared to envisage national production at a particular price disability (determined perhaps with reference to a normal rate of protection) the schedule traces the various alternatives open to him.

Table 53 presents such schedules calculated on the basis of the above function. Again, they should be regarded as little more than illustrative. The point illustrated is however important. For any price differential the attainable level of domestic content increases as volume increases (more precisely it increases with the log of the volume).

In summary international experience suggests that increased scale has important effects upon production costs. Although the statistical and other difficulties encountered mean that no great significance can be attached to any particular estimate, taken as a whole they are broadly consistent and are suggestive of strong economies of scale. They do not appear to conflict with the inferences drawn from the international literature earlier in this chapter.

8.4 The World Bank Mission's View of the New Zealand Motor Car Assembly Industry

The motor industry was extensively considered by the 1968 World Bank Mission to New Zealand[31] which used it as a prime example of the cost disability held to be inherent in an industrialization policy directed towards import substitution. The Mission's comments have helped shape the contemporary public assessment of the economic performance of the New Zealand motor assembly industry and their opinions are frequently cited either as authority justifying "rationalization" of the industry or in opposition to proposals to increase local content.[32]

Because of this it is important to consider the World Bank Mission's conclusions in the light of this study. Attention is confined to the main structure of the Mission's argument and to substantive points which appear uncertain or wrong. Since the Mission's visit, the automotive section of their report has been reprinted as a chapter of Baranson's study "Automotive Industries in Developing Countries"[33] and as this contains a number of revisions (although no change in argument), it is also considered.

The Mission's commentary opens (paras. 73-77) with a brief description of the industry, its growth, the shape of the tariff, import licensing and the various incentive schemes. On the latter, the Mission noted the low leverage exerted by the 1961 scheme and commented unfavourably on that of 1965. It wrongly reports (para. 77) that domestic content was "just over 30 per cent" by 1961 and "had increased to 40 per cent by mid 1963" and was in 1967 "the same as existed in 1963". The inference of a 10 per cent rise in domestic content between 1961 and 1963 is wrong (domestic content rose from 35·1 per cent in 1959-60 to 36·3 per cent in 1962-63) but presumably flows from a literal interpretation of the ministerial press statement quoted earlier in this report.[34] The inference that content was static from 1963 on is also wrong as domestic content increased to 38·5 per cent in 1966-67.

Although in a sense minor, this misapprehension was probably important. The Mission noted that in July 1967 "the Ministry of Industries and Commerce issued a letter to the automotive industry calling for further increases of domestic content to 50 per cent" para. 77). Believing that local content had already once in the decade been hiked by 10 per cent over two years, and believing from experience in other countries that the consequence of increased content was increased prices, the Mission was moved to put in a strong counter argument to the newly-proposed increase in local content.

At this point the Mission commented on the comparative cost of local assembly. We have already noted these estimates but as they are central to the Mission's analysis and policy inferences they are quoted once again.

"A vehicle which would cost NZ $2,000 c.i.f. may cost about NZ $3,200 when produced domestically. The 60 per cent is however only the nominal excess cost. At domestic content of 40 per cent, the *net* savings of imports are about NZ $800. If it costs NZ $2,000 in domestic resources to save NZ $800 worth of imports, the ratio of domestic to international costs in vehicle production is about 250 per cent on a net basis." (para. 78)

This paragraph is repeated in modified form in Baranson's study.[35] The figure of NZ $2,000 for domestic resources is replaced by NZ $1,880 to take account of an additional assumption that the 60 per cent imported content ($1,200) is subject to a 10 per cent duty. As a result the ratio of domestic to international costs is modified to 235 per cent.

As noted earlier, the Mission's estimate of the nominal excess cost of locally-assembled vehicles and of the ratio of domestic to international costs in vehicle production are radically different from those derived from cost data made available for this study. The relevant comparative data are shown in Table 54. Because of some cloudiness of definition, and because the company data

Table 54:

A COMPARISON OF COST ESTIMATES

| | World Bank | Average of twelve examples from seven companies | |
		Unadjusted data	Adjusted data
Ratio of ex factory cost of New Zealand assembled car to c.i.f. cost cost of imported car	1.60	1.08—1.22	1.14—1.17
Cost in NZ $ of saving $ of overseas exchange	2·35—2.50	1.12	1.31

Source: World Bank Report (1968) and section 4.2 of this report. For derivation of entries see note 36.

has some shortcomings which I have attempted to adjust, we are forced to compare ranges of data.

The comparison is startling. Whereas the World Bank estimated that a New Zealand assembled car cost 60 per cent more than one assembled overseas, this study puts the differential in the range of only 8-22 per cent. Even more dramatic is the different assessment of the cost of saving a dollar of overseas exchange, a measure to which the World Bank accorded prime importance. Whereas the Bank estimated the cost to be $2.50 (or $2.35 as weighted by Baranson) this study finds the cost of saving a dollar of overseas exchange to be only $1.12 on data supplied (or $1.31 on that data as adjusted).

The two sets of estimates are thus in conflict. The Bank's estimates appear to reflect, in part at least, the application of internationally derived estimates of comparative manufacturing costs without making sufficient allowance for transport costs. This is confirmed by Baranson who also noted in a letter to the author that the Mission "was only able to get some estimate of cost differentials (for one company), which obviously gave a distorted view of the New Zealand case."[37] It is also necessary to note that the Mission's estimates are self-contradictory. Although the domestic content of the car considered is stated in paragraph 78 to be 40 per cent, the same paragraph suggests that $2,000 of domestic resources enter into a vehicle costing $3,200. If this were so the implicit domestic content, expressed in New Zealand dollars, would be 62¼ per cent, not 40 per cent as reported.

All in all it is safe to conclude that the estimates advanced in para. 78 of the World Bank Mission's report present a seriously distorted picture of the economic performance of the New Zealand industry, and do not provide a satisfactory base from which to pass judgement on it.

Paragraph 79 describes the fragmentation of the industry and the tendency of the no remittance scheme to aggravate this.

There follows a brief but important discussion of the relationship between costs of production and domestic content, a subject to which Baranson has paid considerable attention. On this point the Mission concluded (para. 80):

"At low production volumes, costs rise as a function of domestic content. This tendency is unmistakable in other non-industrial countries with national production volumes two or three times that of New Zealand. Judging by the experience of Argentina, where the domestic cost ratio is somewhat more favourable than that of New Zealand, the increase of domestic content from 40 to 50 per cent may cost around 300 per cent of the marginal savings of imports. Chart III (reproduced here as Chart 14) shows what New Zealand may expect in terms of cost increases at successive stages of manufacture."

The same Chart appears in Baranson's "Automotive Industries in

CHART 14.   AFTER WORLD BANK REPORT   Page 39

COST COMPARISONS AS A FUNCTION OF
DOMESTIC CONTENT. LIGHT TRUCKS

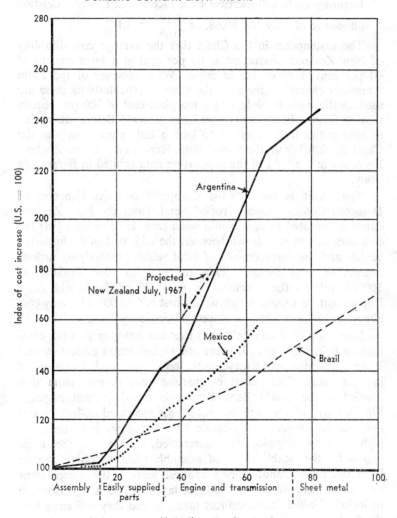

National content (per cent)

157

Developing Countries" along with the data on which it is based.[38] That report also contains, as a footnote,[39] the following explanation of the 300 per cent marginal cost estimate.

"In the 40 to 50 per cent domestic content range, it is estimated costs will increase by a factor of 3·1 for 10 percentage points of local content—the combined result of increased costs for domestic manufacture and low deletion allowance. Thus for every NZ $1 of c.i.f. value it has been estimated that manufacturing costs will increase by a factor of 2·1 over a deletion allowance of only NZ $0.68, or $\frac{2.10}{0.68} = 3.1$."

The assumption in the Chart that the average cost disability of New Zealand production is 60 per cent at a local content of 40 per cent is of course in error. What however of the Latin American examples shown in the Chart, particularly as these are used as the basis for inferring a marginal cost of 300 per cent in moving from a 40 to 50 per cent local content? Before attempting to answer this it is necessary to look a little more closely at the Chart reprinted from the World Bank Report on the New Zealand Economy in the light of the supporting data printed in Baranson's study.

The Chart is titled "Cost Comparisons as a Function of Domestic Content, Light Trucks", and, from the New Zealand data incorporated in it, it would seem reasonable to infer that the cost comparison was drawn between the c.i.f. cost of an imported vehicle and the domestic cost of local vehicles embodying various degrees of local content. Thus the plot for New Zealand, at 160:40, reflects the statement in para. 78 of the World Bank Report that "a vehicle which would cost NZ $2,000 c.i.f. may cost about NZ $3,200 when produced domestically."

Inspection of Baranson's report reveals however that the comparison is in fact drawn between the United States ex-factory and Latin American ex-factory costs, both measured inclusive of indirect taxes. The actual comparison thus departs from that implied in the World Bank Report in two important respects. First the cost of the imported vehicles is measured ex-factory and not c.i.f., an important limitation because, as we have seen, the high cost of shipping fully-assembled vehicles is the main reason for the establishment of assembly plants at points remote from the main manufacturing centres. Second, the comparisons are drawn inclusive of total indirect taxes. While it is reasonable to include United States indirect taxes, in that they will enter into the final price paid by Latin American importers, it is not reasonable to include Latin American taxes. In the latter case we are interested in assessing the resource cost of domestic manufacture. Resources used include imports as well as labour and capital, but they do not include indirect taxes imposed by the Latin American Government. Although such taxes will enter into the final price of the vehicle they do not constitute a resource cost but merely effect a transfer of income within the community. This point is important because such taxes are typically high in Latin America.

Fortunately Baranson's data enable us to assess the importance of these two elements although this can only be done for the final plots on the schedule shown for each of the three countries. The effect of adjustment for these two factors is shown in Table 55. Whereas the comparison drawn in the World Bank Report suggests costs 2·54, 1·71 and 1·64 higher, in Argentina, Brazil, and Mexico

Table 55:
BARANSON'S COST ESTIMATES—LIGHT TRUCKS—JANUARY 1967
U.S. $ equivalent

		Argentina	*Brazil*	*Mexico*
Truck produced in U.S.				
(1)	U.S. production costs	1448	1552	1421
(2)	U.S. indirect taxes	186	200	183
(3)	U.S. ex-factory inclusive of taxes	1634	1752	1604
(4)	Freight	835	835	200
(5)	Cost c.i.f. of vehicle procured overseas	2469	2587	1804
Truck produced in Latin America				
(6)	c.i.f. value of imported components	593	155	902
(7)	Latin American production costs	2186	1828	1444
(8)	Latin American ex-factory cost net of indirect taxes	2779	1983	2346
(9)	Indirect taxes	1290	1013	284
(10)	Latin American cost inclusive of indirect taxes	4069	2996	2630
Ratio Latin American/U.S. ex-factory cost inclusive of indirect taxes (10) ÷ (3)		2.49*	1.71	1.64
Ratio Latin American ex-factory cost net of indirect taxes (Imported c.i.f. cost (8) ÷ (5))		1.13	0.77	1.30
Cost of Saving a $ of overseas exchange (7) ÷ ((5) — (6))		1.17	0.75	1.60
(* This figure differs slightly from that printed in World Bank Report.)				

Source: Derived from data in Baranson (1969), p. 34.

respectively, than in the United States, our comparison suggests that the more relevant ratios are 1·13, 0·77 and 1·30.

Similar results are obtained when the local cost of saving a dollar of overseas exchange is calculated. This measure, which was advocated as a central yardstick by the World Bank Mission is derived by dividing local production costs by the difference between the c.i.f. cost of a fully-assembled import, and that of

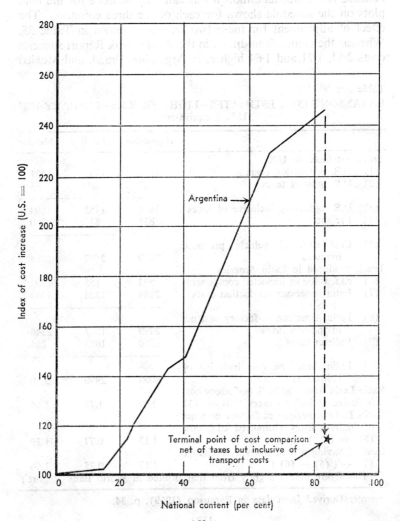

CHART 15.   THE EFFECT OF TAXES AND TRANSPORT COSTS ON THE WORLD BANK SCHEDULE

Index of cost increase (U.S. = 100)

Argentina →

Terminal point of cost comparison net of taxes but inclusive of transport costs

National content (per cent)

160

the imported components embodied in a locally-produced vehicle. On this basis, to which the level of indirect taxes in Latin America is clearly irrelevant, ratios of 1·13, 0·75, and 1·60 are derived. The Argentinian example is illustrated in Chart 15.

Clearly the performance of the Latin American car industries is much better than implied by the Chart in the World Bank Report.

The policy maker is not however primarily concerned with the success or failure of past policy. His interest is in future developments. In considering a proposed increase in local content it is relevant to consider the marginal cost of saving a dollar of foreign exchange over the range contemplated rather than the average cost over the whole operation. Given the nature of production economies in the industry and assuming that the industry undertakes the most economic operations first, we can expect a steadily rising marginal cost schedule as local content is increased. It is likely that at higher levels of content the marginal cost of adding local content is considerably higher than the overall average. Unfortunately the Latin American data advanced by Baranson does not enable assessment of the marginal cost net of indirect taxes but Chart 16 illustrates the relationship between marginal and average costs. For the initial increment of content (at the left hand end of the schedules) marginal cost equals average cost. As marginal costs increase average costs also rise, but more slowly (being weighed down by the lesser marginal costs at lower levels of content). The Chart also assumes that initially marginal costs are below unity (because of freight savings) and that for some easily-sourced parts local costs are no more than the landed cost of imported components. Beyond this point marginal costs are assumed to rise progressively as production enters areas subject to greater economies of scale.

In this connection a direct comparison of manufacturing costs in Argentina and the U.S.A. would be of relevance. It is necessary to emphasize however that the World Bank Report Chart does not make such a comparison. Indeed it is difficult to conceive of any problem to which the comparison drawn in the Bank's Chart does relate. For most purposes it would seem to be irrelevant, certainly it is to the point under discussion by the Bank.

The Bank Mission was on firmer ground when it suggested that the marginal cost of increasing local content was likely to be high. The estimate advanced in paragraph 80 that an "increase of domestic content from 40 to 50 per cent may cost around 300 per cent of the marginal savings on imports" was however justified in terms of Argentinian experience. The magnitude suggested is thus

161

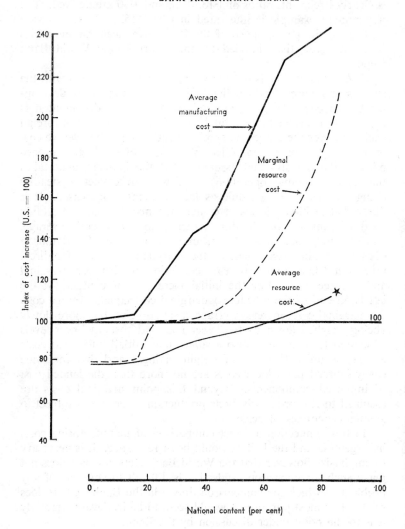

clearly open to question and on the evidence discussed in the following paragraphs is probably too high.

Inevitably what data we have on the marginal cost of substituting New Zealand content relates to past experience and thus to lower levels of content than referred to by the Bank. As the marginal cost of substituting local content will increase progressively, past experience will tend to understate the cost of further increments in content. They are however of interest in that they are suggestive of the order of magnitude involved.

Baranson, in a footnote to his study, notes that "one firm estimated it costs NZ $38 per vehicle to manufacture locally an additional five per cent domestic content, for which they were given a deletion allowance of NZ $18 per vehicle".[40] Implicitly the marginal cost of increasing local content was in this instance 210 per cent of the deletion allowance.

In section 8.1 of this study we noted that examples given by local assembly companies suggested that local component prices were on average about 1·60 to 2·00 times as great as the deletion allowance granted by the overseas supplier. In the same section we noted a wide range of price comparisons advanced by component manufacturers; with a concentration of examples in the vicinity of a ratio of 1·25. The pricing point at which these were drawn varied, but more usually related to prices quoted by overseas component suppliers rather than to the deletion allowance. Deletion allowances will usually be lower than the average cost of the item deleted and if, as suggested by Baranson, they are typically about one third lower, the above quoted ratio of 1·25 could well be equivalent to a ratio of nearly 2 when expressed in relation to deletion allowance. The information advanced by component manufacturers thus seems reasonably consistent with an estimate of something close to 200 per cent as the marginal cost, expressed in relation to the deletion allowance, of New Zealand local content at present levels.

Earlier in chapter 4, table 22, we concluded that on average New Zealand assembly and component costs were about twice as large as the difference between the United Kingdom value of a fully assembled car and the United Kingdom value of the C.K.D. pack.

These estimates are broadly consistent and suggest the cost of substituting local content to the level achieved in New Zealand has been something of the order of 200 per cent of the deletion allowance. This compares with the Bank's estimate of 300 per cent as the marginal cost of local production in the 40-50 per cent content range. Although there is no logical contradiction between them the difference is large and suggests that the latter may be pitched high.

This inference is supported by the function relating domestic content to price on the basis of the Renault company's international experience. That suggested that within the range 40-50 per cent local content, the cost ratio between local and overseas production was 1·79 in plants producing 20,000 vehicles, 2·05 in plants producing 10,000 vehicles, and 2·51 in plants producing 5,000 vehicles.

All in all it is reasonable to conclude that the Bank's estimate of a 300 per cent marginal cost disadvantage in the 40-50 per cent content range should not be taken as established. The Argentinian data on which the estimate was originally made is, as we have seen, subject to severe limitations. Further the estimate appears high when related to the data adduced in the previous paragraphs.

Moreover, inasmuch as the Bank Mission's estimates relate to deletion allowances rather than overseas manufacturing costs they show the cost of local production in an extreme light. Assuming that deletion allowances average two-thirds of average overseas manufacturing costs a 200 per cent ratio of local costs to deletion allowance would imply a ratio of local to overseas manufacturing costs of one and one-third.[12] Although deletion allowances, which in effect measure the short term supply price of the deleted component, are clearly relevant to the comparison made by the Bank it is appropriate to recall that overseas tariff bodies have generally seen the practice as justifying additional protection to offset it. In looking at longer run prospects for local manufacture it may well be appropriate to make the comparison with the likely level of long run manufacturing costs at home and overseas.

Taken as a whole the World Bank Mission's assessment of the motor industry in New Zealand has severe limitations. The effect of these is to weaken the force of the policy recommendations advanced by the Mission in para. 82 of its Report.

"The alternative to further import substitution is specialization in selective components and parts for export to manufacturing affiliates in nearby countries. Eventually, it may be feasible to reduce the number of models and brands assembled locally and to roll back domestic content to a level where the cost premium is well below 60 per cent."

There is sense in the suggestion for international specialization within the industry and in the suggestion that the number of models and brands should be reduced. The final reference to the possibility of rolling back the level of domestic content to a level where the cost premium is well below 60 per cent is however well out of line with reality and would seem to reflect the uncritical application to New Zealand of inferences uncertainly derived from overseas experience.

164

9. DEVELOPMENT POLICIES FOLLOWED OVERSEAS

The post-war years have seen a big increase in the number of countries manufacturing motor cars. New and substantial manufacturing industries have grown in Japan, Spain, Australia, Brazil, Argentina and in Eastern Europe. In addition many countries have begun assembly and most of these have encouraged greater use of local content. These changes have caused a substantial shift in the location of the world industry. Whereas in 1953 the United States produced 75 per cent of all cars, Western Europe a further 24 per cent, and the remainder of the world only 1 per cent, by 1967 these shares had changed to 45 per cent, 41 per cent, and 14 per cent respectively. Even more spectacularly the number of lines assembling cars produced by the major international corporations increased from 170 in 1960 to 430 in 1968.

Almost invariably growth has been encouraged by government interventions, by way of tariff, import controls, or direct licensing, to provide a highly protected environment for the domestic industry. The only important exception is the rapid growth of the Belgian assembly industry within the context of the E.E.C. Also, most of the newly developed automotive industries (those of Japan and Eastern Europe are the exceptions) are dependent to some extent upon the major international corporations of North America or Western Europe. In almost every case the new industries depend upon vehicles designed in the Western metropolitan economies, and usually the local manufacturing company is a subsidiary of one of the international corporations. From the point of view of the parent corporation local development of assembly and manufacture commonly forces departures from the international production pattern that would be considered optimal in the absence of government interventions. To the corporation economies of scale suggest concentration of production in the home base and as a general rule the transfer of particular operations to distant and limited markets is sub-optimal.

For the country attempting to develop an indigenous industry economies of scale are felt in a different way. Usually the domestic consumer will have enjoyed a wide choice amongst the cars produced by the major corporations, which will usually have had well-established distribution systems. Because first stage assembly enjoys considerable freight advantages a government may easily

165

induce a corporation to undertake it, and if one is prepared to, then others are likely to follow, if only to protect their position in the market. Once established the assembler will easily be exposed to pressure encouraging progressive substitution of local components. In this way an array of local assembly plants is established but, as local content increases and production extends to components in which economies of scale are important, this diversity exaggerates the disabilities inherent in production for a small market.

The response to this problem has varied from country to country. The following sections describe in broad terms the pattern in five countries. Three of them, Australia, Canada, and South Africa, originated as British colonies, as did New Zealand, and for their white population have living standards similar to that in New Zealand. They are however bigger. The other two countries, Brazil and Yugoslavia are chosen as being illustrative of developments in countries with lower living standards. The five examples also illustrate the main alternative forms of protection. Some general comments on these follow the country studies.

Australia

The Australian motor car industry is now the world's eighth largest, with an annual production of about 300,000 units. Its growth has been actively encouraged by government since the first tariff on motor bodies in 1902. In 1917 the importation of complete cars was banned as a wartime measure. In 1920 duty on bodies was more than doubled and subsequently concessional rates were introduced for unassembled body panels and chassis. As local manufacture developed protection was accorded to the more important hang-on-parts. The 1930 Scullin tariff encouraged local manufacture of more basic parts such as gears, axle shafts, propellor shafts, piston pins and rings, valves, coupling discs and king-pins.

The Commonwealth Government was anxious to promote further manufacture and in 1939 offered a bounty of £30 on engines (of 15 h.p. or over) produced in Australia. Legislation passed in 1940 authorized an agreement with Australian Consolidated Industries, under which the latter would promote a company manufacturing 20,000 engines and chassis annually. These initiatives proved abortive.

In 1944 the motor companies were invited to submit manufacturing proposals and told that if satisfactory proposals were not received Cabinet was agreed that "the Government should set up a Corporation to manufacture a complete car". This threat drew a positive response. General Motors-Holden committed themselves to all but full local manufacture and Ford, Chrysler, and International Harvester agreed to a progressive increase in Australian content. In its turn the Government made it clear that firms moving towards higher Australian content would receive larger exchange entitlements and favourable tariff treatment. It was no coincidence that all four companies were American-based. The post-war dollar shortage meant that they were severely handicapped relative to their United Kingdom competitors whose market share increased from 40 per cent pre-war to 80 per cent in 1949. Generally the British-based companies were slow to develop manufacture.

General Motors-Holden produced their first car in 1948 and achieved an output of 7,725 units in their first year. By 1951 annual production was running at 50,000 and by 1958 it had increased to 100,000. In 1968 150,000 units were produced and by then two million Holdens had come off the line.

In 1958 following a Tariff Board report a new tariff structure was introduced. This somewhat extended and raised the level of protection accorded to the industry. Some additional components were protected and for the first time built up units became subject to a simple ad valorem duty. Engines, chassis components, and front end panels received continued duty-free entry when brought in as original equipment.

With the removal of import controls in the early 1960's the tariff became the sole instrument of protection. Australian content fell and there was an increased tendency to import in c.k.d. form. A further tariff inquiry was called. This recommended concessional entry of non-competitive imported parts provided that manufacturers attained specified levels of content, the latter varying according to the volume of production. This proposal has already been discussed in section 8.2. In the event it was adopted in a substantially modified form.

The 1964 plan comprised two main parts. Under Plan A, manufacturers who undertook to achieve 95 per cent Australian content within five years were accorded duty-free entry for all imported components. Alternatively manufacturers could, under Plan SV, receive limited duty concessions if their content was 45 per cent, 50 per cent or 60 per cent, provided their assembly of the model concerned did not exceed 2500, 5000, or 7500 vehicles a year respectively. Effectively the Government ignored the three middle steps of the schedule recommended by the Tariff Board, which had provided for a progressive increase in content up to 90 per cent with an annual production of 40,000 vehicles.

The effect of the scheme was to provide a strong incentive, for manufacturers producing models in annual volumes of more than 7500, to put them forward for inclusion under Plan A. But, given the nature of production economies in the industry Plan A proved most attractive in respect of models produced at high volumes. The manufacturer of models in the range 7500—25,000 approximately was placed at a disadvantage relative to three groups, namely; fully assembled imports (dutiable at 35 per cent British Preferential and 45 per cent Most Favoured Nation), models produced in volumes less than 7500 (which received some tariff concessions but incurred relatively little cost disability through local purchasing), and finally those vehicles produced in high volume (which benefited from economies of scale in component purchase and in production). The tariff and local content plans thus provided a watershed in the range 7500 to 25,000 vehicles and in practice this proved most disadvantageous to producers of the more popular light cars including principally the Volkswagen, the B.M.C. 850 and 1100, the Ford Cortina, the Hillman Hunter and later the Holden Torana. Following reduced sales in the face of Japanese competition Volkswagen in 1967 reverted to the status of assembler and disposed of its engine plant. The others continued under plan A with difficulty and late in 1968 the Government announced modifications to the tariff system.

First, for cars in production of less than 25,000, manufacturers are offered duty concessions on remaining imports provided they reach 85 per cent local content. Second at the other end of the watershed the system has been changed so that an assembler whose production exceeds the volume specified for his level of content loses concessional entry only on imports in excess of that volume. It is hoped that this will discourage assemblers from introducing a further model, or from importing fully-built-up units, rather than expanding production to a point where increased content could be achieved.

Despite these changes there is still something of a watershed separating the assemblers from the producers. This pattern has the advantage of forcing all cars with a high sales volume to move to a high local content while leaving room for a range of models produced in smaller numbers. Choice is maintained but not at the expense of inducing production of a wide range of models at the most uneconomic level of production. While this policy has proved effective for the larger cars it has not yet been fully effective in the light car field. Whether it will do so without further modification depends on whether one or two Australian models achieve a volume of sales sufficient to realize production economies, and so increase their competitiveness.

The 1969 pattern of production is shown in Table 56. In addition to Australian-produced cars, 68,100 cars were assembled from imported parts. This latter assembly industry is comparable to that in New Zealand and presumably shares any disabilities inherent in small scale and fragmented production. Its survival suggests that at present the resultant additional costs are similar to those incurred in full manufacture at present volumes. It will be interesting to see if this pattern persists as the market expands.

Table 56:
AUSTRALIAN PRODUCTION, 1969   000 UNITS

A Australian manufactured			
95 per cent content		*85 per cent content*	
Holden	139·0	Austin 1800	12·2
Falcon/Fairlane	72·0	Morris Mini	12·5
Valiant	47·4	Morris	
Torana/Viva	18·7	1100/1500	13·5
		Cortina	16·9
Total	277·1	Hillman Hunter/	
		Arrow	13·8
		Total	68·8

B Australian assembled					
60 per cent content		*50 per cent content*		*45 per cent content*	
Toyota Crown	8·3	Renault R10	2·9	Dodge Phoenix	0·7
Toyota Corona	9·1	Capri	3·3	MG "B" Sports	1·1
Toyota Corolla	9·7	VW 1600	4·4	Peugeot 404	1·9
Datsun 1000	9·0			Rambler Rebel	0·6
Datsun 1600	6·7	Total	10·6	Renault R16	2·1
VW "Beetle"	6·5			Triumph Spitfire	0·1
				Triumph 2000	1·6
Total	49·3			VW Country Buggy	0·2
				Total	8·2

Summary

	Number of models	Total Production
Manufacture and assembly	9	345·9
Assembly only	17	68·1
	26	414·0

Source: Australian Industries Development Association Bulletin No. 207. April 1970, page 19.

Canada

The Canadian automotive industry dates from 1904 when the Ford Motor Company began putting bodies and wheels on chassis ferried across the river from Detroit. The industry is essentially an extension of that in the United States. Most cars are of American origin and all the major units are American owned. Throughout its growth the Canadian industry has been protected by tariff and other means. In view of the proximity of the American base industries it is not surprising that Canada has proved an innovator in protective techniques.

In 1926 the tariff on vehicles was reduced so as to bring Canadian car prices more into line with their American counterparts. To preserve protection on local assembly the tariff on non-competitive components was reduced and, most importantly, provision made for the partial drawback of duty on components if at least 50 per cent of the final factory cost of the car was incurred in the British empire.

The 1936 tariff revision developed this principle. Parts of a kind not made in Canada could be imported duty free provided specified levels of content, which varied according to the number of cars produced, were achieved. The required content was 40 per cent for runs of less than 10,000, 50 per cent for production in the range 10,000—20,000 and 60 per cent for higher levels.

Whereas Canada was one of the world's major car exporters (partly because of her ability to supply American designed cars within the Commonwealth at British Preferential duty rates) her relative position declined following the second world war. Moreover, Canada which had been a net exporter of vehicles, became a heavy net importer. This trend led to the appointment in 1960 of Professor Bladen as a one-man royal commission. As noted in section 8.2 Bladen proposed a substantial change in the schedule relating Canadian content to the volume of production. More importantly he suggested that exports of automotive parts and vehicles should be counted as Canadian content in determining eligibility for drawback of duty. Effectively the remission of import duties would subsidise and encourage Canadian exports of parts.

In 1962 and 1963 the Canadian Government implemented plans under which "duties were remitted on all imports of motor vehicles and original equipment parts to the extent that the company in question increased the Canadian content of its exports of all automotive products above that of the base period."[1] The result was a rapid increase in Canadian exports to the United States, from $Canadian 11 million in 1962 to $89 million in 1964. This led to numerous complaints from American component manufacturers and petitions for countervailing duties.

Following extensive discussions which culminated in meetings between the American President and the Canadian Prime Minister, the U.S.—Canadian Automotive Agreement was signed in January 1965. This had two main features; first, the removal of tariffs on automotive parts and motor vehicles traded between Canada and the United States by manufacturing companies, and second, firm assurances from the Canadian subsidiaries of the three major American producers that they would maintain their present ratio of Canadian vehicle production to vehicle sales, that they would increase Canadian value added by specified amounts, and that they would report quarterly to the Canadian Minister of Industry.

The agreement has had a spectacular effect. Between 1964 and 1968 U.S. exports to Canada increased from $711 million to $2,870 million whilst Canadian exports increased from $99 million to $2,435 million. As a consequence the Canadian automotive trade deficit with the United States declined from $611 million to $435 million. Although a major part of the increase in trade resulted from increased trade in parts, the absolute increase in trade in completed automobiles was even larger.

Table 57:

U.S.—CANADIAN AUTOMOTIVE TRADE, $ MILLION CANADIAN

	1964	1968
Canadian imports from U.S.		
Vehicles	61	1081
Parts	649	1789
Total:	711	2870
Canadian exports to the U.S.		
Vehicles	26	1686
Parts	73	749
Total:	99	2435
Canadian net imports from U.S.	611	435

Source: Based on Canadian Trade Statistics—analysis supplied by Canadian Government Trade Commission, Wellington.

The removal of tariffs has enabled the big three producers to rationalize the pattern of production between U.S. and Canadian plants. At the time of the agreement a staff report to the U.S. Senate Committee on Finance described the Canadian industry as follows:

"Although Canada produces and consumes the same automobiles under much the same conditions as does the United States, costs and prices are significantly higher than in the United States. This is so even in the face of lower Canadian wages and certain other Canadian cost advantages.

"A principal reason is the lower volume of Canadian output . . . Canadian manufacturers typically operate at levels too low to permit them to get the full advantage of such economies. For example, the Ford Motor Co. now makes some 60 different models of five distinct passenger car lines at its assembly plant in Canada. Just across the river on the U.S. side, Ford's great River Rouge assembly plant produces only three models at the Mustang line. Similar disparities exist for the other producers; in only a few auto parts and in none of the vehicles is the volume of Canadian output large enough to bring costs down to American levels."[2]

The agreement has permitted a major change in this pattern. The substantial trade in finished vehicles reflects concentration of production on both sides of the border. Automotive parts manufacturers have been able to stop many small production runs and to concentrate the range of products at the same time as increasing total production and exports.

As a consequence of these changes the margin between Canadian and U.S. wholesale prices has reduced from 8·5 per cent in 1965 to 3·8 per cent in 1969.[3] Perhaps most spectacularly the United Automotive Workers Union (which along with Ford had in 1960 suggested an analogous scheme to Bladen) was able to negotiate parity of wage rates between auto workers in Canada and the U.S. At the time of the agreement Canadian rates were 20 to 25 per cent lower in Canada than in the U.S.

"The automotive trade agreement threw open a single market to the plants in both countries. Vast programs of expansion and reconversion thoroughly transformed the Canadian branch of the industry, giving it the latest technologies and enabling it to produce the larger runs for an expanded market that in turn made possible the same economies of scale that had long prevailed in U.S. manufacture. U.A.W. members on both sides of the border were working for the same companies, doing the same jobs at the same machines, producing the same product for the same market."[4]

From the Canadian Government's viewpoint the keystone to the agreement was the commitment by the major automotive companies to increase Canadian value added in proportion to Canadian sales, and, in any event to increase Canadian value added to specified levels. Effectively the traditional protective device of the tariff which had induced Canadian assembly of most cars produced in the United States, was replaced by corporation to government undertakings, which committed the former to expand Canadian production, but left them free to shape that production at will. Unilateral tariff setting was replaced by direct negotiation with the international corporations.

South Africa

The early history of the South African industry is very similar to that in New Zealand. The first major assembly plants (Ford and General Motors), were established in the 1920's and a further five plants began operation in the period 1939-49. Initially activity was confined to assembly, with incorporation of elementary local components.

In 1960 the Board of Trade and Industries investigated the industry and concluded that the time was ripe for rationalization and for an increase in local content. With a normal capacity of about 118,000 vehicles, and a 1959 output of 83,000, the industry was assembling 24 makes of car and 102 models. The local content was low, about 35-40 per cent on the New Zealand basis of comparing all local expenses (including factor rewards) to total ex-factory cost. On the usual South African measure, of local content in terms of material purchases only, the Board estimated that local content was only about 18 per cent.

As noted in a previous section the Board spent some time examining economies of scale in the industry and suggested that the preconditions of successful manufacture would be a reduction in the number of models produced, perhaps to six basic models, and standardization of components. It saw a considerable potential for standardization in the case of engines, gear boxes, axles and front suspension, steering gear, brakes, wheels, and many other items.

The Board saw three main means by which government could encourage increased South African content. The first, the direct licensing of selected manufacturers as in South America, Spain and India was characterized by the Board as mercantilist, and opposed by it. The second, adoption of a progressive schedule of components that must be sourced locally, had been floated with the manufacturers, who opposed it, as did the Board. Instead, the Board favoured use of the tariff to provide direct protection to assembly and to local components and suggested a scheme of tariff rebates for manufacturers prepared to achieve set levels of local content.

In arguing the case for a rebate system the Board said:

"All the local assembly plants are closely affiliated with overseas manufacturers of cars, either as branches or as contractors, and they are therefore interested primarily in the maintenance of the status quo and where all firms are interested in the maintenance of the existing position, it cannot be in the interest of any of them on his own to initiate the next forward move. There can therefore be no assurance that the South African content of cars will be gradually but progressively increased by the imposition of the appropriate tariff alone."[5]

In March 1962 the government outlined its local content policy which, in addition to the existing protection of local assembly by differential tariffs provided for:

1. tariff protection for certain locally made components (in practice 20 per cent ad valorem),
2. the granting of an increasing number of import permits for individual models as local content increased, and
3. the rebate of excise duty as local content increased.

In September 1963 approval was granted for engine manufacturing programmes which provided:

Initially for the assembly of imported engines, leading to: machining of engine components from imported castings, then to: the use of local engine castings when available.

Such engines would count as local content from the first stage, even though there were no local components, and would qualify for excise rebates and increased import permits.

In July 1964 the original 1962 incentive scheme was modified substantially and it has been subject to further change since then. As at mid 1968 assemblers were offered freedom from import control on cars for which they undertook to maintain a minimum local content of 45 per cent by weight, increasing to 55 per cent by the end of 1969, and to 70 per cent by the end of 1970. Imported components for such cars, which would be declared "manufactured" would benefit from rebates of duty. Motor cars which are not declared manufactured remain subject to strict import controls.

Favourable duty and excise conditions together with the attractive prospect, first of more liberal import licensing and subsequently of complete freedom from such control, have provided a very strong incentive to assemblers to undertake the necessary increases in local content. It is likely also that experience in other countries suggested to the companies the dangers of staying outside schemes designed to increase local content. The results have been spectacular. By 1968 32 car models, drawn from 12 of the international motor corporations, were classed as manufactured. As at the end of 1967 26 of these, each supporting on average four variants, were under assembly at one or other of the nine major assembly plants.

The accounting of locally assembled engines as local content has provided a strong incentive to such assembly. British Motors (in 1964), Ford, General Motors, Volkswagen, Renault, and Chrysler have all built engine assembly and machining plants which now total eight in number. Only British Motors had, by mid 1968, proceeded the further step of producing engine block castings. General Motors began simple panel pressing in 1962 and Volkswagen followed in 1967 but to date only Datsun-Nissan has undertaken a full range of body pressings.

Obviously the Board of Trade and Industries' view that production should be limited to about six basic models has not prevailed. Instead of the 20,000 unit production considered by the Board as the minimum that could be produced on an economic basis the average annual production of South African manufactured models was only 4,500 in 1967. The like figure for production in Australia was 35,000, in the United Kingdom 60,000 and in France 145,000.

To date there is apparently little evidence that the restricted level of local production has seriously affected prices but the increase in local content has not been all that great and there are some special factors:

"South Africa is in a better position than most countries to undertake local manufacture. It has cheap raw materials, relatively cheap labour and sufficient technical ability. The danger is that these advantages are likely to be outweighed by the difficulties outlined above, which result in spiralling prices. There is as yet little evidence of local manufacture causing large scale price increases though many assemblers cited rising local costs as a factor in higher prices."[6]

Further, it is reported that the investment required to bring all the committed models to 70 per cent is proving too great and there have been moves to put back the target date.

It is too early to judge the success of the South African programme. Given the present and prospective size of the market a move to local manufacture was clearly attractive. What has been less so is the extreme fragmentation within the manufacturing programme but it is not possible to judge from the information available what the cost of this has been.

Brazil

Apart from some small scale assembly there was no Brazilian automotive industry before 1956. Since then imports have been restricted to manufacturers who were prepared to increase local content rapidly. A target of 90-95 per cent local content by weight was set for 1960 and since 1964 the average content has been more than 98 per cent.

Although there are eleven approved manufacturers, production is heavily concentrated, with Volkswagen producing 51 per cent of all vehicles, and 61 per cent of motor cars. The next biggest company is Willys Overland and together these produce 70 per cent of all vehicles and 74 per cent of motor cars. Recent links between Ford and Willys Overland, and Volkswagen and Vemag (a local company building DKW and Auto-Union cars) will increase this strong concentration. In 1967 production totalled 225,400 vehicles including 132,000 motor cars.

There has been some considerable experimentation by drawing engines and body designs from different sources but it appears that the present tendency is towards conforming to the production models of the major corporations. This is so even when the producing company is financially independent of the overseas corporations. In such cases it is likely to use tooling based on some overseas design and in some cases to use plant that has gone out of production overseas. It is now generally accepted that the initial growth phase of the industry is over and that it is unlikely that there will be any further entrants to the market or that there will be an attempt to manufacture a fully Brazilian designed car in the near future. As noted in section 8.4 the data presented in Baranson's report on the automotive industries in developing economies shows that for the one Brazilian truck instanced the ex-factory cost net of taxes was 28 per cent higher in Brazil than in the United States but that when freight costs were taken into account the local resource cost of saving a dollar of overseas exchange was only $0.75. The figure serves to confirm that Brazilian production costs are not a major problem. It is likely that this favourable performance is due in part to the concentration of production evident in Brazil.

Yugoslavia

The Yugoslavian motor industry is a post-war growth and not until 1953 did annual production of all vehicles pass 1000 units. In 1960 total production was less than 16,000 but by 1967 it had increased to 55,600 including 42,300 motor cars. Twenty per cent of total production was exported. Motor car production is concentrated in one plant, Crvena Zastava ("Red Flag") which manufactures under licence from Fiat of Italy which since 1968 has had a 10 per cent investment in the enterprise. Some small-scale assembly of other West European cars is undertaken in other plants. In 1966 the CZ plant produced or assembled four models of motor car at volumes of 25,650, 5,700, 800, and 750. Production of the two main models is expected to reach 50,000 and 20,000 units in 1969. Overall the local content was in excess of 70 per cent in 1966.

A considerable expansion is planned for the CZ plant. By 1972 production should reach 130,000 units. A feature of the expansion is provision for international specialization. In addition to the basic dependence on the Italian firm for research and design, agreement has been reached on the exchange of parts with Poland and for the use of Yugoslav components in cars manufactured in the U.S.S.R. The CZ plant already exchanges foundry products with a similar plant in Rumania. As well as participating in this East European specialization Crvena Zastava has an agreement with Fiat under which the latter will market internationally an annual average of $5 million of Yugoslav vehicles and parts during the ensuing decade.

By these means the Yugoslav industry should be able to achieve an annual level of production which will enable significantly lower unit costs of production than would be likely if its total output was directed at the domestic market. It is also worth emphasizing that this production is through one plant and has to date been heavily concentrated in terms of models produced.

Summary

The above examples could be extended, almost indefinitely, to illustrate various aspects of national development policies but enough has been said to enable the main features to be drawn. Most countries now encourage local assembly, and many have advanced well towards full manufacture. Because of the encouragement given by way of import licensing and the tariff, because of freight savings, and because past experience has shown the dangers of staying out of the market, most of the international motor corporations are induced to establish plants.

At this stage it is worth recalling the schedule, relating domestic content to marginal and average costs of local production, which was advanced in section 8.4. This suggested that for most developing economies transport savings alone would provide sufficient offset to the additional costs incurred in local assembly, but, that as local content is increased the developing economy faces a progressively steeper increase in the marginal cost of substituting local for imported components.

The threshold for entry is thus low and experience shows that most companies are easily induced to undertake local assembly. Further, any savings consequent on assembly can be used to offset some increased costs. The use of some local components is thus easily encouraged and at this point there is relatively little conflict between the fragmented nature of the industry and production economies. That problem comes later when consideration is given to the local manufacture of components subject to substantial economies of scale. At this point, and assuming that the size of the domestic market and the state of technology are fixed, the government will have four courses open to it.

1. Accept the status quo and apply little pressure towards an increase in local content.
2. Encourage a significant increase in content across the board, in which case some price increase is likely.
3. Encourage some few firms to increase local content substantially and offer in return the prospect of an increased share of the market.
4. Seek some form of international arrangement facilitating exchange of parts or of completed products, and so enlarge the market.

Inasmuch as the government can be assumed to have three policy aims, an increase in domestic content, the maintenance of choice, and price stability, none of the first three can be seen as an ideal solution.

Not all objectives are however equally important and in particular the maintenance of choice may often reflect less a decision on the part of government than an inability to secure a more rational pattern of production. It seems unlikely for example that the South African authorities sought to have assembled locally, cars produced by each of the world's fourteen largest motor corporations.

"The policy of encouraging local manufacture has achieved its limited aims. New investment has been generated and local content has increased spectacularly. This has been done more easily than expected, perhaps too easily, and too many manufactured models are already being produced. . . . The dangers consequent upon fragmentation are well known, yet an "open-door" policy was from the start bound to encourage many more models than were necessary. Committed to an outdated policy the government still officially welcomes each unwelcome addition to the list of manufactured models."[7]

On the other hand it may be that a government does attach weight to the maintenance of choice. The price of this may be some reduction in the increase in local content or some upward movement in protection, costs, and in prices to the consumer.

We can assume however that in general governments attach relatively greater importance to price stability than to the maintenance of a full range of choice. Indeed inasmuch as choice is influenced by price, the actual pattern of sales is in some degree subject to the policy makers' discretion. Thus although the Holden is clearly the most popular car within Australia this choice is influenced by the framework of tariffs, and is presumably quite different from that which would be made in an open international market. The restriction is not as absolute as Henry Ford's on colour, but in substance the Australian policy maker is saying "Australians can buy any cars they like provided that most of them are Australian".

Assuming that it is prepared to forego some element of choice, and assuming the presence of a considerable number of assemblers, the government's problem is in essence to devise a scheme which will motivate some, but not all, companies to undertake manufacture. There are three examples of success in these terms within the earlier country studies: Australia, particularly in the early Holden phase; Brazil, where Volkswagen has half the market; and Yugoslavia, where the Crvena Zastava (Red Flag) is dominant. These successes reflect varying forms of intervention—in Yugoslavia the use of state power within a socialist system of ownership, and in Brazil a deliberate restriction of the number of manufactures by strict import licensing. Despite differences both involved direct government decision on the number of manufacturers. In Australia the initial concentration upon Holden arose because General Motors responded more positively to the original government invitation. There was not then, nor later, any suggestion that others would not be permitted to develop similar projects if they chose and the 1960's have seen the manufacture of rather more models than seem likely to survive.

Nevertheless relative to South Africa, and to many others, the Australian policies seem to have been effective in limiting the number of entrants. Why is this? The essential elements of the two schemes are shown in Table 58. (It is necessary to note that because of the different stages of growth of the two industries there is some difference in the use of the term assembler, nevertheless it is true that for both countries the status of manufacturer implies use of a locally assembled or manufactured engine).

The essential differences between the two schemes are those

Table 58: ESSENTIAL FEATURES OF SOUTH AFRICAN AND AUSTRALIAN INCENTIVE SCHEMES

	South Africa	Australia
Tariff (a) Protection for assembly	(a) Very high tariff on assembled imports (b) Differential duty of 90 or 230 cents per lb on imports according to whether they are broken down to specified degree	(a) 35 per cent tariff (Preferential) on assembled imports (b) Concessions for entry of 25—30 per cent for assemblers provided local content 45, 50, or 60 per cent depending on whether production did not exceed 2500, 5000 or 7000 respectively
(b) Encouragement of further manufacture	1962 Increase in import permits and excise rebates as local content increased 1963 Approval for engine manufacturing programmes. Engines to count as local content even if local activity limited to assembly.	1964 Plan A. Duty free entry on all components if manufacturer undertook to move to 95 per cent content within 5 years 1968 Plan A modified to provide concession in case of models for which content not expected to pass 85 per cent
(c) Protection for specific components	Typical rate 20 per cent	Typical rate 27½ per cent
Import Licensing	1964 Models with 45 per cent content and for which assembler would undertake to increase to 55 per cent in 3½ years classified as manufactured models and freed from controls. Those remaining as assembled models could expect no growth and fully built up imports were severely restricted.	All imports free from quota

specifying the required increase in local content and those dealing with import licensing. In the South African instance assemblers were offered a reduction in excise and an increase in import allocations with the latter being subsequently extended to full exemption from controls. Assemblers could receive this benefit if they increased content from 45 to 55 per cent (by weight), a feat which could be achieved by and large by simple assembly of imported engine parts. In Australia the offer was limited to duty free entry on remaining parts for models moving to 95 per cent local content (by value).

In South Africa the assembler who undertook engine assembly enjoyed unrestricted importing while the assembler who did not remained under firm control. In Australia all sections of the trade were exempt from control so that firms contemplating the jump to 95 per cent content had to be mindful of competition from fully built-up and locally-assembled cars of overseas origin. Furthermore the tariff protection against such imports was generally less than in South Africa.

All in all the size of the reward, both absolutely, and in relation to the required increase in content, was far greater in South Africa than in Australia. As a result, South Africa now has 32 "manufactured" models and eight engine plants. If the republic wishes to further increase local content (and this will be in an area where economies of scale are greater than in engine assembly), it will again find itself faced with the full array of international corporations, each of which will, by virtue of its investment to date, have a greater interest than before in staying in the field.

The fourth alternative in our earlier listing of the major policy alternatives was to expand the market through the international exchange of parts. Both the Canadian and Yugoslavian examples illustrate this. The Canadian-United States automotive agreement represents the furthest development of this process to date, and like other examples it emphasizes the key place of the international corporations. The changes made permit a rationalization of production within the major corporations rather than between separate units of the Canadian industry. Similarly the Yugoslav example reflects rationalization within the framework of Fiat based plants. Closer to home, the arrangements entered into under article 3.7 of the Australian New Zealand Free Trade Agreement permit rationalization between sister companies in Australia and New Zealand.

Historically the world automotive industry has been dominated by the major automobile corporations and given present technology this is likely to continue. The smaller economies interested in developing motor manufacturing capacity will inevitably find themselves dependent to some extent on the major corporations. Indeed even a country as large and traditionally self-sufficient as the Soviet Union has drawn heavily on the West European and Japanese automotive industry for the design of cars and factories in recent years.

The corporation is thus a natural unit within which rationalization can occur. The question is can such rationalization be achieved consistently with the interests of the national states desiring to develop automotive production within their country? The Canadian example suggests that they can but that a fairly radical change is necessary in the smaller economies' definition of its policy objective. Prior to the changes in 1962 Canadian tariff policy had encouraged an increase in the local content of all models sold in Canada. Coupled with the corporations' desire to maintain, for competitive reasons, an array of models on the market, this led to a considerable fragmentation of production with resultant diseconomies. In an attempt to reduce this unwanted fragmentation Bladen proposed that exports should be treated as local content, thus permitting an increased exchange of parts. More fundamentally, the final agreement provided for the maintenance not of local content, but of the ratio of production to sales, and in addition, for increases in Canadian value added. The Canadian Government was thus assured of an increase in automotive production within Canada, but permitted the corporations to meet this in terms of their total production rather than in relation to each particular model. The encouragement to fragmentation was thus removed.

It is of interest to note that the Australia-New Zealand and Yugoslavia-Fiat arrangements also depend upon generalized value constraints. In the Australia-New Zealand arrangement there is a fixed relationship between the trade flows in either direction, and in the Yugoslav instance specified export values are set.

It is likely that this generalized type of agreement will assume increasing importance in future because it offers much to both parties. The corporations find themselves subject to less detailed control and are thus better able to arrange production as seems most appropriate and economical. The government on the other hand is reasonably assured that local production will reach set levels. No doubt the future will reveal problems in this type of operation. The Canadian type agreement accepts the international corporation as the prime focus of the industry and makes even less likely than before the development of an indigenous car. This may

182

well be appropriate in the Canadian situation but a similar scheme applied in Japan in the 1950's could well have prevented the independent development of what is now the world's second largest motor car industry.

10.   A SUGGESTED POLICY

10.1   Introduction

Although this study has been mainly concerned to examine production economies in motor car assembly and manufacture its ultimate purpose has been to illuminate the policy issues inherent in the promotion of an essentially large-scale industry in a small economy. The rationality of any protective policy depends however on more factors than present production economies alone. The future may bring radical changes in technology and in size of market. In addition other considerations such as the consumers' demand for choice and the government's trade relations may suggest acceptance of what is, in terms of production economies alone, a sub-optimal pattern.

It is obviously not possible to foresee developments in motor car manufacture with certainty but in two areas at least change is likely. Increasing use of plastics and new forms of power units could conceivably affect the optimum volume of production but the evidence is not such as to support a presumption that this will be so. The new technology may be cheaper, and in some cases is clearly so at low volume, but this gives no cause to assume that it will be less subject to economies of scale than present technology. Again, it is possible that changes in transport such as the development of bulk car carriers and changes in Trans-Tasman transport techniques, could radically reduce the freight saving that has followed from local rather than overseas assembly. It seems equally possible however that economies in production will outpace those in transport, so that the relative advantage of local assembly might increase.

All in all we have no good grounds for assuming that production economies will change in any particular direction during the coming decade. We may be reasonably sure however that they will change. In the face of uncertainty the policy maker is best advised to hedge his bets. The possibility of change thus suggests that the level and technique of protection should not be set in a way which would inhibit future changes in policy.

In contrast to this uncertainty it is clear that the demand for cars will increase during the next decade. New Zealand already has, see Table 59, a high level of car ownership but the restricted supply of new cars has held down the level of new registrations to about two-thirds of that in Sweden and Australia and about three-fifths of that in Canada. As a result the average New Zealand car is older than those in countries with comparable income standards.

Table 59:

MOTOR CAR REGISTRATIONS

	Canada	Sweden	Australia	New Zealand
Number of cars owned per thousand persons, 1967	283	250	274	293
Annual new registrations per thousand persons, 1965-68	35	28	29	20
Average number of new registrations 1965-68, per thousand cars owned 1966	128	116	110	71

Source: Derived from official national and U.N. statistical publications.

It is reasonable to assume that in a freely supplied market New Zealanders would turn their car stock over at a rate closer to those in the other countries shown, although the less extreme New Zealand climate, the relatively higher level of car prices and the relatively lower incomes in New Zealand suggests a somewhat slower rate. In the second half of the 1960's the demand for new cars in New Zealand was probably at least a third higher than the average level of new registrations, which was just below 60,000 units per annum in the five years ended 1969.

Neither is the demand for cars static. In its 1969 Roading Survey the National Roads Board forecast that the total number of vehicles would increase to 1,360,000 in 1972-73 and 1,667,000 in 1978-79. If the proportion of cars to total vehicles remains the same as in 1968-69 (83 per cent) then these forecasts imply total car registrations of 1,130,000 and 1,385,000 respectively. If we further assume that new car purchases rise to 9 per cent of the existing stock by 1972-73, and to 11 per cent by 1978-79 (i.e. the present Australian level) then the annual level of new car registrations would be of the order of 100,000 in 1972-73 and 150,000 in 1978-79.

These estimates are of course approximate but they clearly suggest that if during the 1970's the car market becomes freely supplied the annual level of registrations will be very much greater than in the 1960's. Free supply means in effect the exemption of c.k.d. packs from import control. Regardless of whether or not this can be sustained it seems reasonable to assume that it will be attempted. At that point we are likely to see a substantial increase in output from the New Zealand assembly industry.

Of itself such an increase in output should enable some reduction in production costs. In earlier sections it was reported that estimates made by the assembly companies suggested that a doubling in output would lead to a $12\frac{1}{2}$ per cent fall in operating costs (or 2 per cent in ex-factory cost) to which would need to be added economies in component manufacture.

Alternatively we can ask what increase in content could be achieved without an increase in final price if the annual level of production was doubled? The Renault-based data (see Table 53) suggested that a doubling in output would generally permit an increase from 40, to between 60 and 70 per cent in local content without any increase in price. The equation is arbitrary but is one of the few pieces of quantitative evidence in this critical area.

More generally, and looking ahead to the end of the 1970's it seems reasonable to foresee an industry in which five major producers between them produce about 150,000 motor cars. The two largest might well be assembling in excess of 40,000 units. At this point they would be well beyond that at which their Australian and South African counterparts were induced to undertake engine assembly. Assuming similar encouragement in New Zealand, it is reasonable to suppose that one or more companies would take a similar step.

A major increase in content, of the order of 10 per cent or more, could result only from engine assembly or local body panel manufacture. For the conventional car the most likely area is engine assembly incorporating some local parts such as pistons but depending on overseas-machined engine blocks. Economies of scale in both engine machining and body panel pressing are very high and would discourage them, as also would New Zealand's lack of experience in most aspects of steel manufacture. For cars of less conventional design it is possible that other items would take precedence over engine assembly, as for example with the near flat steel panels pressed for the Trekka utility and the fibreglass body envisaged in some projects.

An extension into areas such as these could not be expected unless Government were prepared to extend to them protection similar to that accorded at present to motor car assembly and most manufacturing. The foreseeable increase in volume thus offers a choice. The resultant economies can be used either to reduce the cost of the final product, or to offset the cost of extending protection to a further phase of manufacture, or to make some progress in both directions.

A similar choice is available to the policy maker in respect of the array of vehicles produced. As was seen in Chapter 6 there are two aspects to this, the multiplicity of models and the larger number of assembly plants. Tentative estimates were made which suggested:

1. That a reduction, from 34 to 15, in the number of models assembled would, by lowering direct wage costs, lower the ex-factory cost of the average car by $1-1\frac{1}{2}$ per cent.
2. That a reduction in the number of assembly plants, to two of equal size, would, by reducing operating costs, lower the ex-factory cost of cars by about 3 per cent.

These estimates made no allowance for lower local material and component costs, which comprise 15 per cent of the ex-factory door value of a vehicle. In Chapter 7 it was seen that such costs could be expected to fall if the number of models was reduced. A reduction to about half the present number might reduce component costs by about 10 per cent and the ex-factory cost by about $1\frac{1}{2}$ per cent.

These three estimates are additive and suggest that an ambitious "rationalization" could reduce the ex-factory cost of New Zealand-assembled cars by as much as 6 per cent. Against this would have to be weighed the implicit reduction in consumer choice. Also Government would have to consider the consequences of reducing the number of producers in terms of internal competition and trade relations. A possible resolution of this problem would be to relax controls on the import of fully assembled cars.

The questions of consumer choice, cost and domestic content are thus interrelated. We can summarize the policy maker's dilemma as in Chart 17. In this the three assumed policy aims are represented by the three circles, whilst the areas of overlap show the conditions under which the relevant policies can be met. It is clear that any pair of objectives can be met simply by abandoning the other. Thus choice can be maintained and content increased if prices are allowed to rise. The only conditions under which all three aims can be met are increases in market size or improvements in technology. As we have seen the latter has to be assumed neutral but the former can be expected to increase and so facilitate change. Furthermore, if as seems likely, policy makers and consumers would be prepared to accept some reduction in choice then the potential for reduced production costs and/or increased content would be enhanced.

One other point needs to be recapitulated before considering the appropriate pattern of protection. We have seen that it is normal practice when items are deleted from the c.k.d. pack for

CHART 17. THE INTER-RELATED POLICY AIMS

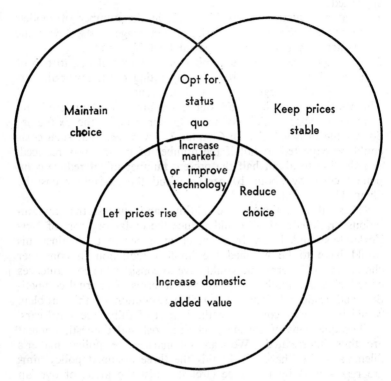

less than the full cost of the item to be allowed as a credit. Overseas tariff authorities have usually seen deletion allowances as justifying a somewhat higher level of protection than would otherwise be accorded, and evidence was advanced in this study which suggested that the longer term supply price of deleted components might well be higher than the initial deletion allowance. Nevertheless the deletion allowance does measure the short to medium term supply price for the component. To forego this by imposing a higher than usual level of protection is to lose a temporary advantage with the longer term aim of building a domestic car manufacturing industry. The proposals subsequently advanced envisage a fully supplied local market subject to more competitive pressures than at present and the imposition of a substantially higher tariff on imported components. Both changes should discourage any tendency to over-price c.k.d. packs through inadequate deletion allowances. At the same time rationalization and an increased volume of production should enable cheaper production of local components. Because much will be in flux if the proposed policy changes are adopted it does not seem appropriate to make any additional changes simply to offset the possible inadequacy of deletion allowances. It would however be appropriate to review this question subsequently and if deletion allowances proved to be inadequate to correct this either by negotiation with the companies or by imposing an additional duty.

10.2 A Policy for the Next Decade

Assuming that demand for cars will increase to something like the level described, and in the light of the production economies described, what would be a rational policy for the next decade? In discussing this it is not proposed to traverse the general argument for and against protection. It is assumed in this context that Government will be prepared, and in the opinion of the author should be prepared, to accord to the motor industry protection comparable to that accorded other manufacturing industries. Given these assumptions it is reasonable to conclude that some increase in local content will be achievable during the next decade consistently with Government's general economic objectives. In this context the policy problem becomes one of shaping the tools of protection and determining its appropriate level.

In structural terms policy should promote an industry in which most cars on sale are assembled in New Zealand and incorporate elementary hang-on parts manufactured in New Zealand. An increase in local content should be encouraged and it would be useful if some of the models produced in greater volume could embody a significantly higher New Zealand content than at present. The development of the component industry should be encouraged, particularly of units able to realize economies of scale through international exchange of parts. At the same time the mode of protection should be changed to permit greater flexibility in the industry and to permit the cost of developing it to be compared with competing calls for resources from within the manufacturing sector and beyond.

This last change could be most easily accomplished by transferring the main burden of protection from import licensing to the tariff. Import licensing by protecting the market share of each assembler has inhibited competition and change in the industry. Also by its nature it disguises the level of protection. It is suggested that import licensing of c.k.d. packs should cease.

Continued assembly of most cars sold in New Zealand would most easily be assured by retaining import controls on fully-assembled cars at least in the short run. As at present however there would be a need for some assembled imports of marques not assembled in New Zealand and of specialized variants of models assembled here. In the longer run however, the main protective load will have to be carried by the tariff which should continue to provide an incentive to assembly.

The most generalized method of encouraging production of components for local use would be to impose a flat tariff on all materials entering into motor cars, regardless of their stage of manufacture, and on motor cars themselves. Such a tariff by imposing the same rate at all points would ensure a uniform effective level of protection, equal to the nominal rate, for all stages of manufacture.

In practice flat tariffs present several problems. In New Zealand, as elsewhere, protective tariffs are usually applied only to competing imports, whilst non-competing goods are admitted duty free or at concessional rates. It is not easy to weld a flat tariff for one industry into such generally stratified tariffs. Further, and depending on the level of protection, a flat tariff could cause a large increase in tariff rates with untoward effects on trade relations and domestic price levels. Finally because duty is levied on c.d.v. rather than c.i.f. values, and because ad valorem freight costs vary markedly between asembled and unassembled cars a flat tariff would not in practice confer equal protection to assembly and to manufacture.

Because of these difficulties (some of which are not insurmountable) a flat tariff does not appear ideal. It is nevertheless appropriate to provide a similar level of protection to all stages of manufacture. Such a result can be got by a fairly simple modification. As has been seen a tariff which imposes a higher rate of duty on a final product, than on the components used in its manufacture, accords a rate of effective protection which is higher than the tariff on the final product. Thus the present 20 per cent (British Preferential) duty on fully assembled cars, coupled with the $6\frac{1}{4}$ per cent duty on imported components accords effective protection of over 40 per cent to New Zealand assembly. The level of effective protection is also affected by the degree of local manufacture. In general, if the tariff on a final product is fixed, then to maintain a constant rate of effective protection (at a level higher than the tariff on the final product), the rate of duty on components will need to fall progressively as local added value increases.

The general formula describing the relationship is as follows:

$$t = aT - b\frac{v}{m}$$

where t = the tariff rate on imported components
   T = the tariff rate on assembled cars
   v = domestic added value
   m = import cost
   a, b = parameters determined inter alia by the incidence of freight costs and the desired level of effective protection.

NOTE: Appendix C.1 details the derivation of the above formula.

The function is shown schematically in Chart 18 where it is contrasted with a flat tariff giving the same level of effective protection.

A tariff which declines progressively as local content increases can thus be used to confer a constant effective level of protection to all stages of manufacture without imposing the uniformly high tariffs implicit in a flat tariff schedule and so offers an attractive alternative. Before discussing its possible shape and level it is necessary to examine the major remaining alternative.

The present New Zealand tariff offers a concessional rate of duty on c.k.d. packs, provided that the conditions stated in the Customs determinations are met. A more generalized system, which related the concession to the level of domestic content and the volume of production operated in Canada from the mid-1930's until 1962 and a similar one now operates in Australia.

The New Zealand system is illustrated schematically in Schedule C. Because the duty concession is tied to specific conditions the marginal protection accorded to firms for meeting them is very high. Once met however the low tariff on components (from British Preferential sources) offers little encouragement to increased use of local components. As a result the average rate of effective protection falls steadily as local content increases.

It was this difficulty which led Canada and subsequently Australia to introduce volume related local content schedules. Under these, firms whose output passed set levels had to achieve higher levels of local content under penalty of loss of the concession. The effect of such schemes is illustrated in Schedule D. Within any band the marginal incentive to increase content is determined by the rate of tariff on components but in passing from one band to another the possible withdrawal of concessional entry imposes a very high marginal rate of protection. As a result the

CHART 18. THE MAIN TARIFF ALTERNATIVES

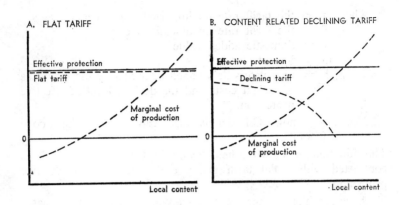

A. FLAT TARIFF

Effective protection
Flat tariff

Marginal cost
of production

0

Local content

B. CONTENT RELATED DECLINING TARIFF

Effective protection
Declining tariff

Marginal cost
of production

0

Local content

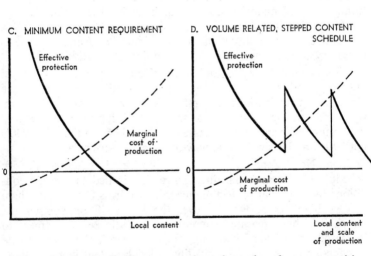

C. MINIMUM CONTENT REQUIREMENT

Effective
protection

Marginal
cost of
production

0

Local content

D. VOLUME RELATED, STEPPED CONTENT
SCHEDULE

Effective
protection

Marginal cost
of production

0

Local content
and scale
of production

average level of effective protection rises sharply on transition
from one band to another and then falls gradually. This discon-
tinuity has proved difficult in practice, manufacturers being under-
standably reluctant to increase production if that would lead to a
loss of concessional entry. In Australia authorities have attempted
to overcome this by changing the system so that concessional
entry is foregone only in respect of vehicles in excess of the stated
limits. This change replaces the saw-toothed schedule of effective
protection by one which first rises and then falls within each

content band, and thus reduces one major disadvantage of content/volume related systems. Two major objections remain.

The rationale for requiring manufacturers to increase content as their volume of production increases derives from economies of scale. As volume increases the cost of producing to the current level of content falls and this saving is used to offset the cost of increasing content. Regardless of the exact shape of such schedules their general effect is to deny to the larger producers some or all of the benefits that might be expected to accrue from an increased scale of operations. To this extent they militate against rationalization within the industry, a serious objection given the present fragmented nature of the New Zealand industry.

To specify a content/volume schedule requires arbitrary judgement in a very uncertain area. As this study has shown, what is known about the interaction of price, content and volume, is at best approximate. Policy makers of necessity make many judgements in the face of uncertainty but in the present case the extent of this is so great as to suggest following a simpler course.

For these reasons a content/volume type schedule does not appear appropriate. It is suggested instead that use should be made of a declining tariff of the type discussed previously.

Any tariff is essentially a protective instrument which encourages import substitution. To apply one to a domestic motor industry is to tend to fragment what is essentially an international industry. As has been seen there is considerable scope for rationalization of component production between associated companies in different countries. It would be useful to design the tariff in such a way as to promote rather than hinder this. For this reason it would be sensible to replace the usual local content measure with one of added value which could, as in Canada, be met either by producing for the local market or for export. To do this would be to extend to the export of automotive components an incentive equal to that accorded to import substitution. This incentive would be substantial and if adopted it would be appropriate to consider excluding the automotive industry from the various general export incentives schemes, which operate at present.

Finally, one consequence of introducing a generalized incentive scheme would be to make the present system of tariff determinations redundant. To protect existing component suppliers it would however be sensible to retain the present determinations as a transitional measure, but they should not be extended, and in time should be relaxed.

10.3 Suggested British Preferential Tariff

Table 60:

THE SUGGESTED BRITISH PREFERENTIAL TARIFF

Assembled motor cars   30 per cent ad valorem
Unassembled motor cars (as defined by Customs determination)
The rate of duty shall be:

27 per cent ad valorem *less* 10 times the ratio of domestic added value to the c.i.f.e. cost of imports.

i.e. Rate of duty, per cent, ad valorem $= 27 - 10 \dfrac{\text{(domestic added value)}}{\text{(c.i.f.e. cost of imports)}}$

NOTES: 1. Domestic added value is defined as the wholesale cost (exclusive of duty) of motor cars assembled in New Zealand less the c.i.f.e. cost of imported components plus the value of any automotive export certificates held by the company.
        2. An automotive export certificate is a freely negotiable certificate, issued by the Customs Department, and having a face value equal to the f.o.b. value of any automotive products exported from New Zealand by any party, less the assessed import content of such exports.
        3. Duty shall be paid on a provisional basis at time of import subject to adjustment in the subsequent year.
        4. The tariff formula outlined above is based on that shown in Appendix C, section 1.

In the light of the preceding discussion the tariff presented in Table 60 is suggested. It has four main features.

1. It provides a constant rate of protection to all stages of motor car assembly and manufacture. The author has worked on the asumption that the appropriate rate of effective protection is 35 per cent. This is probably lower than that accorded many manufacturing industries but is advanced as an appropriate medium term aim.
2. The duty paid on fully assembled cars is set at 30 per cent.
3. Assemblers are entitled to a duty concession which increases as the ratio of New Zealand added value to imports increases. The appropriate rate of duty is derived from the given formula the effect of which may be judged from the following schedule:

Level of domestic content per cent	*B.P. duty rate on components* per cent
30	23
40	20
50	17
60	12
70	4

4. New Zealand added value is defined to include both the local content of cars assembled and sold in New Zealand and the local added value of exported automotive products.

The approximate impact of the proposed tariff can be gauged from the data relating to the average cost of production advanced earlier in this study. On the basis of the average data for 12 examples from seven companies the results shown in Table 61 have been derived.

Table 61:

THE IMPACT OF THE PROPOSED TARIFF

	Overseas Assembled	New Zealand Assembled at present level of N.Z. added value	New Zealand Assembled at hypothetical level of N.Z. added value
Average company data (index wholesale price exclusive of duty of overseas assembled car=1000)			
c.d.v. value	710	562	450
c.i.f. value	882	616	492
New Zealand added value	118	415	585
wholesale price (exclusive of duty)	1000	1031	1077
Level of New Zealand added value (per cent)	12	40	54
Ratio of New Zealand added value to ci.f.e. import value	0·134	0·674	1·189
Duty (on company data index base)			
Present B.P. Tariff	142	35	28
Proposed B.P. Tariff	213	114	68
Wholesale price inclusive of duty (on company data index base)			
Present B.P. Tariff	1142	1066	1105
Proposed B.P. Tariff	1213	1145	1145

NOTES: 1. The first three rows of data are derived (by scaling) from Table 17 for the first two columns. The third column is hypothetical.
2. Duty under present tariff is calculated at B.P. rates and differs from company average which included some M.F.N. duty.

A comparison of the wholesale prices shown in the last rows of the first two columns of Table 61 shows that at present added value levels the proposed tariff gives a similar margin of protection (i.e. 1213 — 1145 = 68) to that provided by the existing tariff (i.e. 1142 — 1066 = 76). The difference between them appears as New Zealand added value increases, as can be seen by comparing the second and third columns of the table. Under the present tariff an assembler reducing his import content from the average level of 563 to say 450 would gain a duty concession of only 7. Under the proposed tariff such a reduction would (assuming no change in the final selling price) lead to a duty reduction of 46. As a result the assembler would be competitively able to increase local added value by 170, at domestic prices, rather than 133 as under the present British Preferential Tariff. An increase of 170 in New Zealand added value in substitution for an import saving of 124 implies a cost of saving one dollar of overseas exchange of $1.37. (This implies an effective protective rate, in this range, of 37 per cent rather than 35 as proposed. The difference arises from rounding errors and could be removed by finer specification of the duty formula).

The proposed tariff is thus much more appropriate as a means of encouraging a continuing increase in local automotive component manufacture. One unintended consequence of the proposed tariff structure would be to increase the wholesale price of all cars. To offset this it is proposed that, at the time of introduction of the duty formula, sales tax on all cars should be reduced accordingly.

In the above proposals the policy focus is changed from local content to added value. This achieves two things. By taking account of exports it reduces the bias to import replacement inherent in most incentive schemes. It also reflects an attempt to match the national tools of protection to the international corporate structure of the industry by encouraging international exchange of parts. The effect of the proposals is very much the same as those developed under the United States-Canadian automotive agreement with the significant difference that these proposals can be implemented unilaterally, as was envisaged in Bladen's original proposal. As in Canada, the central focus is on the level of domestic added value. This should give the international corporations and their New Zealand subsidiaries and associates full opportunity to develop international specialization through the exchange of parts. The potential for such development may well be less in the case of New Zealand's small and remote economy; a consideration which heightens the importance of ensuring that the tariff structure does not present an obstacle.

The proposed automotive export certificates are intended to assist the industry to respond to this change in emphasis. Whereas it is reasonably easy for sister companies within an international corporate structure to adopt to changing national policies it is not so for less closely associated companies. Under the existing array of export incentives there has been a slow, and varied, evolution of arrangements between assembly companies and exporting component manufacturers. The automotive export certificates which it is proposed would be freely negotiable between firms would facilitate trade arrangements involving unrelated firms.

One question remains—that of national preferences. This study has been concerned with allocative efficiency and the motor industry. In such terms the present differential between the British Preferential and Most Favoured Nation tariffs makes no sense. But of course, the justification for it must be sought in wider terms of trading policy. All that need be said here is that the differential should be reduced to the minimum consistent with those other considerations. In terms of present agreements with Britain, New Zealand is bound to maintain a 10 per cent minimum preference on motor cars and is obliged to consult before the existing margins are altered. New Zealand has on several occasions offered to reduce the extent of the preference in exchange for concessions on exports to Most Favoured Nation countries. The quiescent response suggests that this offer is unlikely to meet with any substantial counter concession. In this case there would seem to be little point in continuing to misallocate scarce overseas funds on the scale implicit in the preferential tariff. It is suggested that Most Favoured Nation tariffs on motor cars be lowered towards the British Preferential tariffs by the maximum extent consistent with treaty undertakings.

A more difficult question of national preferences concerns Australia with whom New Zealand has an expanding bilateral trade in automotive parts. The main stimulus to this has come from the New Zealand-Australia Free Trade Agreement and in particular from the operation of Article 3.7 of that agreement. The proposed removal of import controls from unassembled cars would remove the main present incentive to trade under article 3.7. The proposed increase in the British Preferential Tariff would provide ample scope for concessional entry but it must be recognized that any such concession with respect to Australia would weaken the general incentive provided by the tariff to an increase in New Zealand added value. Australia is in any event likely to share the main benefits of whatever increase might occur in international specialization as a result of the proposed tariff structure.

It is perhaps necessary to comment in this context that the United States-Canadian automotive agreement does not provide an appropriate analogy. For New Zealand, Australia is not the major supplier of motor car components, the corporate structure is not linked so closely between the two economies, and the New Zealand industry is at a much lower stage of development than that in Canada. For these reasons it would seem that initially any concessional reduction in duty in favour of Australia should be small.

As has been commented many times the organizational focus of the motor industry is the international corporation. The proposals outlined above have been designed as a package which can be implemented by a single nation, but which will leave to the corporations the maximum freedom of manoeuvre consistent with national policy aims. These have been set as consistently as possible with the general protective structure at present in force in New Zealand and are made to turn upon one highly generalized measure—the desired rate of effective protection accorded to New Zealand added value. The proposals made do not offer New Zealand the early prospect of a New Zealand car but they do offer a steady expansion in automotive production. At the same time they hold out the hope of more economic production through increased specialization.

Table 1:

IMPORTS OF MOTOR CARS

	000 Unassembled (c.k.d.)	000 Assembled	Total
1927	..	..	10·9
1928	..	..	16·5
1929	..	..	23·4
1930	..	..	14·3
1931	..	..	3·4
1932	..	..	3·0
1933	..	..	2·9
1934	..	..	11·7
1935	6·4	11·3	17·7
1936	11·7	12·6	24·3
1937	18·6	11·7	30·3
1938	19·4	9·0	28·4
1939	16·8	4·7	21·5
1940	5·0	0·1	5·0
1941	0·2	—	0·2
1942	—	—	—
1943	—	—	—
1944	—	—	—
1945	—	0·1	0·1
1946	4·9	2·3	7·2
1947	14·0	5·3	19·4
1948	6·8	4·2	11·0
1949	11·2	0·8	12·0
1950	13·8	2·7	16·6
1951	12·8	14·1	26·9
1952	17·8	21·4	39·2
1953	17·7	3·2	20·9
1954	28·8	11·4	40·2
1955	31·8	14·6	46·4
1956	29·1	7·2	36·2
1957	36·2	5·3	41·5
1958	25·1	4·0	29·1
1959	25·2	1·1	26·3
1960	29·8	2·6	32·4
1961	32·8	2·6	35·4
1962	34·6	3·3	37·9
1963	53·3	5·8	59·1
1964	56·3	8·0	64·3
1965	58·1	7·9	66·0
1966	52·7	7·5	60·3
1967	47·0	5·7	52·8
1968	43·7	4·3	48·0
1969	50·7	3·9	54·5

Source: Trade Statistics, Monthly Abstract of Statistics.

Table 2:

PRODUCTION IN THE MOTOR VEHICLE
ASSEMBLY INDUSTRY

	Value of Production $m	% Change	Volume of Production 1949-50=1000	% Change
1946-47	5.5	n.a.	n.a.	n.a.
1947-48	14.4	164	n.a.	n.a.
1948-49	16.2	13	n.a.	n.a.
1949-50	17.2	6	1000	n.a.
1950-51	21.7	27	1149	15
1951-52	26.2	20	1334	16
1952-53	30.9	18	1289	—3
1953-54	32.8	6	1335	4
1954-55	42.6	30	1744	31
1955-56	51.3	20	2152	23
1956-57	51.9	1	2028	—6
1957-58	58.0	12	2173	7
1958-59	48.8	—18	1748	—20
1959-60	42.5	—11	1501	—14
1960-61	55.6	31	1941	29
1961-62	61.3	10	2109	9
1962-63	64.5	5	2176	3
1963-64	83.4	29	2935	35
1964-65	95.9	15	3316	13
1965-66	97.9	2	3269	—1
1966-67	102.3	4	3129	—4
1967-68	86.9	—15	2657	—15
1968-69	86.4	—1	2482	—7

Source: Industrial Production Statistics.

Table 3:

NUMBER OF MOTOR VEHICLES ASSEMBLED

Production Year	Cars	Buses	Vans	Trucks	Lorries, Vans, Trucks, etc.
1946-47	3,467	46	n.a.	n.a.	2,676
1947-48	10,408	104	n.a.	n.a.	4,474
1948-49	9,977	91	n.a.	n.a.	6,283
1949-50	9,731	86	n.a.	n.a.	6,668
1950-51	13,444	116	2,162	4,823	8,473
1951-52	15,712	43	1,935	6,466	series ends
1952-53	15,480	47	1,244	6,399	
1953-54	20,676	115	990	3,577	
1954-55	26,895	156	1,148	5,470	
1955-56	32,315	82	1,691	7,431	
1956-57	32,117	119	1,325	5,967	
1957-58	36,168	117	1,380	5,291	
1958-59	26,103	152	2,557	5,493	
1959-60	24,434	337	3,096	2,722	
1960-61	29,988	100	2,685	5,464	
1961-62	32,708	82	4,066	5,294	
1962-63	36,357	n.a.	4,452	4,093	
1963-64	51,538	n.a.	4,276	4,630	
1964-65	58,219	n.a.	5,151	4,890	
1965-66	56,953	n.a.	3,381	4,962	
1966-67	53,353	n.a.	5,180	5,683	
1967-68	48,872	n.a.	3,282	3,363	
1968-69	44,624	n.a.	2,958	2,997	

Source: Industrial Production Statistics.

Table 4:
COST OF MOTOR VEHICLE PRODUCTION 1967-68

	Total cost $000	Parts per 000	Approximate cost per vehicle produced[2] $
MATERIALS			
Imported components[1]	54,607	629	984
Timber and plywood	14	—	—
Paint, enamel, thinners	1,051	12	19
Batteries	392	4	7
Tyres	3,018	35	54
Tubes	184	2	3
Radiators	681	8	12
Body solder	117	1	2
Hardware	345	4	6
Glass	1,158	13	21
Trimmings—plastic	2,159	25	39
other	262	3	5
Other materials	1,800	21	32
Contract and commission work	692	8	12
Total materials	66,480	765	1,197
OTHER EXPENSES			
Electricity and fuel	596	7	11
Insurance	188	2	3
Repairs and maintenance	494	6	9
Management and office expenses	1,612	19	29
Interest	113	1	2
Rent	200	2	4
Depreciation	1,314	15	24
Total other expenses	4,517	52	81
SALARIES AND WAGES	9,159	105	165
MANUFACTURING SURPLUS	6,715	77	121
VALUE OF PRODUCTION	86,872	1,000	1,565

Source: Industrial Production Statistics 1967-68.

NOTE: 1. Data published in the Industrial Production Statistics on c.k.d. components and number of vehicles includes amounts relating to industry 466, motor body building. The above entry for c.k.d. components used in industry 464 is drawn from the Monthly Abstract of Statistics, August 1969, page 9.
2. The total average cost per vehicle produced, $1,565, refers to the average value of cars, vans and trucks produced, and this is split proportionately in line with the allocation of total cost. In fact the total includes in addition undisclosed numbers of other vehicles but these will be small in number and are unlikely to significantly affect either the average value of vehicle or the composition of that cost.

COSTS OF MOTOR VEHICLE PRODUCTION
IN THE POST-WAR PERIOD

	Imported c.k.d. components	Other materials	Other expenses	Salaries and wages	Manu-facturing surplus	$m. Value of Production
1946-47	4·4		0·3	0·6	0·1	5·5
1947-48	11·5		0·6	1·3	1·0	14·4
1948-49	12·2	1·2	0·6	1·4	0·9	16·2
1949-50	12·2	1·7	0·6	1·7	0·9	17·2
1950-51	14·9	2·6	0·7	2·1	1·4	21·7
1951-52	18·0	3·0	0·8	2·6	1·5	26·2
1952-53	21·8	3·3	1·2	2·9	1·7	30·9
1953-54	22·0	4·4	1·3	3·1	2·1	32·8
1954-55	29·2	4·5	1·3	4·2	3·4	42·6
1955-56	34·3	5·4	1·9	4·9	4·8	51·3
1956-57	35·2	5·3	1·9	5·1	4·5	51·9
1957-58	39·3	5·9	2·0	5·8	4·9	58·0
1958-59	32·1	5·1	1·9	4·6	4·1	47·8
1959-60	27·7	5·1	1·9	4·2	3·6	42·5
1960-61	36·1	6·8	2·1	5·5	5·1	55·6
1961-62	39·1	8·0	2·4	6·3	5·6	61·3
1962-63	40·6	8·4	2·3	6·8	6·4	64·5
1963-64	51·8	11·0	2·5	8·5	9·5	83·4
1964-65	61·3	13·9	3·0	9·8	8·0	95·9
1965-66	60·1	14·3	3·6	10·5	9·4	97·9
1966-67	62·9	14·3	4·4	10·6	10·1	102·3
1967-68	54·6	11·9	4·5	9·2	6·7	86·9
1968-69	53·7	12·3	5·2	8·3	6·9	86·4

Source: Industrial production statistics.

Table 6:

COSTS OF MOTOR VEHICLE PRODUCTION
IN THE POST-WAR PERIOD

	Imported c.k.d. components	Other materials	Other expenses	Salaries and wages	Parts per 000 Manufacturing surplus	Value of Production
1946-47	807		55	111	27	1000
1947-48	799		40	90	71	1000
1948-49	754	71	34	84	57	1000
1949-50	711	101	35	99	53	1000
1950-51	686	122	33	96	63	1000
1951-52	698	116	32	98	56	1000
1952-53	705	108	38	93	56	1000
1953-54	670	133	39	94	65	1000
1954-55	685	105	31	98	80	1000
1955-56	668	106	36	96	94	1000
1956-57	677	103	36	98	86	1000
1957-58	678	103	35	100	84	1000
1958-59	672	107	39	95	86	1000
1959-60	652	120	45	98	85	1000
1960-61	649	122	38	99	92	1000
1961-62	637	130	38	103	92	1000
1962-63	629	130	35	105	100	1000
1963-64	622	132	30	103	114	1000
1964-65	639	145	31	102	84	1000
1965-66	614	146	37	108	96	1000
1966-67	615	140	43	103	99	1000
1967-68	629	137	52	105	77	1000
1968-69	622	142	61	97	79	1000

Source: Derived from data in Table 5.

Table 7:

NO REMITTANCE IMPORTS
The no-remittance import scheme was introduced in May 1950. The first published figures on imports under the scheme relate to 1955.

Year	Imports Approved
1955	1998
1956	2321
1957	1427
1958	2409
1959	2527
1960	3981
1961	7727
1962	6584
1963	11426
1964	12606
1965	14121
1966	14426
1967	14928
1968	10286
1969	9035

Source: Annual Report of the Customs Department.
Appendices to the Journals of the House of Representatives. Paper H 25.

Table 8: WORLD MOTOR CAR PRODUCTION AND ASSEMBLY 1967

PRODUCTION

North and South America		Western Europe		Eastern Europe		Africa	Asia and Oceania	
United States	7436·8	West Germany	2295·7	U.S.S.R.	251·4		Japan	1375·8
Canada	720·8	France	1751·8	Czechoslovakia	111·7		Australia	296·3
Brazil	140·6	United Kingdom	1552.0	East Germany	111·5		India	38·9
Argentina	133·7	Italy	1439·2	Yugoslavia	47·9			
		Spain	280·9	Poland	27·7			
		Sweden	194·0					
		Netherlands	49·5					
		Austria	1·2					

ASSEMBLY

North and South America		Western Europe		Africa		Asia and Oceania	
Mexico	86·0	Belgium	481·9*	South Africa	142·6	New Zealand	50·0
Venezuela	42·2	Ireland	38·5	Rhodesia	8·3†	Philippines	12·6
Peru	11·5	Portugal	35·8	Morocco	9·6	Taiwan	4·0
Columbia	0·7*	Denmark	26·5	Algeria	6·0	Iran	5·3*
		Netherlands	25·5	Tunisia	0·4	Korea	5·0
		Switzerland	18·6	United Arab Republic	0·2	Turkey	3·0
		Greece	0·5†	Ghana	0·1	Israel	2·6
						Indonesia	0·6‡

Source: United Nations Statistical Yearbook 1968.

* 1966 data
† 1965 data
‡ 1964 data

NOTE: 1. Production figures include production of completely knocked down packs for export. Assembly figures do not represent additional output.

NOTE: 2. The division of countries into producers or assemblers follows U.N. practice. Figures for Australia, Argentina, Brazil and Yugoslavia include local assembly of overseas produced cars.

Table 9:

THE WORLD'S FOURTEEN LARGEST MOTOR COMPANIES AND COUNTRIES
IN WHICH THEIR CARS WERE ASSEMBLED CIRCA 1967
(initial figures refer to 1966 production of all vehicles, in millions)

	Number of companies	General Motors	Ford	Chrysler	Volks-wagen	Fiat	B.M.H.	Renault	Toyota	Cit-roen	Nissan	Peu-geot	Ameri-can Motors	Daimler-Benz	Volvo
		6·7	4·5	2·4	1·7	1·5	0·9	0·7	0·6	0·5	0·5	0·4	0·3	0·3	0·2
Argentine	12	x	x	x	x	x	x	x		x	x	x	x	x	
Bolivia	1														
Brazil	7	x	x	x	x			x	x					x	
Canada	7	x	x	x	x			x	x						x
Chile	11	x	x	x	x	x		x	x	x	x	x	x		
Colombia	4	x	x												
Costa Rica	8		x			x	x	x	x	x	x		x		
Dominican Republic	1								x						
Guatemala	2						x								
Mexico	7	x	x		x			x	x		x	x	x		
Paraguay	7	x	x	x		x		x	x			x	x		
Peru	12	x	x	x	x	x	x	x	x		x	x	x	x	
Trinidad	5	x	x	x	x		x	x							x
Venezuela	10	x	x	x	x	x		x	x		x		x	x	
United States	4	x	x	x									x		
Australia	11	x	x	x	x		x	x	x		x	x	x		x
Cambodia	2							x		x					
Ceylon	1						x								
Formosa	2								x						
India	6	x		x		x	x				x			x	
Indonesia	5	x	x	x		x					x		x	x	
Japan	2								x		x				
South Korea	2		x						x						
Malaysia	12	x	x	x	x	x	x	x	x		x	x		x	x

207

Table 9—continued

Country	Number of companies	General Motors 6·7	Ford 4·5	Chrysler 2·4	Volkswagen 1·7	Fiat 1·5	B.M.H. 0·9	Renault 0·7	Toyota 0·6	Citroen 0·5	Nissan 0·5	Peugeot 0·4	American Motors 0·3	Daimler-Benz 0·3	Volvo 0·2
New Zealand	11	X	X	X	X	X	X	X	X		X	X	X		
Pakistan	3	X	X	X											
Philippines	12	X	X	X	X	X	X	X	X		X	X	X	X	
Thailand	6		X	X		X			X		X			X	
Austria	3					X				X		X			
Belgium	9	X	X		X	X	X	X		X				X	X
Great Britain	4	X	X	X			X								
Denmark	5	X	X	X			X							X	
Finland	1		X												
France	4						X	X		X		X			
Germany	5				X		X	X					X	X	
Ireland	10	X	X	X	X	X	X	X	X		X	X			
Italy	2						X	X							
Malta	2						X						X		
Netherlands	5		X	X		X		X		X					
Portugal	12	X	X	X	X	X	X	X		X	X	X		X	X
Spain	7		X	X	X	X	X			X				X	
Switzerland	4	X	X	X						X					
Yugoslavia	2					X	X								
Iran	6			X		X	X						X	X	X
Israel	2			X			X								
Turkey	9		X	X	X	X	X	X		X				X	X
Bulgaria	2					X		X							
Czechoslovakia	1							X							
Hungary	2					X					X				
Poland	1														X

Country	No.	30	36	34	16	30	35	33	21	13	22	17	16	22	13
Rumania	1							x							
U.S.S.R.	1							x							
South Africa	14	x	x	x	x	x	x	x	x	x	x	x	x	x	x
Algeria	1						x								
Angola	4		x			x		x			x				x
Camaroons	1						x								
Ethiopia	2						x								
Ghana	9	x	x	x		x	x	x	x		x			x	
Guinea	1													x	
Ivory Coast	4		x	x		x		x							
Kenya	2							x	x			x		x	
Madagascar	1								x						
Morocco	9	x	x	x		x	x	x		x	x				
Mozambique	3	x	x				x	x						x	x
Nigeria	5	x	x			x	x				x	x		x	x
Rhodesia	5	x	x			x	x	x				x		x	
Tunisia	3		x			x					x				
United Arab Republic	1					x									
TOTAL	**338**	30	36	34	16	30	35	33	21	13	22	17	16	22	13

Sources: Company production totals from "The Growth of the World Automotive Industries and the Business Policies of its multi-national Companies to 1968." General Report 1 to the International Metal Workers' Federation Conference 1968. Location of Assembly plants from "Repertoire Mondial Des Usines D'Assemblage De Vehicules Automobiles." Chambre Syndicale Des Constructeurs D'Automobiles, November 1968.

209

APPENDIX B

TARIFFS ON MOTOR CARS AND COMPONENTS
A. MOTOR CARS—HISTORICAL SUMMARY

	Ordinary (per cent)	Foreign (per cent)	
1907 Tariff Act			
213 Motor car bodies	20	+10	
434 Chassis for motor vehicles whether attached or not	Exempt from duty		
1915 Finance Act			
194A Motor cars (no distinction drawn between bodies and chassis)	10	+10	

	British Preferential 10%	Intermediate 20%	General 25%
1921 Customs Amendment Act			
XI Motor vehicles	10%	20%	25%
plus on Single seated bodies	£ 5		£ 7.10.0
Double seated bodies	£10		£15. 0.0
Canopied bodies	£15		£22.10.0

	British (per cent)	Intermediate (per cent)	General (per cent)
1926 Customs Amendment Act			
XI Motor vehicles	10	25	30
plus, if imported with body suited for passengers,			
on first £200 value of whole vehicle	10	15	15
on remainder of value	5	7½	7½
1934 Customs Amendment Act (per cent)			
Unassembled motor cars	5		50
Assembled motor cars	15		60

	British Preferential	M.F.N. (per cent)	General
1948 General Agreement on Tariffs and Trade Act			
Unassembled motor cars	5	40	50
Assembled motor cars	15	50	60
1961 Customs Acts Amendment Act			
Unassembled motor cars	6¼	45	65
Assembled motor cars	20	55	75

Sources: Various official documents.

NOTE: Dates given refer to year of legislation, not necessarily year of first application.

B. 1970 TARIFFS ON SOME MATERIALS AND COMPONENTS OF INTEREST TO THE ASSEMBLY INDUSTRY

Tariff Chapter or item number		British Preferential	M.F.N.	General
		(per cent unless otherwise specified)		
32	Tanning and dyeing extracts			
32.09.09	Paints other	27½	47½	60
.11	Enamels	27½	47½	60
.16	Other pigments	27½	50	60
40	Rubber			
40.11	Rubber tyres and tubes			
.01–03	As may be approved by the Minister per 100 lb.	Free	$ 5.83	$ 5.83
40.11.05 & .07	Other per 100 lb.	$10	$15.83	$15.83
40.14.02	Moulded rubber mats	27½	55	55

APPENDIX C
NOTES ON FORMULAE
1. THE RATE OF EFFECTIVE PROTECTION

The rate of effective protection accorded by a tariff is defined by:

$$E = \frac{T(m + v') - tm}{v'} \tag{1}$$

where E = the rate of effective protection
T = the tariff on imports of fully assembled cars
t = the tariff on imported components
m = the value of imported components
v' = the extent of local value that could be added in the absence of a tariff. i.e. $(m + v')$ = the import cost of a fully assembled car, and v' = deletion allowances plus freight savings.

Equation (1) states that the rate of effective protection is equal to the difference between the amount of duty on an assembled car and that on an unassembled car expressed as a proportion of the value that could be added in local assembly in the absence of a tariff. Equation (1) assumes that tariffs are levied on the full import cost rather than on c.d.v. as in practice. To take account of this we can use:

$$E = \frac{TF(m + v') - tfm}{v'} \tag{2}$$

where F = ratio c.d.v./c.i.f. for assembled cars
f = ratio c.d.v./c.i.f. for components.

In common usage the domestic content of a vehicle is measured in domestic prices, i.e. at prices determined within the protected market. The relationship between domestic content as usually measured, and the extent of value that could be added in local assembly in the absence of a tariff is:

$$v' = \frac{v}{1 + E} \tag{3}$$

where v = domestic content measured at domestic prices.

By substituting (3) in (1) it can be shown that:

$$E = \frac{TFv + m(TF - tf)}{v - m(TF - tf)} \tag{4}$$

This function was used to calculate the values shown in Table 26 on the assumptions stated in that table.

It can be similarly shown that:

$$t = \frac{TF}{f} - \frac{v}{mf}\left(\frac{E - TF}{1 + E}\right) \tag{5}$$

This supports the function shown on page 191. If the policy maker is prepared to set values for E and T, and if F and f can be assumed as fixed (an approximate but not unrealistic assumption in the short run) then we have:

$$t = k_1 + k_2 \frac{v}{m} \tag{6}$$

This function provides the basis for the tariff proposals advanced in Table 61, which were derived on the following assumptions, all variables being specified in ratio form.

E, the effective rate of protection	= 0·35
T, the tariff on the assembled cars	= 0·30
F, the ratio of c.d.v./c.i.f.e. cost for assembled cars	= 0·80
f, the ratio of c.d.v./c.i.f.e. cost for unassembled cars	= 0·90

The former two specifications involve arbitrary policy judgements whereas the latter were derived from the data quoted in Table 17. On this basis we have:

$$t = \frac{TF}{f} - \frac{v}{mf}\left(\frac{E - TF}{1 + E}\right)$$

$$= \frac{0.30(0.80)}{0.90} - \frac{v}{m}\left(\frac{1}{0.90}\right)\left(\frac{0.35 - 0.30(0.80)}{1 + 0.35}\right)$$

$$= \cdot267 - \frac{v}{m}\quad(0.0905)$$

2. THE LEARNING CURVE

(a) The learning curve is specified as

$$m_i = aQ_i^b \tag{1}$$

where m_i = marginal direct labour cost per unit in establishment i
         Q_i = volume of production in establishment i
         a, b = parameters

Cole suggested as typical of the cases studied a value of -0.322 for b. This implies a 20 per cent fall in 1 with each doubling in Q_i.

(b) The following relationships are implicit in (1)

$$M_i = \frac{a}{b + 1}\,Q_i^{b + 1} \tag{2}$$

and

$$\overline{m_i} = \frac{a}{b + 1}\,Q_i^b \tag{3}$$

where M_i = total direct labour cost in establishment i

        $\overline{m_i}$ = average direct labour cost in establishment i

(c) The values in Table 36 were calculated by comparing estimates of total costs for different configurations as specified in the left-hand column of the Table. For each configuration total costs were estimated by

$$\sum_i M_i = a' \sum_i Q_i^{b + 1}$$

$$(a' = \frac{a}{b + 1})$$

As the final estimates are expressed in ratio form no estimate of the parameter a' was required.

3. HALDI AND WHITCOMB COST FUNCTION

(a) The function is specified as

$$C_i = aX_i^b$$

where C_i = total operating cost of establishment i
        X_i = output capacity of establishment i
        a, b = parameters

(b) The values in Table 40 were calculated by comparing estimates of total costs for different configurations of the industry as specified in the left-hand column of the Table. For each configuration total costs were estimated by

$$\sum_i C_i = a\sum_i X_i^b$$

As the final results are derived as ratios no estimate of the parameter a is required.

    (c) NOTE: Because Haldi and Whitcomb's equation refers to total rather than average cost, the parameter b above is equivalent to that of $b + 1$ specified above in the learning curve.

APPENDIX D
REFERENCES AND NOTES

Chapter 2.—A Brief History of the Industry

1 "Progressive New Zealand. 1840-1924", edited by L. S. Fanning. Christchurch, Dominion Advisory Council; Vivian E. Page, 1924. pp 191-2.
2 Sloan, A. P., "My Years with General Motors". Doubleday, 1964, p. 316.
3 "Report of Import Licensing Committee", Parliamentary paper J.4 1950.
4 Press Statement, 9 June 1961.
5 *Dominion,* 19 March 1970, "Nova car had provisional backing: Minister".

Chapter 3.—The Industry Today

1 Wilkins M. and H. F. E., "American Business Abroad—Ford on Six Continents". Wayne State University Press, Detroit, 1964, p 378.
2 This point is discussed in T. K. McDonald "Regional Development in New Zealand". Contract Research Unit Paper, N.Z. Institute of Economic Research. 1970.
3 Northern Wellington, Nelson, and Canterbury Metal Trades Employees (In Motor Assembly Works) Award, 23/2/70.
4 Board of Trade and Industries "Report No. 613 Investigation into the Motor Industry in South Africa", 1960, para 28.
5 Committee on Industrial Organization, Dublin, Report on the Motor Vehicle Assembly Industry, 1962, p 47.
6 T. Barna "The replacement cost of fixed assets in British manufacturing in 1955", Journal of the Royal Statistical Society, Volume 120, Part 1, 1957, p 24.
7 General Motors, Trentham publicity brochure, 1967.
8 Regression Estimates Relating the Proportion of Total Assembly Costs Accounted for by C.K.D. Materials, local Materials, and Manufacturing Surplus, (as given in Appendix A, Table 6) to time.

In each instance the variable under consideration (Y) is related to time (t) by the equation

$$Y = a + bt$$

The results of the regressions are set out in tabular form below giving estimates of a and b, and, of the correlation coefficient (R^2), the standard error of estimate for the equation (s), and the standard error of estimate with respect to b (s_b).

Y	Time Period	a	b	R^2	s	s_b
c.k.d. materials	1948-49—1968-69	723·2	—5·5	0·87	13·8	0·50
Local materials	1948-49—1968-69	93·8	2·4	0·62	12·0	0·43
„ „	1948-49—1958-59	100·9	1·0	0·05	15·8	1·51
„ „	1958-59—1968-69	81·9	3·1	0·75	6·3	0·60
Manufacturing surplus	1948-49—1968-69	59·4	2·0	0·52	12·1	0·44

9 Richard and Nancy Ruggles "Concepts of Real Capital Stocks and Services" in "Output, Input and Productivity Measurement". National Bureau of Economic and Social Research. Princeton 1961, p. 390.
10 George J. Stigler "Economic Problems in Measuring Changes in Productivity". N.B.E.R. (1961), as above, p. 48.

Chapter 4.—The Comparative Cost of New Zealand Assembly

1 Parliamentary Paper H.48 1963. "Report to the Minister of Industries and Commerce on Criteria for Industrial Development". N.Z. Tariff and Development Board, June 1963.

2 Parliamentary Paper B.4 1968. "The World Bank Report on the New Zealand Economy 1968".

3 This ratio is very similar to that noted by Charles E. Edwards in "Dynamics of the United States Automobile Industry"—University of South Carolina Press; Edwards noted that four assembled cars, or the components for ten or eleven cars, could be packed in one rail freight car.

4 This issue is discussed in paras 83-85 of "New Zealand Overseas Trade" —a report by the Producer Board's Shipping Utilization Committee and the New Zealand Trade Streamlining Committee, London 1964.

5 World Bank Mission Report cited above, pp 61 Annex II. "The Criterion of Domestic Costs of Foreign Exchange".

6 A recent presentation is W. M. Corden "The Structure of a Tariff System and the Effective Protective Rate", the Journal of Political Economy, June 1966, pp. 221.

7 Inter-Industry Study of the New Zealand Economy 1959-60. Part 3. Table 3.7 (Cumulated Primary Input Coefficients for Capital Formation by Industries) shows the following estimates for industry 27, motor vehicle assembly:

Salary and wages	0·389
Other value added	0·214
Imports	0·283
Total:	0·886

Import costs are equal to 32 per cent of the total.

8 P. Hampton "The Degree of Protection Accorded by Import Licensing to New Zealand Manufacturing Industry". Publication No. 12, 1965, Agricultural Economics Research Unit, Lincoln College.

W. Candler and P. Hampton, "The Measurement of Industrial Protection in New Zealand", Australian Economic Papers, June 1966.

More comprehensive estimates will be published in a forthcoming N.Z.I.E.R. research publication prepared by P. G. Elkan.

It will be noted that there is a marked difference between Elkan's estimate of the effective level of protection enjoyed by the motor vehicle assembly industry in 1964-67 and the post devaluation estimate made earlier. The two authors have corresponded about the possible reasons for this difference and have concluded that whilst differences in technique will account for some part of the difference, the major part is accounted for by two factors. The most important is a difference in industry coverage. This study has examined the comparative cost of local motor car assembly, including the cost of locally manufactured components. Elkans study distinguishes between assembly and component manufacture, the latter being included, along with other products, in the "other transport products" industry. A weighting of Elkan's results according to the deflated value of net output in the two industries gives an overall rate of effective protection of 44 per cent. Secondly, these figures would be further reduced if allowances were made for the effect of devaluation. The estimates thus do not appear to be in serious conflict, as was to be expected as Elkan used some of the price data advanced earlier in this chapter.

Chapter 5.—Policy Instruments Affecting the Motor Assembly Industry

1 Letter of Minister of Customs to the motor trade, 1 July 1963.

2 The price control authorities acceptance of the wholesale price as agreed

by Customs is interesting. The Customs Department is presumably interested in the maximization of revenue, and so of wholesale price. Similarly the combined wholesale and retail margin will increase as the wholesale price increases because even although this entails higher sales tax that in turn permits a higher margin. Conceptually, the system would lead to a maximum combined wholesale and retail margin at the point where increasing price reduced demand to match supply, an outcome hardly consistent with the motives of price control.

Chapter 6.—Motor Car Assembly

1 See for example John H. Goldthorpe "Attitudes and Behaviour of Car Assembly Workers". The British Journal of Sociology, September 1968.
2 Reno R. Cole. "Increasing Utilization of the Cost-Quantity Relationship in Manufacturing". Journal of Industrial Engineering, American Institute of Engineers, May-June 1958, Vol. IX, No. 3, p. 173. A fuller description appears in Appendix C, part 2.

Chapter 7.—The Effect of Scale in Assembly

1 Haldi and Whitcomb; "Economies of Scale in Industrial Plants". The Journal of Political Economy, August 1967, Part I. The estimate is derived from the data presented in Table 1, p. 376.
2 Bain J. S.; "Barriers to New Competition". p. 245.
   Maxcy G. and Silberston A.; "The Motor Industry". p. 79.
   Edwards C. E.; "Dynamics of the United States Automobile Industry". pp. 154-163.
   Jurgensen H. and Berg H.; "European Motor Industry—Mergers versus Competition". Inter-Economics, September 1968, p. 268.
   Board of Trade and Industries; Report No. 613. "Investigation into the Motor Industry in South Africa, 1960". para. 101.
   Bladen V. W.; "Report of Royal Commission on the Automotive Industry". p. 27.
   Committee on Industrial Organization, Ireland. "Report on the Motor Vehicle Assembly Industry". p. 70.
   Maxcy G.; "The Motor Industry", in Hunter A. ed. "The Economics of Australian Industry". p. 499.
3 Mass Production, October 1967, Manufacturing the Volkswagen, p. 90.
4 Japan Economic Journal, Industrial Review of Japan 1969, p. 30.
5 Maxcy G.; op. cit., p. 513.
6 In 1965-66 salary and wage payments plus other non material expenses totalled 144 parts per 1000 in New Zealand. In South Africa, in 1958, the same costs comprised 128 parts per 1000; and in Ireland, in 1960, they comprised 159 parts per 1000. A similar figure is suggested by Baranson for assembly of light trucks in the United States. (Baranson, p. 40). A conflicting estimate is however given by Maxcy and Silberston (p. 63), where they estimate final assembly costs to be only 5 per cent of the unit factory cost of a mass produced car. This latter estimate is however given in the context of a full allocation of costs to parts of the car and probably excludes cost of assembly of body shell.
7 Haldi and Whitcomb, op. cit., p. 373.

Chapter 8.—Manufacture

1 Tooling includes jigs, dies and machine accessories for the particular item being manufactured. For example, each design of hubcap requires a special die, with which the hubcap is formed.

2 Board of Trade and Industries, op. cit. Para. 73.

3 H. C. Holden. "Future of the Automobile Industry in New Zealand". Paper presented to Society of Automotive Engineers, 1968.

4 Jack Baranson. "Automotive Industries in Developing Countries". I.B.R.D. Report EC-162, Second Edition, 1969. p. 39, footnote 10.

5 Bain, op. cit. p. 245.

6 Maxcy and Silberston, op. cit. p. 93.

7 Pratten and Silberston, op. cit. p. 380.

8 Edwards, op. cit.

9 Jurgenson and Berg, op. cit. p. 267.

10 Farmer, R. N., and Orr, L. D. "Electric Automobiles and the Developing Countries". International Development Review. December 1968.

11 Knight, B. W. "Plastics and the Motor Vehicle". Mass Production, June 1969. p. 58.

12 Rowbotham, E. M. "Plastics in the Motor Industry". Proceedings of the Institution of Mechanical Engineers 1968-69. Vol. 183, Part 2a, No. 4. p. 85.

13 Maxcy, op. cit. pp. 532 and 535.

14 "Fiat unlikely to set up local car plant". Australian Financial Review. 20 Feb. 1969.

15 Pratten and Silberston, op. cit. Both authors are experienced in this field, Pratten having specialized in the economies of large scale production and Silberston being joint author, with Maxcy, of the major study of the United Kingdom automobile industry.

16 United States Senate. "United States—Canadian Automobile Agreement". Hearings before the Committee on Finance, Eighty-ninth Congress, First Session, on H.R.9042.

17 Baranson, op. cit.

18 Pratten and Silberston, op. cit. p. 380.

19 The function $y = ax^b$ (where x = average size of dominant firm, and y = man years per 000 cars) was fitted to the data in Table 48. This yielded estimates of

a	b	R^2	s	s.b
3·27	—0·395	0·97	0·05	0·06

When fitted to the six observations in Table 49, and to all twelve observations, the function yielded the following results

	a	b	R^2	s	s.b
Table 49	3·763	—0·694	0·80	0·13	0·18
All twelve cases	3·384	—0·439	0·92	0·11	0·04

20 Estimates were derived from the following data. In each case production data was weighted motor cars, 1·0, and other vehicles, 1·5. In the case of Australia cars assembled from imported components were weighted 0·6. The two main sources of information on motor vehicle production and the related employment were:—Chambre Syndicale des Constructeurs d'Automobiles "Repertoire Mondial des Usines d'Assemblage de Vehicules Automobiles", November 1968, and various reports prepared for the 1968 conference of the International Metalworkers Federation. i.e. the IMF.

ARGENTINA 1967

Production	Cars	124,587	Chambre Syndicale	p. 13
	Other	50,731		
	Total:	175,318		

Dominant firms	IKA Renault	37,226	,,	,,	p. 15
	Ford	28,659			
	Fiat	40,911			
	General Motors	22,062			
	SAFRAR (Peugeot)	13,315			
	Total:	142,213			
	Mean	28,443			

Employment	Production and assembly	30,000	IMF Regional Report III	p. 5
	Parts and accessories	65,000		
		95,000		

BRAZIL 1967

Production	Cars	132,027	Chambre Syndicale	p. 24
	Other	93,335		
	Total:	225,362		

Dominant firms	Ford	20,010	,,	,,	p. 26
	General Motors	17,158	,,	,,	p. 27
	Volkswagen	116,002	,,	,,	p. 30
	Willys Overland	41,984	,,	,,	p. 32
	Total:	195,154			
	Mean	48,788			

Employment	Production	50,000	,,	,,	p. 25
	Components	120,000			
	Total	170,000			

SPAIN 1967

Production	Cars	276,258	Chambre Syndicale	p. 131
	Other	88,447		
	Total:	364,705		

Dominant firms	Barreiros Deisel	43,295	,,	,,	p. 138
	Citroen	36,739	,,	,,	p. 139
	Fasa Renault	72,351	,,	,,	p. 135
	Seat (Fiat)	160,658	,,	,,	p. 133
	Total:	313,043			
	Mean	78,261			
Employment	Production	50,000	,,	,,	p. 132
	Components	70,000			
	Total:	120,000			

INDIA 1967

Production	Cars	33,354	Chambre Syndicale	p. 88
	Other	37,285		
	Total:	70,639		

Dominant firms	Hindustan	22,230	,,	,,	p. 89
	Mahindra	6,608	,,	,,	p. 90
	Premier	13,131	,,	,,	p. 91
	Tata Mercedes	19,190	,,	,,	p. 92
	Total:	61,159			
	Mean	15,290			

Employment	Manufacturing, assembly, parts and accessories	75,000	IMF Regional Report V p. 11 on basis of Indian Labour Ministry Statistics

AUSTRALIA 1967

Production	Cars	298,000	Chambre Syndicale	p. 69
	Other	48,000		
	Total:	346,000		
	(Assembly)	44,000		

Dominant firms (production only)	British Leyland	45,671	,,	,,	p. 72
	Chrysler	45,000	,,	,,	p. 73
	Ford	65,226	,,	,,	p. 74
	General Motors	151,838	,,	,,	p. 76
	Total:	307,735			
	Mean	76,934			

Employment Construction and			Australian Official	
(1966-67) assembly	24,807		Yearbook 1968 p. 1114	
Motor bodies	38,202			
Accessories	19,113			
	82,122			

YUGOSLAVIA 1966

Production	Cars	36,936	Chambre Syndicale p. 173
	Other	11,897	
	Total:	48,833	

Dominant firms (1967)	Crvena Zastava	32,934	„	„	p. 173
	FAP	3,000	„	„	p. 174
	T.A.M.	4,700	„	„	p. 175
	Total:	40,634			
	Mean	13,545			

| Employment (1966) | Total: | 60,000 | IMF Regional Report II p. 6 on basis of Yugoslav estimate |

21 All wage data used in Table 53 was derived from information in the ILO Yearbook of Statistics 1968.

(a) Average wage earnings, for male and female, were drawn from Table 19B. These related variously to industry 38, Transport equipment, industries 34-38, metal industries, or some narrower grouping within this range. For most countries data related to the average earnings for males and females combined. Where wage earnings were given separately for the two sexes these were combined using employment data relating to all manufacturing industries given in Table 2A. Where earnings were specified hourly or weekly, estimates were calculated from data on weekly hours worked, from Table 13, scaled by the factor $\frac{365}{4 \times 12}$.

(b) The derived monthly earnings were converted to \$US by means of the exchange rates given in Table 28.

22 U.S. Senate, op. cit.

23 U.S. Senate, op. cit., p. 450. Information in report of U.S. Tariff Commission. The data relates to twelve models comprising the major models of each of the big three in 1964.

24 U.S. Senate, op. cit., p. 360. Evidence by Secretary of Labor. Average hourly earnings U.S.A. \$3.41, Canada \$Can. 2.86 = \$2.65.

25 Official Yearbooks for Canada and the United States give data for value added and employment.

26 Calculated on the following basis:
Let VW = QP
where V = volume of factor input

221

$$W = \text{rate of factor reward}$$
W = rate of factor reward
Q = volume of output
P = price of output
and subscripts c and u refer to Canada and the United States.

Then $\dfrac{V_c W_c}{V_u W_u} = \dfrac{Q_c P_c}{Q_u P_u}$

and $\dfrac{\dfrac{Q_u}{V_u}}{\dfrac{Q_c}{V_c}} = \dfrac{P_c}{P_u} \cdot \dfrac{W_u}{W_c}$

The left hand side measures the ratio (R) of output per unit of factor input in the U.S. to that in Canada. The first item on the right hand side is 1·14, and the second (allowing for only 60 per cent Canadian content and assuming the remaining 40 per cent to be rewarded at U.S. rates) is derived as $\dfrac{1 \cdot 29}{0 \cdot 4(1 \cdot 29) + 0 \cdot 6(1 \cdot 0)} = 1 \cdot 156$

Thus R $= 1 \cdot 14(1 \cdot 156) = 1 \cdot 32$

[27] Maxcy and Silberston, op. cit., p. 93.

[28] Baranson, op. cit.

[29] World Bank, op. cit., p. 36.

[30] The results of the regression calculation were

Coefficient	Value	Variance	Standard Deviation	95% confidence limits	
Constant	0·309	0·00119	0·0345	0·240	0·378
D	0·00318	0·00000	0·00082	0·00155	0·00481
LQ	—0·248	0·00171	0·0413	—0·331	—0·166

$R^2 = 0 \cdot 75$ R^2 corrected 0·69
D.W. statistic 0·72
Log variables expressed to base 10.

[31] World Bank, op. cit., pp. 36-39.

[32] Witness the following:
"Few would disagree with the general criticism of the economic defects of the industry expressed in the World Bank Mission's recent report on the New Zealand economy."
    Adrian Blackburn in the first of a series of five articles on the "problems and prospects facing the much-criticised New Zealand car assembly industry." *Auckland Herald*, Sept. 2, 1968.
"The World Bank Report . . . reveals . . . thinking, which, even if it contains its share of somewhat simplistic economic assumptions, displays a concern for particularities as well as the ensuing generalities. The simplistic quality is most apparent in the wholehearted recommendation of development within the framework of international comparative advantage, and the sensible but pious hopes about rationalising the car assembly industry."
    A. E. McQueen. Review of the report. *Pacific Viewpoint*, May 1969, p. 125.
"Forcing an increased domestic content on the New Zealand motor assembly industry could only result in a sharp increase in the cost of motor vehicles (said) the Dominion President of Federated Farmers, Mr P. S. Plummer. "This is a ridiculous proposition and completely

ignores the factual appraisal of the automotive industry made by the World Bank Mission last year," Mr Plummer said.
Dominion, Jan. 1969.

33 Baranson, op. cit., pp. 59-65.

34 See page 22.

35 Baranson, op. cit., para. 108 and footnotes.

36 There is some uncertainty as to the point at which Baranson's comparison was drawn. The general sense of his text suggests use of comparable pricing points for overseas and locally assembled cars. In practice the c.i.f. price used for imported cars excludes subsequent handling and freight charges which would properly be included in arriving at a figure comparable to ex-factory cost for a locally-assembled car.

The entries in row one depend on a comparison of the following data from Table 20.

$$\frac{\text{Price ex-factory}}{\text{Price ex-wharf—Duty}} \quad \frac{1000}{1084 - 154} = 1{\cdot}08 \quad \frac{959}{998 - 154} = 1{\cdot}14$$

$$\frac{\text{Price ex-factory}}{\text{C.I.F.E. value}} \quad \frac{1000}{820} = 1{\cdot}22 \quad \frac{959}{820} = 1{\cdot}17$$

(columns headed: Unadjusted / Adjusted)

The alternative entries in the first column of row 2 are drawn from Baranson (1969) and World Bank (1968) respectively. The company figures are those in last row of Table 22.

37 Letter September 1969. The company named is one of those which supplied data to the author. The company ratios are in general above the average of the twelve examples but are remote from those instanced in the Mission report.

38 Baranson, op. cit., pp. 31 and 34.

39 Baranson, op. cit., p. 63.

40 Baranson, op. cit., p. 64, note 9.
The three variables are interconnected as follows

$$\frac{\text{Average cost N.Z. production}}{\text{Average cost overseas production}} = \frac{\text{Average cost N.Z. production}}{\text{Deletion allowance}} \cdot \frac{\text{Deletion allowance}}{\text{Average cost overseas production}}$$

i.e. $1.36 = 2{\cdot}0 \times 0{\cdot}68$

Chapter 9.—Development Policies Followed Overseas

The major sources of material for this section were:

Chambre Syndicale des Constructeurs d'Automobiles. "Repertoire Mondial des Usines d'Assemblage de Vehicles Automobiles". November 1968.

Jack Baranson. "Automotive Industries in Developing Countries." IBRD report EC-162. 1969.

Preparatory Documents to the International Metal Workers World Auto Conference. May 1968.

Additional material for particular countries

AUSTRALIA

Australian Financial Review. Various articles.

Australian Industries Development Association. "Government Policy and the Automotive Industry." Two part survey appearing in the Association's Bulletin, January/February and April 1970.

Australian Tariff Board. "Report on Automotive Industry", June 1957, and "Report on Motor Vehicles", September 1965.

Federal Chamber of Automotive Industries. Australian Automotive Year Book 1969.

Hartnett. "Big Wheels and Little Wheels".

Maxcy, George. "The Motor Industry" in Hunter, Alex (Ed.) "The Economies of Australian Industry".

McEwen, John. Press statement of 18 December 1968.

Motor Vehicle Registration Statistics 1968.

Stubbs, Peter. "The Australian Motor Industry", article in Current Affairs Bulletin, Volume 35, No. 9, 1965. University of Melbourne.

BRAZIL

Geschelin, Joseph. Articles in Automotive Industry. Various issues 1967.

Wilkins, Gordon. Article in Engineering. January 1969.

CANADA

Bladen, V. W. "Report Royal Commission on the Automotive Industry". April 1961.

Sun Life Corporation. "The Canadian Automotive Industry".

U.S. Senate. "United States-Canadian Automobile Agreement". Hearings before the Committee on Finance, United States Senate 89th Congress First Session on H.R. 9042.

SOUTH AFRICA

Board of Trade and Industries, Report No. 613. "Investigation into the Motor Industry in South Africa". 1960.

Griffiths, Ieuan L. "The South African Motor Industry". Supplement to the Standard Bank Review.

[1] U.S. Tariff Commission Report. Reprinted in U.S. Senate 89th Congress. Hearings before the Committee on Finance on H.R. 9042, 1965, p. 384.

[2] U.S. Senate, op. cit., p. 42.

[3] Communication from Canadian Government Trade Commission, Wellington.

[4] International Metalworkers Federation, World Auto Conference 1968. Regional Report IV, p. 7.

[5] "Investigation into the Motor Industry in South Africa". Board of Trade and Industries, Report No. 613, 1960, para. 189.

[6] Ieuan L. Griffiths. "The South African Motor Industry". Supplement to the Standard Bank Review, June 1968.

[7] Griffiths, op. cit., p. 17.

N.Z. INSTITUTE OF ECONOMIC RESEARCH Inc.

LIST OF MEMBERS

MAY 1971

Air New Zealand Ltd.	Auckland
Ajax G.K.N. Ltd.	Lower Hutt
Alex Harvey Industries Ltd.	Auckland
W. M. Angus Ltd.	Lower Hutt
Armstrong & Springhall Ltd.	Wellington
Arthur Ellis & Co. Ltd.	Dunedin
Associated British Cables Ltd.	Christchurch
Associated Engineering N.Z. Ltd.	Panmure
Auckland Savings Bank	Auckland
Australia and New Zealand Bank Ltd.	Wellington
Australian Mutual Provident Society	Wellington
Australian Provincial Assurance Society Ltd.	Wellington
Australian Tourist Commission	Melbourne
Australasian Temperance & General Mutual Life Society Ltd.	Wellington
BALM Paints (N.Z.) Ltd.	Lower Hutt
Bank of New South Wales	Wellington
Bank of New Zealand	Wellington
Barr Burgess & Stewart	Dunedin
Battelle Memorial Institute	Columbus USA
Battery Makers of N.Z. Ltd.	Lower Hutt
Beazley Group of Companies	Mt. Maunganui
Berlei Industries Ltd.	Auckland
Blundell Bros. Ltd.	Wellington
Bond's Hosiery Mills (N.Z.) Ltd.	Wellington
BP (New Zealand) Ltd.	Wellington
Broadcasting Corporation N.Z.	Wellington
Broadlands Dominion Group Ltd.	Auckland
Bryant & May Bell & Co. Ltd.	Wellington
Butland Industries Ltd.	Auckland
Buttle Wilson Rutherfurd & Co.	Auckland
Cable Price Downer Ltd.	Wellington
Cadbury Fry Hudson Ltd.	Dunedin
Calder Mackay Co. Ltd.	Christchurch
Caltex Oil (N.Z.) Ltd.	Wellington
Campbell & Ehrenfried Co. Ltd.	Auckland
Canterbury Frozen Meat Co. Ltd.	Christchurch
Charles Haines Ltd.	Wellington
Christchurch Press Co. Ltd.	Christchurch
Ciba Co. Pty. Ltd.	Wellington
Claude Neon Lights of N.Z. Ltd.	Auckland
Coates Bros. (N.Z.) Ltd.	Penrose
Coca-Cola Export Corporation	East Tamaki
Colonial Mutual Life Assurance Society Ltd.	Wellington
Comalco Industries Pty. Ltd.	Melbourne
Commercial Bank of Australia Ltd.	Wellington
Consolidated Brick & Pipe Investments Ltd.	Auckland
Consolidated Metal Industries Ltd.	Auckland
Consolidated Plastic Industries (N.Z.) Ltd.	Auckland
Cory-Wright & Salmon Ltd.	Wellington
Coulls Somerville Wilkie Ltd.	Dunedin
Crothall & Co. Ltd.	Christchurch
Dalgety and New Zealand Loan Ltd.	Wellington

Daysh Renouf & Co.	Wellington
Dental & Medical Supply Co. Ltd.	Wellington
de Pelichet McLeod & Co. Ltd.	Hastings
Dominion Fertiliser Co. Ltd.	Dunedin
Dominion Life Assurance Office of New Zealand Ltd.	Wellington
Dunlop New Zealand Ltd.	Wellington
East Coast Farmers Fertiliser Co. Ltd.	Napier
Ellis Hardie Syminton Ltd.	Auckland
Europa Oil (N.Z.) Ltd.	Wellington
F & T New Zealand Ltd.	Wellington
Farmers' Co-op Auctioneering Co. Ltd.	Hamilton
Farmers' Trading Co. Ltd.	Auckland
Fibremakers (N.Z.) Ltd.	Papatoetoe
Firestone Tire & Rubber Co. of New Zealand Ltd.	Christchurch
Fisher & Paykel Ltd.	Auckland
Fletcher Group Services Ltd.	Auckland
Ford Motor Co. of New Zealand Ltd.	Lower Hutt
Formica (N.Z.) Ltd.	Papakura
Forsyth Barr & Co.	Dunedin
Francis Allison Symes & Co.	Wellington
Gear Meat Co. Ltd.	Wellington
G.E.C. (New Zealand) Ltd.	Wellington
General Motors New Zealand Ltd.	Wellington
Glaxo Laboratories (N.Z.) Ltd.	Palmerston North
Godfrey Phillips (New Zealand) Ltd.	Wellington
Golden Bay Cement Co. Ltd.	Wellington
Gollin & Co. Ltd.	Wellington
W. Gregg & Co. Ltd.	Dunedin
Hamilton Hindin Greene & Co.	Christchurch
Russell Hancock	Wellington
Hawke's Bay Farmers' Co-op. Association Ltd.	Hastings
R. & W. Hellaby Ltd.	Auckland
His Master's Voice (N.Z.) Ltd.	Wellington
Holeproof Mills Ltd.	Auckland
I.B.M. World Trade Corporation	Wellington
J. Ilott Ltd.	Wellington
Imperial Chemical Industries (N.Z.) Ltd.	Wellington
International Computers (New Zealand) Ltd.	Wellington
Ivon Watkins-Dow Ltd.	New Plymouth
Japan External Trade Organisation	Auckland
John Burns & Co. Ltd.	Auckland
Joseph Lucas (N.Z.) Ltd.	Auckland
Kaiser Aluminum & Chemical Corporation	Oakland
Kempthorne Prosser & Co.'s N.Z. Drug Co. Ltd.	Dunedin
Kirkcaldie & Stains Ltd.	Wellington
Kodak New Zealand Ltd.	Wellington
Lactose Co. of New Zealand Ltd.	Hawera
Leopard Brewery Ltd.	Hastings
Lincoln Industries Ltd.	Penrose
Mace Engineering Ltd.	Christchurch
McAlpine Refrigeration Ltd.	Auckland
McKenzies (N.Z.) Ltd.	Wellington
McSkimming Industries Ltd.	Dunedin
Mason & Porter Ltd.	Panmure
Mason Bros. Ltd.	Auckland
Milne & Choyce Ltd.	Auckland
Mobil Oil New Zealand Ltd.	Wellington
Mutual Life & Citizens Assurance Co. Ltd.	Wellington
L. D. Nathan & Co. Ltd.	Auckland

National Bank of New Zealand Ltd.	Wellington
National Cash Register Co. (N.Z.) Ltd.	Wellington
National Insurance Co. of New Zealand Ltd.	Dunedin
N.M.A. Co. of N.Z. Ltd.	Dunedin
National Mutual Life Association of Australasia Ltd.	Wellington
News Media Ownership Ltd.	Wellington
New Zealand Apple & Pear Marketing Board	Wellington
New Zealand Breweries Ltd.	Wellington
N.Z. Cement Holdings Ltd.	Dunedin
New Zealand Dairy Board	Wellington
New Zealand Farmers' Co-op. Association of Canterbury Ltd.	Christchurch
New Zealand Farmers' Fertiliser Co. Ltd.	Auckland
N.Z. Forest Products Ltd.	Auckland
New Zealand Insurance Co. Ltd.	Auckland
New Zealand Meat & Wool Boards' Economic Service	Wellington
New Zealand Motor Bodies Ltd.	Petone
New Zealand Motor Corporation Ltd.	Wellington
New Zealand National Airways Corporation	Wellington
New Zealand Newspapers Ltd.	Auckland
New Zealand Refrigerating Co. Ltd.	Christchurch
New Zealand Shipping Co. Ltd.	Wellington
N.Z. Steel Co. Ltd.	Auckland
New Zealand Sugar Co. Ltd.	Auckland
N.I.M.U. Insurance Co.	Wellington
Jas J. Niven & Co. Ltd.	Wellington
Norwich Union Life Assurance Society	Wellington
C. & A. Odlin Timber & Hardware Co. Ltd.	Wellington
Overseas Containers N.Z. Ltd.	Wellington
P. A. Management Consultants Ltd.	Auckland
Pacific Steel Ltd.	Otahuhu
A. S. Paterson & Co. Ltd.	Wellington
S. W. Peterson & Co. Ltd.	Wellington
Philips Electrical Industries of N.Z. Ltd.	Wellington
Pilkington Bros. (New Zealand) Ltd.	Lower Hutt
Port Craig Timber Group of Companies	Invercargill
Rolf Porter	Auckland
Prestige (N.Z.) Ltd.	Wellington
Producers' & Citizens' Co-operative Assurance Co. Ltd.	Auckland
Provident Life Assurance Co. Ltd.	Wellington
Prudential Assurance Co. Ltd.	Wellington
P.T.Y. Industries Ltd.	Putaruru
Pye Ltd.	Auckland
Qantas Airways Ltd.	Auckland
Reckitt & Colman (New Zealand) Ltd.	Avondale
Reid New Zealand Rubber Mills Ltd.	Auckland
Repco Manufacturing Co. (N.Z.) Ltd.	Upper Hut
Reserve Bank of New Zealand	Wellington
Rex Consolidated Ltd.	Auckland
Rheem New Zealand Ltd.	Tawa
Robert Holt & Sons Ltd.	Napier
Rothmans Tobacco Co. Ltd.	Napier
Royal-Globe Life Assurance Co. Ltd.	Wellington
Salmond Holdings Ltd.	Wellington
A. M. Satterthwaite & Co. Ltd.	Christchurch
W. D. Scott & Co.	Auckland
Security Dealers Ltd.	Auckland
Self Help Co-op Ltd.	Wellington
Shell Oil New Zealand Ltd.	Wellington
South British Insurance Co. Ltd.	Auckland

Steel & Tube Co. of New Zealand Ltd.	Wellington
Tappenden Industries Ltd.	Auckland
Tasman Pulp & Paper Co. Ltd.	Kawerau
R. & E. Tingey & Co. Ltd.	Wellington
Todd Motors Ltd.	Wellington
Totalisator Agency Board	Wellington
Tourist Hotel Corporation of New Zealand	Wellington
U.E.B. Industries Ltd.	Auckland
Unilever (New Zealand) Ltd.	Petone
Union Carbide New Zealand Pty. Ltd.	Auckland
Union Steamship Co. of New Zealand Ltd.	Wellington
United Dominions Corporation (South Pacific) Ltd.	Wellington
J. Wattie Canneries Ltd.	Hastings
Wellington City Corporation	Wellington
Wellington Publishing Co.	Wellington
Whitcombe & Tombs Ltd.	Christchurch
Williams & Kettle Ltd.	Napier
Williamson Jeffery Ltd.	Dunedin
W. D. & H. O. Wills (New Zealand) Ltd.	Auckland
Wilson & Horton Ltd.	Auckland
Wilson (N.Z.) Portland Cement Ltd.	Auckland
Winstone Ltd.	Auckland
Woolworths (New Zealand) Ltd.	Wellington
Wormald Bros. Industries (N.Z.) Ltd.	New Lynn
Wright Stephenson & Co. Ltd.	Wellington